3   Dawn of a New Era

1209   1215   1215

Newsweek Books New York

Editor Maurice Ashley

1215

1240

1265

3 Dawn of a New Era

1273   1275   1320

Library of Congress Catalog Card No. 73-81684.
ISBN: Clothbound edition 0-88225-062-0
ISBN: De luxe edition 0-88225-063-9

Printed and bound in Italy
by Arnoldo Mondadori Editore - Verona
Linking passages written by Adrian Brink.

1337   1348   1368

1378   1381   1387   1402

Contents

Introduction

The thirteenth century in European history was economically buoyant and culturally progressive. Foreign trade was expanding in a spectacular way both in the Baltic Sea, based upon the northeast German towns which were later consolidated into the Hanseatic League, and in the Mediterranean, where the rival Venetians and Genoese exhibited their genius for commerce with the East. Towns of fifty or sixty thousand inhabitants were to be found and Paris was in the process of becoming a nobly designed capital city. It has been estimated that the population of Europe was as large then as it was to be four centuries later.

Europe was Christian and aggressively so. The Moslems had been repulsed in the south of Spain—the battle of Las Navas de Tolosa (July 16, 1212), where King Alfonso VIII of Castile defeated the Almohades from North Africa, was one of the decisive battles in medieval history. The heretics known as the Albigenses in southern France were suppressed and a Crusade was planned against Egypt. That fantastic character, Emperor Frederick II, "the Wonder of the World," succeeded in making himself King of Jerusalem in 1229.

After the conquest of Constantinople (1204) in the Fourth Crusade—a damaging blow to the Greek Church—the power of the Roman Church reached its apex under Pope Innocent III, a skillful politician as well as a determined evangelist, who had been elected in 1198 at the early age of thirty-seven. He made lavish use of the weapons of excommunication and interdict (a ban on church services) to further his ends. King John of England was obliged to become his vassal; his wishes were imposed on Philip Augustus of France; the Emperor Frederick II acknowledged him as overlord of Sicily. At the Fourth Lateran Council, held under Innocent's presidency, the traditional teaching of the Roman Church was reaffirmed, including the doctrine of the Trinity and the miracle of the Eucharist.

Innocent III welcomed, a little tepidly, the institution of the friars under the leadership of the Italian St. Francis of Assisi and the Spaniard, St. Dominic. These Christian missionaries had no fixed abodes but traveled the world preaching the Gospel. St. Thomas Aquinas, who was a Dominican friar and the prince of scholastic philosophers, wrote two great books in the middle of the century expounding the Christian faith and trying to reconcile the doctrines of the Bible with the arguments in the known works of the Greek philosopher Aristotle.

These works of Aristotle had been rediscovered in the previous century and contributed to a Renaissance in Europe. Universities, or *studia generalia*, had then come into being. The University of Paris dates from about 1150 and the University of Oxford from about 1168. Cambridge, which split away from Oxford in 1209, had its first college, Peterhouse, set up in 1284, while University College, the earliest Oxford college, dates from 1249. Emperor Frederick II founded the University of Naples in 1224, and the Sorbonne dates from 1257. This century was also a splendid age for Gothic building. In England, for example, both Salisbury Cathedral and Westminster Abbey were rebuilt, and in Germany the cathedral of Magdeburg was constructed. Thus Europe was a strong, united and cultured Christian community.

The only menace to Christian Europe came from the Mongols. These nomads of the steppe, which stretched from the Hungarian plains to the Great Wall of China, lived by war. A quarter of their total population of a million formed an extraordinary army of sharp-shooting warriors. Mounted on swift ponies, they devastated much of the world. Cavalrymen armed with arrows of varying lengths, they had an efficient signaling system with black-and-white flags.

They proved invincible. Even the early Russian hero, Alexander Nevski, conqueror of the Swedes, acknowledged their military supremacy. Under the Great Khan, Genghis, they overran North China, invaded India, took Moscow and Kiev and crossed the river Dnieper. They won a victory at Liegnitz in Silesia in the midcentury and occupied Hungary, but after the death of Genghis Khan, they withdrew to their treeless homelands. For they were plunderers rather than settlers. However, Genghis Khan's grandson, Kublai Khan, later overthrew the Sung dynasty in South China and founded an empire with a new capital city built at Peking. Here the Venetian traveler Marco Polo visited him, entered his service and was deeply impressed by the administration and culture of Mongol China. But in the middle of the fourteenth century an upstart peasant named Chu Yuan-chang led a revolt against the Mongols and succeeded in founding the Ming dynasty. Chu was a cruel despot, but he promoted painting, pottery, textile weaving and printing. Another Mongol warrior, Timur, reunited the various clans, annexed Persia, occupied Delhi, sacked Baghdad and defeated the Ottoman Turks at the battle of Ankara (1402). He died in 1405, just as he was preparing to attack the Chinese.

A later threat to European civilization from nomads of the steppe came from the Ottoman Turks, who subdued the Balkans and were to harrass and embarrass Europe for over six hundred years. But, like the Mongols, they failed to penetrate into the heart of Europe at this time. Nevertheless Christian Europe was unsettled in the fourteenth century. The authority of the papacy was undermined. First, Clement v moved from Rome to the independent city of Avignon and thus began what is know as "the Babylonian captivity," which lasted for seventy years. This was followed by "the Great Schism" which culminated in there being no fewer than three ecclesiastics all claiming to be the properly elected representatives of God on earth.

So it was that the authority of the papacy was shaken. Learned men such as Dante, the magnificent Florentine poet, William of Ockham, Marsiglio of Padua and Dr. John Wycliffe of Oxford each wrote books implicitly attacking the pretensions of the Roman Church on intellectual grounds. Politically Europe was divided against itself, the adherents of Pope and King, the Guelfs and the Ghibellines, fighting each other throughout Italy. In the same century the Hundred Years War between England and France began. The French were defeated at Sluys, Crécy and Poitiers before a peace was signed at Bretigny in 1360, allowing the English to retain Aquitaine. The Black Death, the killing bubonic plague, which reached Europe from the Levant in the middle of the century led to a reduction in the size of the European working population (perhaps by one-third); this scarcity of labor brought about an economic depression and much social unrest, exemplified by the Peasants' Revolt of 1381 in England. Thus philosophic doubt, endemic war and social distress injured the unity of fourteenth-century Europe in contrast to the political and cultural progress in the previous century. Yet the fourteenth century could boast the names of Giotto, the first master painter, Dante and Chaucer, both of whom wrote in the vernacular, and Roger Bacon, a Franciscan, who was one of the first western European scientists. Only in China was there a comparable culture.

In this volume sixteen milestones of history are described, covering, with linking passages, every aspect of world events from the sealing of Magna Carta and the establishment of parliaments in England to the Peasants' Revolt; from the conquest of North China by Genghis Khan to its victorious reconquest by the peasant Chu; from the triumphant meeting of the Lateran Council under Innocent III to the damaging "Great Schism" of the papacy in 1378. Thus is presented a lively and illustrated chronicle of the world as it was from seven hundred to six hundred years ago.

MAURICE ASHLEY

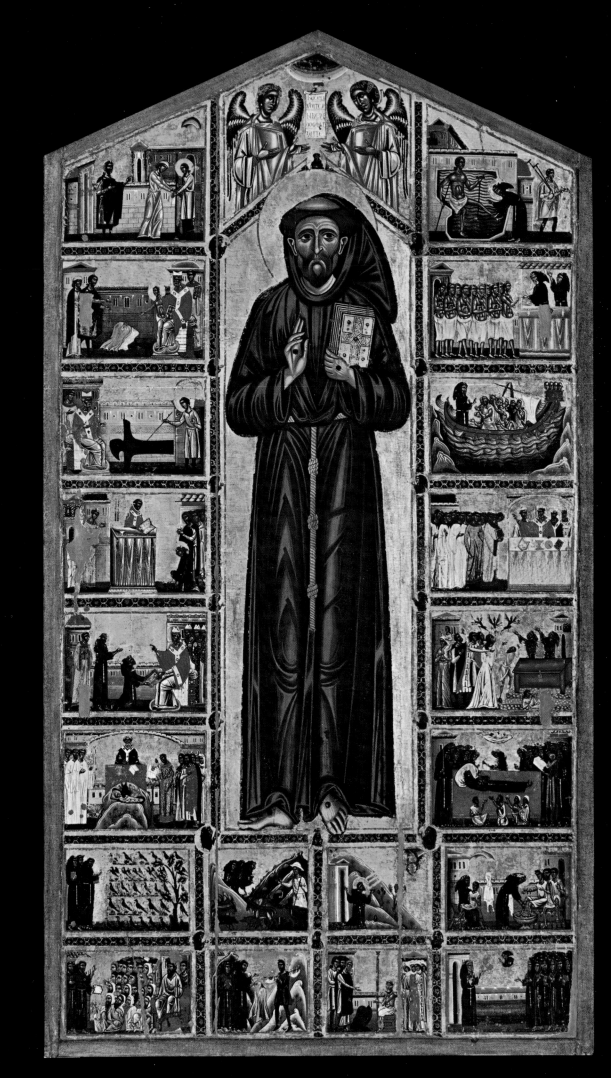

The Order of St. Francis

At a time when disillusionment with the Church was widespread, the Franciscan movement restored popular faith in religion. The genius of the Order's founder, Francis of Assisi, cannot be underestimated. By living a truly Christian life—by his humility, his love of man and nature, and his joyous religious fervor—he did more than anyone else to keep alive the ideals of a Church devoted to the good of mankind.

In September, 1224, a certain Agnello, a native of Pisa, landed in England with eight companions. They were a motley crew, dressed in the tunics and hoods of beggars with ropes tied about their waists. The local inhabitants mistook them for circus performers from France but soon learned that they were Franciscan friars, followers of Francis of Assisi. The Rule they followed called for a life of obedience, poverty and chastity. The newcomers explained that they were not monks, for they did not live in monasteries: their cloister was the world. Thirty years later there were forty-nine communities numbering 1,244 friars in England alone. And all over Europe the story was the same, men and women had flocked to join these joyous groups of gray-habited friars who came from central Italy preaching a message that was to transform the religious life and attitudes of the West.

The Franciscan movement emerges as one of the more successful attempts to restore popular faith in the Church at a time when it was under severe attack, and there can be little doubt that it redeemed an age and set guidelines for the future. The world Francis was born into held little hope for the vast majority of people. They lived out their lives in ignorance and poverty, exploited by their overlords and with little expectation of any advancement or improvement in these conditions. The religious fervor of the age was tainted with a cynicism engendered by corrupt practices within the Church, and heretical movements were widespread. It was said that the reigning pope, Innocent III, had a recurring nightmare, that Church, state and society were doomed to collapse. At a time when Christian orthodoxy appeared to be in dire straits, Francis and his friars burst upon the scene, seeking to reform the Church by resurrecting the doctrines of humility and love.

To the rich, they said that it was better to be a tenant in God's world than an owner in this; to the poor, that in God's eyes every man was equal. Francis preached the brotherhood of man, and translated the message of the Gospels into the language of the troubadours—an indication of his natural gaiety of spirit. It was said that any sinner who looked into his eyes saw an image of what he could be as opposed to what he was; for what he was, there was only compassion. To the current concept of a God of wrath, who would punish all those who strayed, the Franciscans countered with the mild rebuttal that there were no goats, only lost sheep.

Francis was born in Assisi in Umbria in late 1181 or early 1182, the son of Pietro and Pica Bernardone. He was baptized Giovanni but was called Francesco (Francis) either because his father was a frequent traveler to France or because of his penchant for French romances and songs of the troubadours. Pietro was a wealthy cloth merchant, and he, his wife and their three children were a typical well-to-do Italian family.

After a somewhat indifferent education Francis began helping in the family business. He was slightly below average in height, slim, with a dark, long, thin face. Intuitive, poetic, intelligent, he possessed a will of steel. Outside the family circle his social life was certainly intense. His biographers see him in this period of wine and roses as the darling of the town—chivalrous, courteous, affectionate, generous and gay. He loved stories of chivalry and yearned to distinguish himself as a knight.

When he was twenty, he rode off to the war with neighboring Perugia but was captured and imprisoned for a year. He returned to Assisi still ablaze with chivalrous feelings and set off to enlist in the papal army. But after traveling only a short distance, he decided that he was pursuing the wrong sort of chivalry and returned home. He was vaguely unhappy with his past and uncertain about his future. He turned to prayer and contemplation. Gradually the idea took hold of him that he should follow literally the poverty of Christ. He declared to his friends that he intended to wed "a fairer

An early portrait of Francis of Assisi. Founder of the first mendicant order, the Friars Minor, he restored popular faith in the Church at a time when it was under severe attack.

Opposite St. Francis in triumph: a medieval panel in the Church of Santa Croce, Florence, depicting scenes from his life.

Honorius III approves the Franciscan rule in 1223. A revised version, it lacked the joy, humility and generosity of spirit of the original.

bride than ever you saw, who surpasses all others in beauty and excels them in virtue"—the Lady Poverty.

The next step was to take the pilgrim's path to Rome, whether as a penance, or for guidance is not known. On the steps of St. Peter's he made a momentous decision. He changed clothes with a beggar, sat on the steps with the ragged crowd, and for one whole day learned what it was to belong to the outcasts of society. Back in Assisi, he now sought to serve the unwanted. And the most unwanted of all, the lepers (even lower on the scale than beggars), were numerous. Like everyone, Francis was terrified of them. One evening, riding back to town, he turned a corner and was suddenly face to face with a leper. He dismounted and embraced the sufferer, giving him alms. He remounted and rode to a leper house nearby. He called the lepers together, begged their pardon for his past disgust, and promised to live with them. He kissed each inmate and departed.

While visiting the ruined chapel of San Damiano, on the fringes of the town, Francis knelt in prayer before a Byzantine crucifix. The figure of Christ appeared to tell him: "Go, Francis and repair my house." Francis went and literally did as he had been told. He ransacked his father's shop for the finest bolts of cloth and rode the three leagues to Foligno, where he sold the cloth and his horse and returned to Assisi on foot. He sought out the priest who served the ruined chapel and offered him the money. The priest refused the gift, but Francis left it in the chapel.

Pietro Bernardone, horrified at his son's be-

14

haviour, referred the matter to the town council. Summoned by the town crier to appear before them, Francis appealed to the bishop on the grounds that he was now in the service of God. The appeal was allowed, and in a dramatic scene in the piazza before the bishop's palace, Francis stripped off his outer garments, threw them at his father's feet and declared that his father now was the Father in Heaven. Clothed in a gardener's old cloak, he then went off into the woods singing, convinced that, at last, he was beginning to tread in the footprints of the poor Christ.

But Francis came to realize that the repair of God's house meant more than just the restoration of a ruined chapel. For three years he lived with the lepers, shared his crusts with the beggars, rebuilt three churches, and had nowhere to lay his head. At last his preaching began to attract both fame and followers. The first brothers numbered about eleven. They came from all walks of life, one was a nobleman, others were a crusader, a knight, a peasant, a lawyer and a priest. They were attracted to this singing prophet who taught them to curse nothing or no one, but to praise all things and to offer men love, hope and the promise of salvation.

At dawn, one morning in April, 1209, Bernard, the former nobleman, and Peter, the former lawyer, went to church with Francis, who opened the Gospels and singled out three different precepts: "If thou wilt be perfect, go and sell what thou hast and give to the poor", "Take nothing for your journey"; "If any man will come after me let him deny himself and take up his Cross and follow me." These, said Francis, would form the Rule of the Order.

The brothers dressed in the tunic and hood of beggars. They tied ropes around their waists and wore either sandals or went barefooted. Assisi had learned to tolerate Francis but as his followers grew in number it seemed that the town was becoming a breeding place for beggars. In other Umbrian towns they were equally badly received. It seemed that the time had come to seek the confirmation of papal approval for the Order. In 1209, Francis and his twelve "Penitents of the City of Assisi," as they now called themselves, went to Rome to petition Innocent III. He received the friars, but showed no great enthusiasm for their ideas. Francis declared that the message of the Gospels was to be the literal foundation of the Franciscan Rule. No previous Order had ever sought to make the Gospels literally interpreted, the basis of its way of life. This meant that the new Order would exist without possessions and without revenue. Innocent consulted his advisers. That night, Innocent, in a dream, saw the Lateran Basilica falling, but this time the Church was saved by Francis. Next morning Innocent cautiously gave his approval to the founding of the Franciscan Order.

On their return, the brothers stopped at an old hovel they had found in the woods at Rivo Torto

not far from the Porziuncola, an abandoned chapel restored by Francis. There they stayed working among the peasants and lepers, existing largely on roots abandoned in the fields, for the autumn and the winter. They were half-starved but full of joy. However, the idyll had to end, and they were eventually displaced by a peasant.

Francis returned to his native city to organize additional groups of friars, and founded the first real home of the Franciscan Order at the little chapel of the Porziuncola near Assisi. Here shortly was to come a noble and wealthy young woman for whom Francis was to found his Second Order, that of the Poor Ladies (or Poor Clares). Just before Easter, in 1212, Clare Offreducci stole away from her home in Assisi under cover of darkness, and ran down to the Porziuncola where Francis cut off her hair, clothed her in a gray robe similar to his own, and procured her sanctuary in a nearby Benedictine convent. She was soon joined by her sister, Agnes. Francis brought them to the Benedictine Abbey of Sant' Angelo. The Offreducci family appealed to the bishop of Assisi to recover

The meeting in Rome of Dominic and Francis. Dominic proposed that their orders merge, but Francis felt that the difference in approach was too great.

A painting by Gozzoli showing Francis casting out devils from Arezzo.

the girls, but he remained unmoved, and gave San Damiano to the two sisters as their first convent. Clare was to remain there until she died, while her Order was carried all over Europe by the indomitable women who flocked to San Damiano. The Rule of the Second Order was not written by Francis, but by Cardinal Ugolino, later Pope Gregory IX, and was modeled on the Rule of St. Benedict. It was austere, but not founded on literal interpretation of the Gospel precepts, as was the primitive rule that Innocent III had verbally approved for the First Order. The world of the thirteenth century could never be the cloister for the Poor Ladies, and like all other orders for women, they were strictly enclosed.

Over the next five years (1212–17) Francis recruited many new brethren to his Order. By 1215, they had grown strong in Tuscany and northern Umbria and begun to spread into southern France and Spain. By this time the Franciscans had a definitive name—Friars Minor or Lesser Brethren, the brethren of the poor, the outcast and the unwanted. These were golden days for Francis. He preached a God who was Love enshrined in all his creatures. If there was a worm on a footpath he would move it to safety. In wintertime he would place warm wine and honey at the mouth of a beehive. He preached sermons to the sparrows, and composed the poem which opens all anthologies of Italian poetry, *The Praises of God's Creatures*:

Praised be Thou, my Lord, with all Thy creatures,
Especially our Sir Brother Sun,
Who maketh day, and Thou givest light through him
And he is beautiful and radiant with great splendor
Of Thee, Most High, he beareth significance.
Praised be Thou, my Lord, for Sister Moon and the stars
. . .
Praised be Thou, my Lord, for Brother Wind
. . .
Praised be Thou, my Lord, for Sister Water.

It became obvious to Francis that his ideals should be translated into terms that would make it possible for lay people to live the Franciscan way of life. This was to be called the Third Order (or the Tertiary Order of Minorites). The first plan for it seems to have been drafted in 1214, and the definitive version was formulated about 1221. It was as revolutionary in its effect on the life of the laity as Francis' First Rule had been for his friars. It took Christianity back to its beginnings. The would-be tertiary had to lay aside the sword and could take no oaths of allegiance to a feudal lord or commune. The abolition of the oath of allegiance

Above Gray Friars preaching
to shepherds. Based upon a
literal interpretation of the
gospels, their rule was
dedicated to the ideal of
poverty and work among the
lowly.

Left Francis preaching to the
birds, by Giotto. The
Franciscan spirit profoundly
influenced Christian art,
freeing it from its stylized
Byzantine forms.

to the sovereign lord struck at the very heart of feudalism and came to be a major factor in sowing the seeds of modern democracy. Thousands of pious laymen enrolled themselves in the Third Order—noblemen, townsmen, poets and peasants alike. Dante, himself a tertiary, was to devote a canto to Francis in the *Paradise* of the *Divine Comedy*.

From Giotto to Fra Angelico, the influence of Francis can be seen in the dawning art of Italy. The Franciscan spirit was to humanize Christian art, freeing it from its stylized Byzantine forms. The love for all created things inspired the painting of animals and landscapes and the development of new, more naturalistic techniques.

From 1217 until his death in 1226, Francis was to suffer in mind and body. The very popularity of his

movement was the cause of much of his distress. In a sense, his friars had outgrown their founder. Many did not know him; others resented him, especially the more lettered, who inevitably rose to eminence in the new Order. On the day of judgment, Francis was wont to say, all books will be thrown out of the windows. This matched badly with the aspirations of learned men. At the Chapter of 1219, the intelligentsia of the Order lobbied Cardinal Ugolino to force Francis into line with older established monastic orders. A saddened Francis decided to join the Fifth Crusade, hoping to die for Christ in Egypt.

He reached Damietta and told the crusaders that converting the Saracens was more important than cutting their throats. He walked through the Saracen lines singing the Twenty-third Psalm,

A fresco by Giotto showing St. Francis with the Sultan Saladin. During the Fifth Crusade, Francis walked through the lines of battle in an unsuccessful attempt to convert the Saracens.

charmed the Sultan, was given a horn to summon Christians to sermons, and escorted back to the Christian camp. Unsuccessful in his efforts to convert the Saracens, Francis went to Syria. There, tidings were brought to him in 1220 of a crisis in the Order.

During his absence a Chapter had been called by the more learned superiors who hoped to organize and institutionalize the simple Gospel life that Francis had always preached. Francis requested, and received from the Pope a Cardinal Protector, Cardinal Ugolino, who was to preside at the crucial Chapter of 1221.

At this Chapter Francis presented a written rule, full of the spirit of Rivo Torto. But the opposition, backed by Cardinal Ugolino, argued that it was not legally concise and it was referred back to Francis for redrafting. The final version was to be approved in 1223 by Pope Honorius III. There is little of Francis in it. It remains a canonical text. Omitted are most of the Gospel texts of the pristine rule with its wondrous prayer: "Let us love, honor and adore, serve, praise and bless, glorify, celebrate and thank ... the unchangeable God, invisible, incapable of error, ineffable, incomprehensible, unknowable, blessed, glorified, exalted, great, sublime, merciful, adorable, delectable, entirely and absolutely desirable for ever and ever, from whom proceeds all pardon, all grace and all glory ..."

Francis was disheartened; he felt his faith wavering and that his Order, over which he now had no control, was abandoning him. But nine months later, on the Monte della Verna in Tuscany, Francis had a vision. He prayed that he might share in the Passion of Christ; and when the image of Christ crucified had passed, he found that he bore the wounds of the Crucifixion on his hands, feet and side. Francis was the first to receive the stigmata. For him it was the ultimate seal of Christ's approval. To medieval man it seemed that Christ had come again in Francis, so that he became "the other Christ," and despite any changes in his Order the ideals of Francis were to continue to move and inspire common people.

Francis had only one more year to live. By this time he was almost blind and returned to the Porziuncola to await "Sister Death." He died at dusk on October 3, 1226. He died singing, in sackcloth and ashes in honor of the poor Christ, in the forty-fifth year of his age and the twenty-fifth of his conversion.

Two years after his death, St. Francis was canonized and his followers began to formulate plans for a great church at Assisi. Ironically, it was to be richly decorated by the greatest artists in Italy—to honor the apostle of poverty.

After the death of the first generation of friars, the Order suffered by its very popularity. A flow of donations made the rule of absolute poverty impossible to enforce. Life became more comfortable, and less dedicated men were drawn into the Order's ranks. Yet the friars still went among the

people, and until the end of the Middle Ages their influence remained greater than that of any other clerical group. The genius of Francis cannot be underestimated. By living a truly Christian life and by persuading men and women all over Europe to imitate him, he did more than anyone else to restore popular faith in the Church and to keep alive the ideals of a Church devoted to the good of all mankind.   ALAN KEENAN

Top The town of Assisi in Umbria. In the foreground is the basilica dedicated to St. Francis.

Above Francis appearing to the Friars Minor at Arles, a fresco that reflects the impact of the man on his age.

19

The Franciscans were only one of the orders of friars founded in the thirteenth century. Moved by impulses similar to Francis', a Spanish canon named Dominic Guzman (1170–1221) set up an order to preach against the Albigensian heresy. Like the Franciscans, the Dominicans (or Order of Preachers) were an "active" order; they were not expected to stay in monasteries but were supposed to preach the Gospel and to set an example by their holy lives. Unlike the Franciscans, however, they were expected to study; they were the first religious order to replace manual labor, which St. Benedict's rule laid down as an

A Franciscan friar.

integral part of the religious life, by intellectual labor. Although never as popular as the Franciscans, the Dominican Order spread rapidly throughout Europe. Because of the Order's reputation for orthodoxy and learning, Dominicans were usually chosen to act as inquisitors in heresy trials. Their vigorous approach to heresy and heretics soon caused them to

be known as *Domini canes* (the hounds of the Lord) rather than *Dominicanes*.

There were other orders of friars, and some still survive. The Carmelites were founded in the twelfth century as an order of hermits with headquarters on Mount Carmel near Haifa. But, after the loss of Palestine, the order was refounded as an order of friars. The Augustinian friars were founded in an attempt to control the lives of hermits in central Italy. Other smaller orders, such as the Trinity Friars and the Crutched (or Crossed) Friars, existed also.

Albigensian Crusade

One of the most serious features of life in the late twelfth century in the eyes of the Church was the growth of organized heresy. Heretics had often been condemned in the early Middle Ages; but these isolated individuals presented little threat to the Church. The Albigensians (named after the city of Albi on the Tarn River in southern France) were very different; their ideas bore some resemblance to the Manichean heresy, which had been attacked by early Christian theologians, notably St. Augustine. The immediate source of Albigensian ideas was, however, probably the Bogomil sect, an heretical group, that flourished in Bulgaria and Yugoslavia.

The Albigensians believed that good and evil were two warring principles, that all matter was created by the evil principle, and that all spirit was created by the good principle. They classified believers into two groups: "the perfect" and other "believers." Believers lived a normal life but were expected to receive the *consolamentum* (an act of absolution that could be performed only once in a lifetime) before their death. The *consolamentum* represented a baptism by the Holy Spirit, and after it they were expected to live the life of the perfect, which meant that they must live as vegetarians and abandon marriage, in order to avoid contact with the evil material world. They were even urged to starve themselves to death.

As early as 1022 thirteen priests had been condemned at a council at Orléans for holding ideas such

as these. Later councils defined Catholic doctrine to exclude those who regarded themselves as perfect, or pure (*cathari*), but in the late twelfth century the ideas took a firm hold in Provence in the south of France. The sharp contrast between the lives of the perfect and of the local clergy helped spread the heresy. When Raymond VI, Count of Toulouse, lent his support to the movement, the Church was forced to do more than condemn it.

After his accession to the papacy in 1198, Innocent III tried to convert the Albigensians by sending missionaries, a policy that met with only limited success. He sent a legate, Peter of Castelnau, to coordinate his missionary program, but Peter was murdered in 1208, and Innocent decided to apply the idea of a crusade to the Albigensian heretics, whom he regarded as "worse than the Saracens." Landhungry men from the north of France joined the crusade, and Philip Augustus saw an opportunity to restore royal rule in the south of France. The crusade quickly degenerated into a war of conquest. Raymond and his brother-in-law, King Peter of Aragon, were unable to defend the region. The leader of the crusade, Simon de Montfort, gained control over most of the area, but after Simon's death in 1218, Raymond's forces recovered. Ultimately both sides ceded most of the land to the kingdom of France. The Albigensian heresy faded gradually away during the thirteenth and fourteenth centuries.

St. Dominic burning the books of the Albigensians.

The fortified cathedral at Albi, built immediately after the crusade.

The Greeks

The fall of Constantinople to the crusaders in 1204 did not destroy Byzantine civilization. In a sense it extended it. Greek manuscripts and treasures were taken to Venice, Rome and other Western cities. There was an increasing interest in Greek theology in the West. The Latin kingdoms that were set up in the former empire were influenced by Greek ideas of kingship. There were a number of these states: Count Baldwin of Flanders became Latin Emperor at Constantinople; there was a kingdom of Thessalonica, and a number of principalities and duchies in Greece; Venice acquired many of the Greek islands. The fragmentation of the empire went further. With the disappearance of the authority of the Byzantine emperor many Greek nobles became independent rulers. Descendants of the Comneni set up an empire at Trebizond (Trabzon) and a despotate in Epirus. Most important, Theodore Lascaris, nephew of a former emperor, was crowned emperor in Nicaea in 1206. Most of the surviving courtiers and higher clergy accepted him.

From the first it was obvious that the Latin Empire could not survive. Help from the West was unlikely. The Bulgarians and Serbians threatened the northern frontier and inflicted a crushing defeat on Baldwin at Adrianople (Edirne) in 1205. Meanwhile Theodore (1205–22) and his successor John (1222–54) began to conquer the Aegean islands and suppressed the despotate of Epirus. In 1261 the city of Constantinople fell to the Greeks who were led by the Emperor Michael Paleologus. The restored empire, however, never became more than a shadow of its former self.

d sword

Mongol expansion

The expansion of the Mongol empire took place at a time of change throughout Asia. Hindu India was threatened by the Moslem state of Ghor (in modern Afghanistan), which began sending raiding parties into the principalities of northern India in 1191. The Moslems were held back for a time by Prithvi Raj Rahtor, who gathered an army from all the northern states. But the Hindu alliance failed to hold together, and Prithvi Raj's weakened army was beaten. The whole of northern India was quickly conquered by the armies of Mohammed of Ghor. Mohammed's viceroy in Delhi, Kutbuddin Aibak, soon became the effective ruler of Moslem India; after Mohammed's assassination in 1206, he claimed the title of sultan of Delhi. But Kutbuddin himself was assassinated in 1211. The existence of the sultanate was only formally recognized by the caliph in 1226, by which time Kutbuddin's successor, Iltutmish, who died in 1236, had imposed firm Moslem control

throughout his dominions. It was largely because of Iltutmish's strength that the Mongols invaded Russia; Genghis Khan's army was thwarted in its attempts to invade Delhi and went across Asia as far as the Dnieper instead.

In Japan, too, the early thirteenth century was a period of change. From the tenth century Japanese history had been dominated by a feud between two great feudal clans, the Taira and the Minamoto. This ended in 1185 with the victory of the Minamoto, who were thus free to dominate the politically weak Fujiwara regents. Yorimoto, the leader of the Minamoto, was given the title *Seii-Tai-Shōgun* (Field Marshal who Quells the Barbarians)— although he was in fact more concerned with quelling rival groups who might threaten his clan's ambitions. The period of the civil war had led to the growth of an ideal known as "the way of the horse and the bow," which was not dissimilar to Western chivalric ideas. This was the basis of the later "way of the warrior" (*bushido*). The value of military relationships was emphasized. This influenced the development of a

"feudal" structure, built on land ownership and the relationship between a military leader and his men.

The death of Yorimoto in 1199 left a political vacuum, which his sons proved unable to fill. Instead the Hojo family seized the regency in 1205. This was the beginning of over half a century of peace, which was only punctuated by occasional unsuccessful rebellions and invasions. Despite the continued existence of moribund political institutions, the Hojo were able to govern the whole community. In China the course of history was to be very different; the Mongol invasions provided a new factor.

England: a time of tribulation

Richard 1 (the Lion-Heart), who had died in 1199, had shown more interest in the heavenly crown that he might earn by fighting Saladin than in the crown of his earthly kingdom. He had totally neglected the government of his country. Richard's problems had been increased by the disloyalty of his brother, John Lackland. After Richard's death, John seized the English crown, despite the opposition of his nephew, Arthur, who had the support of the French king, Philip Augustus. John succeeded in capturing Arthur and had him killed, but his concentration on establishing his authority in England left Philip Augustus free to attack Normandy, which

was lost to England in 1204. Even at home John's position was weak. Despite their feudal obligations, the northern nobles refused to help in any attempt to recover Normandy. The monks of Canterbury insisted, with the support of Innocent III, on their right to elect a new archbishop of Canterbury after the death of Hubert Walter in 1205. Although the monks were forced to leave England, they were able to ensure the election of their nominee, Stephen Langton. Meanwhile the King enjoyed the revenues of the archbishopric also. These additional funds were of great value to John in his efforts to recover lost ground in Scotland, Ireland and Wales. In 1208 his revenues were further increased. Innocent III, furious at John's treatment of the archbishop, placed England under an interdict, to which John replied by seizing clerical property.

But John had made too many enemies. By 1212 he had no allies: in England the barons refused help; the Welsh were in revolt; Innocent, having no other weapons left, was planning his deposition; Philip Augustus was planning an invasion. John decided that ideological defeat was less serious than military disaster. He surrendered his kingdom to the papacy. By doing so he assured himself of papal support. He gathered an army, which he sent to France in 1214 to forestall Philip's invasion. The problem of his unruly barons, however, remained.

Minamoto Yoritomo, the first permanent shōgun.

King John hunting stag.

Agreement at Runnymede

In the summer of 1215 King John of England affixed his seal to Magna Carta, a crude bill of rights drawn up by his rebellious barons, and thus unwittingly hastened the decline of omnipotent, "divine-right" monarchs not only in England but in Europe as well. The "firm peace" that was reached at Runnymede proved to be an enduring one : the Great Charter survived subsequent civil wars, numerous rewritings and even annulment by the Pope. In ensuing generations, Magna Carta was reinterpreted and expanded to the point where it became the "irrepealable fundamental statute" of English law. And five and a half centuries later the personal liberties guaranteed by the Charter served as the basis for the Bill of Rights of the United States Constitution.

On June 15, 1215, a remarkable confrontation took place at Runnymede, a meadow located a mile or so to the west of the Thames-side town of Staines and twenty miles southwest of London. This unusual assembly, a formal meeting between King John of England and a party of his subjects who had been in rebellion since the beginning of May, had been called to settle the dispute concerning the King's rule and the general conduct of the government. As such, the gathering at Runnymede was unprecedented in English history.

When the antagonists met on June 15, the broad terms of agreement had already been settled through official envoys. The confrontation at Runnymede was the final stage of a long and complex series of negotiations begun by representatives of the beleaguered King and his rebellious barons on May 25, 1215. On June 19, a final settlement, described in the records of the meeting as a "firm peace," was finally reached.

Nonetheless, King John and his opponents continued to meet at Runnymede through June 23, for the King was compelled to fulfill immediately some of the concessions he had promised. From June 15 to 23, therefore, John and the rebel lords rode out to Runnymede daily; the King and his supporters from his castle at Windsor, the rebel party from the town of Staines.

The rebel party, made up of a group of barons and their supporters, was dominated by England's most powerful landowners, who held title to their estates in return for military and other forms of feudal service to the King. The final settlement therefore assumed feudal characteristics that now seem antiquated and inadequate: the rebels renewed their homage and fealty to the King; the King and his leading supporters swore a solemn oath to observe the terms of the settlement; and the execution of the agreement was secured by a treaty that placed the barons in charge of London, the capital of the realm. The terms of the settlement were written in a charter, one that came to be known, because of its large size,

as Magna Carta, or the Great Charter.

At the time, the charter form seemed the most suitable vehicle for the terms of peace. Charters were frequently used in the early 1200s to record grants of land, rights or privileges; they were the most solemn and formal documents available for such transactions. In 1215 England had no statute laws and but a rudimentary concept of legislation. Hence this part of the settlement took the form of a solemn concession, an apparently voluntary act of self-restraint, whereby John promised to right the wrongs alleged against him and to limit both his own and his successors' actions in the future. Magna Carta was traditional and familiar in form, a fact that seemed to give it strength and permanence.

King John did not actually affix his signature to the Charter; instead it was sealed with the impression of the Great Seal and witnessed by the Archbishop of Canterbury and other great men. The document, written in Latin and which later came to be divided into some sixty numbered chapters, originally was written without such aids to reference and ranged haphazardly over most aspects of government.

First, Magna Carta sought to regulate the feudal relationships between the Crown and its immediate tenants by laying down rules about payments due on the succession to estates, about the custody of wards and their lands, and about the marriages of heiresses. Second, it provided for regular justice in central and local courts and sought to ensure that the King would only act against his subjects by recognized legal procedure. The most famous and most significant chapter of Magna Carta, Number 39, states:

> No free man shall be taken or imprisoned or deprived or outlawed or exiled or in any way ruined . . . except by the lawful judgment of his peers or by the law of the land.

Third, the Charter attempted to regulate the King's financial power, seeking to control his right to tax and the manner in which his officers collected debts or sought to increase royal revenues. Fourth, it demanded that the King restore rights and property

John of England, nicknamed Lackland and Softsword. He lost the English possessions north of the Loire to Philip II of France.

Opposite King John, from his tomb at Worcester Cathedral.

Henry III and later successors of John reissued Magna Carta.

Chateau Gaillard, a great English stronghold in France, which John lost to Philip Augustus of France.

reign (1189–99) fighting abroad, John (1199–1216) was largely resident in England, and was personally responsible for his government. John was an active and inventive monarch, but he was faced with several major problems. The Continental empire accumulated by his father, Henry II (1151–89), was breaking up; Normandy, England's remaining Continental holding, had fallen to the French in 1204.

John responded to his problems with energetic defiance, mustering all the resources of his realm for military and diplomatic victory on the Continent; war plans and war finance dominated his policies. He achieved a settlement with the Pope in 1213, but failed in a great counterattack against King Philip of France in 1214. This defeat led immediately to the outbreak of a rebellion which had been developing in England for some time. The opposition exploited the King's failures abroad—soon after the loss of Normandy he was nicknamed John Softsword—but it fed on the resentment produced by his policies at home. This welling discontent was caused by the King's financial demands, by his exploitation of feudal relationships for his own political and financial interests, and by his increasing readiness to inject political and personal considerations into his exercise of justice. John's subjects were further outraged by his use of patronage, which sharply distinguished those in from those out of favor, and by his reliance on a number of skilled foreign advisers who came to England from the lost lands on the Continent and enjoyed increasing influence and reward as sheriffs, custodians of castles and husbands of native heiresses.

Magna Carta dealt with all these injustices and inequities, but it was not concerned with them alone. King John's transgressions were not novel, and many of the grievances that the Charter dealt with considerably antedated John's reign. Richard I, the King's brother, and Henry II, their father, had also found the task of defending England's Continental possessions to be demanding and expensive; they too had been forced to muster armies and levy heavy taxes. Nor were John's policies really new. He and many of his most important officials had been brought up in the administrative traditions of Henry II's court, and for the most part they simply adhered to those traditions.

that he had seized or acquired by unjust agreements. Fifth, it arranged for the election in every county of juries of knights who were to inquire into the activities of the sheriffs and other local agents of the Crown. Finally, the Great Charter established a body of twenty-five barons—originally twenty-four of the rebel leaders and the Mayor of London—who were to hear and adjudicate complaints and claims against the King under the terms of the Charter.

In all, Magna Carta was a radical, indeed a revolutionary document. "Why," King John is purported to have asked, "do they not demand my kingdom?" The Charter had been inspired by deep and bitterly felt grievances, focused for the most part on King John himself. Unlike his brother and predecessor, Richard I, who spent most of his brief

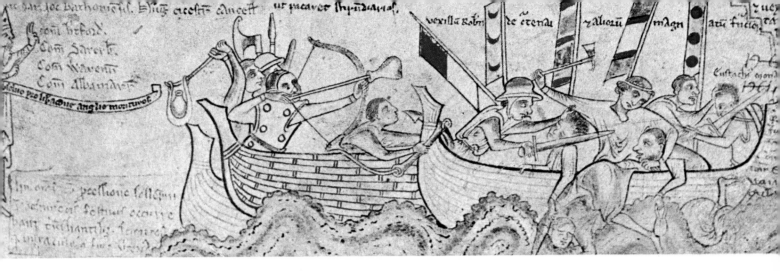

The political theories and assumptions that the Charter embodied were likewise issues of long standing. In the course of the twelfth century men had become increasingly familiar with two notions, both of which they owed in large measure to the increasing law and order provided by the Crown. One assumption derived from a growing readiness to accept and expect regular justice according to routine procedures in a court of law; from that notion emerged the idea of an established custom of the realm. The other concept derived from the fact that kings sold, and subjects bought, rights and privileges. Local communities—first towns and then counties—had rapidly acquired privileges in this way, possessing and defending them in common, and chartered liberties held by individuals or groups had become common features of English feudal society. Magna Carta, which sought to equate the custom of the realm with the rights of all free men, summarized both these trends. English law and political thought were profoundly affected by the Charter, which equated law with liberties and ultimately law with liberty.

The rebellion of 1215 marked a new departure. It was not simply another example of feudal anarchy, but rather a political and legal program, a statement of general rather than individual aims. As the crisis deepened in the early months of 1215, the argument turned increasingly on defining the customs of the realm, and upon erecting a largely fictitious "ancient custom" to challenge the innovations of Henry II and his sons. Out of these arguments grew a list of preliminary demands, which the rebellious nobles submitted to their king in April. John failed to meet the baronial demands, and in May of 1215, the barons went to war. On May 17, the rebels seized London, and the King was forced to open negotiations at Runnymede.

However, the June settlement was only a temporary one. On the one hand, it was a compromise that failed to satisfy the most intransigent of the King's opponents; on the other, it was equally unacceptable to the King himself. In time, inquiries into local government provoked outbreaks of lawlessness. The restoration of lands and privileges to individuals revealed a number of irreconcilable cases soluble only by force of arms. By September the country was drifting into a new civil war. The Charter itself provided the King with a rationale for attack, for although its text asserted that the Charter

had been freely granted, the supporters of the document knew that their demands had been exacted by force. On these grounds, Pope Innocent III, to whom both parties had appealed for arbitration, annulled Magna Carta on August 24, 1215. The civil war that ensued was a bitter affair that continued for a year after John's death in October, 1216. Although the war ultimately involved the French, Magna Carta remained the central issue. Peace was secured only by reissuing the Charter in November, 1216, and November, 1217. These versions owed a great deal to the approval of the Pope and his agents in England. They omitted many of the purely temporary sections of the Charter of 1215 and abandoned the court of twenty-five barons and many of the provisions concerned with financial administration. With John dead and the new king, Henry III—a boy of nine at his accession—less of a threat to the barons' power, these chapters were no longer as essential. It was the 1217 version, slightly amended in 1225, that was incorporated into the law of the land. The 1217 and 1225 versions of the Great Charter were accompanied by a Charter of the Forest specifically concerned with the administration of the royal forests. In subsequent confirmation the two were usually associated.

The Charter's transformation was both curious and unique. Originally, Magna Carta was simply part of a settlement to end a civil war; it was in force only during the summer months of 1215, until its annulment by Pope Innocent. Yet it became, in the words of the great legal historian, F. W. Maitland, "the nearest approach to an irrepealable fundamental statute that England has ever had"; nine of its chapters still stand on the statute book. This transition from peace treaty to "fundamental statute" makes Magna Carta significant.

England was not alone in having such a charter of liberties; they were common features of European politics in the thirteenth and fourteenth centuries. Hungary had the Golden Bull (1222); Germany had both the Confederation with the Ecclesiastical Princes (1220) and the Statute in Favor of the Princes (1232); Aragon, the General Privilege (1283) and the Privilege of the Union (1287); and France, the charters of privileges of Normandy, Burgundy and other provinces (1315). All these concessions sprang from situations analogous to that of England in 1215: war, financial pressure, harsh administration and discontent. No contemporary

A battle at sea between the English and the French.

King John; Magna Carta attacked his power.

The sufferings of prisoners arrested without trial. This was banned by Magna Carta.

would have selected the English Magna Carta as the one most likely to survive, and yet it did while the other charters were soon defunct.

Magna Carta survived and flourished because it became inextricably linked with the processes of English government and political life. As early as 1215, careful measures were taken to ensure its full publication—a copy was sent to each shire, and the sheriff was ordered to read it out in the county court. This procedure was repeated in 1216, 1217, 1225 and again in 1253. As time passed, even greater emphasis was given to publication: a twice yearly reading in the county courts became law in 1265, a twice yearly reading in the cathedrals followed in 1297, and a reading four times a year in the county courts was decreed in 1300. On this last occasion, English was specified as the appropriate language, apparently for the first time. As a result, the Charter was well known, and copies proliferated in monastic or cathedral archives, in legal text books, and even in the hands of the knights who did much of the work of the county courts.

However, the story of the Charter did not end with the feudal politics and law of the thirteenth century. Its longer survival depended on two features of the original document that were preserved in all subsequent reissues: first, the Charter was a grant in perpetuity intended to last for all time; and second, it stated broad general procedures and principles rather than detailed and transitory points of law. Thus each generation could reinterpret the Charter to fit new circumstances. Between 1331 and 1363 Parliament passed six statutory interpretations of the famous Chapter 39, which developed it in directions unimagined in 1215. These interpretations equated the "lawful judgment of peers" with trial by jury, a process that scarcely existed in thirteenth-century England; they identified the "law of the land" with "due process of law," a phrase that would have been all but incomprehensible in 1215; and they replaced the words "no free man" of the 1215 version with "no man whatsoever estate or condition he may be," a change that extended Magna Carta's protection to the villeins, or the majority of the population, who were thus brought within the scope of a provision from which they had been hitherto excluded.

Such reinterpretation became common and was extended to other chapters, particularly in the seventeenth century. Even in contemporary times, lawyers have appealed to the chapter of Magna Carta that states that widows are to have their dower and marriage portion without delay in order to secure the prompt payment of a widow's pension, and to the chapter that permits free entry and exit from the realm in order to challenge the requirement of a passport for foreign travel.

Lawyers have been encouraged in this practice by the peculiar prominence that Magna Carta has acquired in English common law. The Charter was always given pride of place as the first item in the printed collection of statues published in the sixteenth century, and by the late thirteenth century— at a time when men were first becoming acquainted with the notion of statute law—Magna Carta already figured prominently in the manuscript collections of statutes that lawyers were then beginning to compile as books of reference. In a sense, Magna Carta became the origin of statute law. In 1215 this was unintended, at least by the rebel barons; their legal theory did not carry them beyond the idea of chartered privileges. Nevertheless, the 1215 charter contains a number of provisions concerned with the detailed administration of the law that do not seem to have been part of the rebels' demands, and which were probably inserted by the lawyers of the Crown simply in order to reform existing laws. The reissues of 1216 and 1217—particularly the latter—contain additional and more important material of the same kind, concerned with the conveying of land and the sessions of local courts. Much of the Charter of the Forest is made up of similar detailed regulations. Each of these successive documents show progressively better drafting, and all are marked improvements as legal drafts on the 1215 petition,

Philip Augustus unhorsed at the Battle of Bouvines (1214) —one of the series of battles in the endemic war between France and England.

known as the Articles of the Barons, in which the King's opponents first stated their demands.

These revisions of the original Charter were the work of men experienced in the administration of the courts, who used the Charter as a means of legal reform. Hence, Magna Carta was both a program of rebellion and a statement of law. The former characteristic was the more prominent in 1215, the latter in the revisions of 1217 and 1225. The former characteristic led to the demand for its confirmation in later crises; the latter made it a starting point for a growing body of legislation in the thirteenth century. The Provisions of Merton of 1236, the Statute of Marlborough of 1267, and the Statutes of Westminster of 1275 and 1285 were all in part concerned with points of law first formulated in Magna Carta, and as a result the Charter has become embedded in English history as a fundamental law. In the constitutional conflicts of the seventeenth century, Magna Carta was the obvious weapon to use in defending Parliament and the common law courts against the prerogative of the Stuart kings. "I shall be very glad to see," Sir Benjamin Rudyard declaimed in a Commons debate on the Petition of Right in 1628, "that old, decrepit Law Magna Carta which hath been kept so long, and lien bed-rid, as it were, I shall be glad to see it walk abroad again with new vigour and lustre..."

In the hands of Sir Edward Coke, first the Chief Justice and then the bitter constitutional opponent of the Stuarts, the Great Charter was used to attack royal monopolies, prerogative taxation and the prerogative court of the Star Chamber. All these Coke denounced as injurious to the freedom of the individual or to established judicial process. Others used the Charter to justify the principle of habeas corpus and the claim, advanced in the Petition of Right, that there should be "no arrest without cause shown." Coke was the first to equate the "liberties" of the Charter with the liberty of the individual, and it was the legal writings of Coke that carried the Charter to North America and planted the principles that he had found in Chapter 39 in the constitutions of the early colonies and ultimately of the United States. By this time, the Charter was considerably altered; the feudal liberties of the thirteenth century had given way to liberty as conceived by Coke and the American Founding Fathers, but some of the characteristics of the original charter still remained. Coke and his fellows regarded Magna Carta as a statement of fundamental, incontravertible law which itself went back beyond 1215 to the days before the Norman conquest of England. The men of 1215 had made no claim as bold and precise as that, although they had maintained, somewhat falsely, that their program was but a statement of ancient custom. Indeed, it was their myth that provided the foundation for Coke's modern legal structure— which continues to influence much of British, and American, legal thought today.   J. C. HOLT

Magna Carta; an attempt by the barons to increase their power at the expense of the King became in time the foundation stone of constitutional liberty.

27

INNOCENTI

PP III

✠ INNOCENTIVS EPS SERVVS SERVORV̄ DĪ. DILECTIS FIL[
SPECV̄ BEATI BENEDICTI REGLARE VITĀ SERVANTIBVS JN Ṗ
VIRTVTV̄ NVLLV̄ MAGIS EST MEDVLLATV̄. QVĀ ꝙ OFFERTVR A
CARITATIS. HOC IGĪT ATTENDENTES. CV̄ OLI CAVSA DEVOTIONIS ACCE
VR̄E TVE BEATVS BENEDICT̄ SVE CONVERSIONIS PRIMORDIO CŌSECRAVIT. E

Innocent III's Lateran Council

The Fourth Lateran Council, the largest ecumenical council ever held in the West, was the crowning achievement of Innocent III's pontificate. The strong-willed Innocent believed that things of the spirit take preeminence over corporeal things and that the Church rules the spirit while earthly monarchs rule only the body, therefore, all earthly rulers must defer to the Pope. His purposes in calling a council were the restoration of the spirit of worship, the reassertion of the law of the Church and the recovery of the Christian holy places in Jerusalem. The laws and reforms that resulted from the Fourth Lateran Council were to alter the Church profoundly.

In November, 1215, there assembled in the basilica of St. John Lateran at Rome seventy-one archbishops, over four hundred bishops, eight hundred abbots and priors, and numerous envoys from the secular heads of Christendom. They were obeying a summons by Pope Innocent III to attend an ecumenical council—their objective was the reform of the Church and the recovery of the holy places in Jerusalem. The Fourth Lateran Council, the largest ever held in the West, was to be the crowning achievement of this greatest of medieval popes.

At the time, Christendom was less threatened by external pressures. Though the Moors were still at Cordova and across the Tagus from Lisbon, danger from Saracens, Norsemen or Tartars was a thing of the past. Instead the Church faced a different threat—from within its own ranks. A new commercial spirit was rising and towns were growing. With a broader-based prosperity, people were inclining to temporal rather than spiritual pursuits. A less quiescent laity became increasingly critical of the conduct of the clergy, and heresies found fertile ground. In the twelfth century, for example, the Church had been severely weakened by disputes over the buying and selling of clerical appointments and the inroads made by noble families on ecclesiastical property. But perhaps the most serious threat to the supremacy of the papacy was the growing allegiance of the laity to the secular state.

By calling a council, Innocent wanted to restore the spirit of worship, to reassert the law of the Church and to direct energies toward the overthrow of Islam in the East, where from previous crusades there remained scattered Christian castles and islands but no cohesive kingdom.

So large an assembly was calculated to show to the world the enhanced role of the papacy that Innocent wished to uphold. For him the position meant that he was the viceregent of God in a united Christendom and thus Christendom's ultimate head. He proclaimed: "No king can reign rightly unless he devoutly serves Christ's vicar. . . . The priesthood is the sun, and the monarchy the moon. Kings rule over their respective kingdoms, but Peter rules over the whole earth. . . . The Lord gave Peter the rule not only over the universal Church, but also over the whole world."

Though he declared that he did not wish to rule Europe directly—that was the duty of secular rulers—it was clear that the position he took would lead to an immense increase in appeals to the Pope for greater intervention on his part. The occasion of a large gathering at the Lateran stimulated such an increase, to the indignation of the imperialists. For there had also been canon lawyers who argued in the imperial interest that the emperor was typified by the Old Testament figure of Melchisedech, in whom royalty and priesthood were combined. If what they said was true, an emperor should have been presiding at the Lateran over the Council. But, for the moment, in the struggle between empire and papacy, the latter was stronger.

Innocent was the fourth and youngest child of Count Trasimond of Segni. With three uncles who were cardinals (one reigned as Pope Clement III from 1187 to 1191), he had every inducement to devote himself to the Church. From his training in canon law he had a clear idea of what the Church ought to be, and he was a competent organizer. A product of the universities of Paris and Bologna, he had experienced the dialectics of the new Aristotelianism in the one, and the enthusiasm for the rediscovered Roman civil law in the other. In 1198, at the early age of thirty-seven, Innocent was elected Pope. He was the logical choice, having distinguished himself as an administrator and lawyer.

Innocent was a strong Pope. He was determined to reassert the leadership of the papacy, making it the arbiter in every important dispute. He had accepted the claims of Otto of Brunswick to be

Gold Augustalis minted by Frederick II of Sicily. His coronation by Innocent III set the precedent for papal responsibility in the choice of emperor.

Opposite Pope Innocent III. He convened the Fourth Lateran Council which reformed the Church, settled disputed points of doctrine and called the Fifth Crusade into being.

Scenes of monastic life. The Lateran Council tightened control of religious orders through a form of chapter government and by granting bishops powers of supervision.

century each abbey had been a law unto itself, a form of chapter government was instituted in each province. The chapter had to appoint visitors to inspect the abbeys and correct abuses. Beyond this, the Council gave to the bishops the power and duty to visit abbeys, in theory annually; the deposition of abbots was entrusted to bishops, not to the visitors from the chapter. What this could mean may be seen in the fact that Grosseteste, the famous Bishop of Lincoln, deposed eleven heads of houses in one year.

The choice of good bishops was of the greatest importance in the eyes of Innocent III, for it ensured the progress and independence of the Church. The Council drew up rules for the election of bishops, and these are still in force for a papal election. No bishopric was to remain vacant for more than three months; anyone accepting an election carried out by abuse of secular power disqualified himself for future advancement. The rules for elections were extended to abbeys and even to nunneries.

The Council ordered archbishops to hold their own provincial councils once a year in order to look to the reform of the clergy. At such annual meetings they were to read over the Lateran statutes and discuss their observance, making provision for the correction of abuses. Each bishop was required to hold an annual synod and communicate to his clergy what the provincial council had decided. The chain of command was thus instituted, but it took time for it to come alive. Recalcitrant human nature may have resisted the reforming zeal of Innocent, but it must be admitted that a considerable amount of legislation from diocesan synods came about after the Lateran Council.

The Council prohibited bishops from acting as secular judges, but in England at least, they remained in demand for that work. Henry III (1216–72) had, at different times, the bishops of Durham, Chichester and Worcester as his chancellor, and abbots acted as itinerant justices, to the great indignation of Grosseteste, Bishop of Lincoln.

Some bishops kept secular jurisdiction within their dioceses, such as the prince-bishops of Durham and Liège, but in general the decision of the Council, coupled with the growth of canon law and its separation from the civil law, led to greater opportunities for the nonclerical administrator and encouraged the growth of a separate administration dependent only on the monarch. What is more, the practice of appointing two laymen as "keepers" of a diocese on the death of the bishop, a practice enforced in England by regalian right, gave scope to many royal clerks with ambition. The Lateran Council strove to curtail the length of vacancies to bishoprics, but royal greed found ways of holding up appointments and meanwhile drawing off episcopal revenues. The Council also forbade priests to officiate at inquiries or other legal proceedings, thus encouraging more equitable methods of trial.

A priest elevating the Host. Transubstantiation was defined by the Council and made into an article of faith.

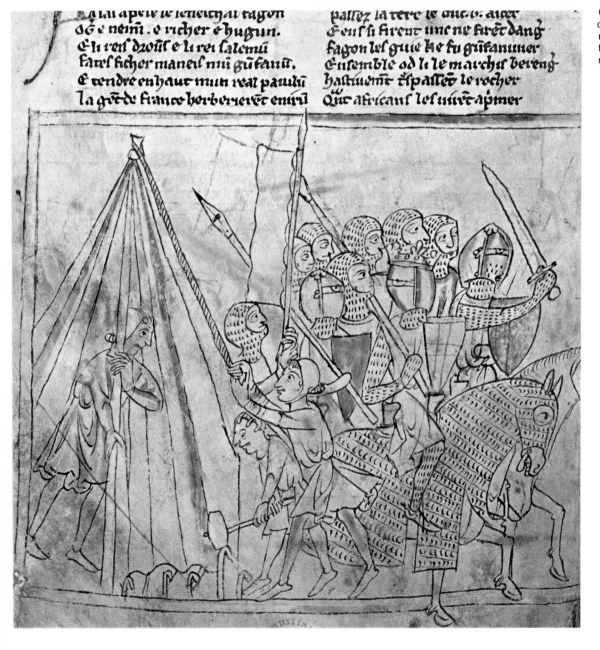

On crusade. Anxious lest the crusading ideal lapse, Innocent made extensive preparations for the Fifth Crusade, but did not live to see it launched.

The final legislation of the Council was concerned with the Fifth Crusade, announced to start on June 1, 1217. What is said to be the first tax on income was imposed on the clergy for three years at a rate of five per cent, while the Pope and cardinals taxed themselves at ten per cent. All trading in munitions of war with the Saracens was forbidden, and Christian princes were told to keep the peace among themselves for four years. Volunteers for the crusade were promised a moratorium on all their debts for the duration of the war, and were assured that while they were absent their property would be under the protection of the Church. One of those who took the Cross in 1215 was the Emperor Frederick II, then aged twenty-one.

Innocent was not canonized after his death in 1216, but he left his mark on the Church. His Council had made into law what had often been

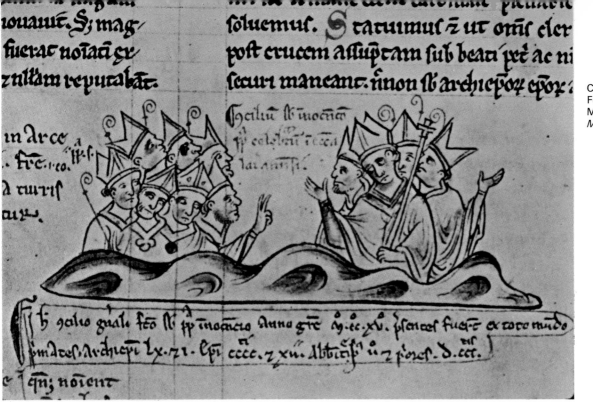

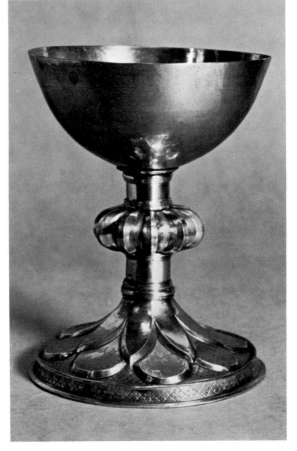

A thirteenth-century sacramental chalice.

preached without sanction in preceding years, and it started a movement of reform in monasteries whose impetus was felt for a century. No record survives of the way in which conciliar drafts were transformed by debate, but their wording often corresponds to what Innocent had written in letters prior to the Council.

There was a streak of melancholy in Innocent's character, evidenced by the tone of his only considerable book of spiritual counsel, *De contemptu mundi*, and by his opening speech at the Council. In the speech he compared himself to King Josiah, who called for religious reforms in the eighteenth year of his reign; and shortly thereafter was killed in battle. Innocent seems to have sensed that he would not live through the crusade he planned— and indeed he died soon after the Council dispersed in 1216.

The Pope loved beauty and order in worship, and his private chapel at the Lateran must have made its own impression on the gathered bishops. He knew that laws depend on the men who carry them out, and the choice of scholar-bishops and reforming bishops, for which he is noted, made the Council he had fostered into a far-reaching instrument of reform.

Without the Lateran Council the great forward movement of the Church that came with the friars would not have been possible. To have two large cohorts of fervent volunteers working alongside the local clergy and bishops inevitably meant that there would be rivalries, but these would have been infinitely worse had there not been a system of canon law to provide solutions. Such a system hardly existed before the Council went to work. The century that followed the Council was freer from major calamities than the preceding centuries since 800. The rise of universities, the flourishing of the law schools, the great buildings, all betoken a new spirit of optimism that was abroad. Innocent III had done his best to translate it into the legislation of the Church. Without the Council the optimism of the times would have been lost in Joachimite fantasies of an approaching millennium; as it was, the crusade sailed as planned (though Innocent had died by then), and the friars went from strength to strength in the new seats of European learning.   JOSEPH CREHAN

Genghis Khan Conquers North China

The Great Wall of China was built to protect the rich alluvial farmlands of the north from the marauding nomads of Asia's barren steppes. But not even the Great Wall could stem the tide of a Mongol advance once the "barbarians" had united under a strong leader. Genghis Khan started by bringing together all the Mongol peoples; by the time he was finished, his heirs were in possession of an empire stretching from China to the Caucasus, and from the far north to the Himalayas.

Genghis Khan proclaiming to the people of Bokhara that heaven has sent him to punish them. He firmly believed in his mission to conquer the world.

Opposite Genghis Khan fighting the Chinese in a mountain pass. He breached the Great Wall and shattered the Chinese myth of invulnerability.

The life of Genghis Khan and the devastating success of the Mongol conquests are intertwined with legend and exaggeration. It was said that Mongol horses were so huge that they ate branches from trees, and that ladders were needed to mount them. Genghis Khan himself was regarded by his foes as a hell-sent monster who led an army so vast that none could withstand its might. In reality, however, he emerges as a highly skilled politician and the leader of an efficient but relatively small fighting force. Within a generation he rose from poor circumstances to rule a nation, and left to his heirs an empire stretching from China to the Caucasus, and from the far north to the Himalayas.

Physically, the Mongols he led were almost indistinguishable from the Chinese, having a similar flat facial appearance, thick skin with few pores and sweat glands, and other features that made them well suited to the sub-zero temperatures of the steppe winter. Culturally, however, the Mongols and the Chinese were worlds apart. The Mongol language belongs to the Altaic group, which includes Turkish and is quite unrelated to Chinese. No written form of their language existed, and consequently the Mongols had no literature or recorded history. In sharp contrast to their sophisticated Chinese neighbors, the Mongol way of life was extremely primitive. Though tolerant and intrigued with other religions, they practised a form of crude Shamanism.

In the harsh, barren Asian steppes agriculture was virtually unknown, and the Mongols' meager existence depended on rearing cattle and sheep which they followed seasonally from pasture to pasture. Since nomadism precludes urban development, they had no cities. They had little material wealth other than their tents and domestic equipment, and no developed art forms. To control and protect their herds, they became expert horsemen and skillful warriors. Riding their hardy little ponies, Mongol children grew up in the saddle and became expert archers. The annual tribal hunt was organized like a military operation, and continual

blood feuds between rival tribes show that the Mongols were almost by instinct a warlike people. Both men and mounts were seemingly resilient to cold, hunger and thirst, and one reads time and time again of the incredible endurance of Mongol warriors—a fact that was repeatedly underestimated by their enemies.

In contrast, the settled population of the rich alluvial plains of North China had everything the Mongols lacked—agriculture, trade routes, towns and wealth. From early times onward they were a natural and easy target for Mongol raids. Even before the birth of Christ, the nomads represented so great a threat as to compel the Chinese to build at colossal expense in terms of materials and manpower, the 1,684-mile Great Wall. The Wall was diligently maintained and was fairly effective in keeping back nomad marauders for more than one thousand years.

On occasion, however, the Wall was breached. At the end of the T'ang period (A.D. 618–907), the Khitan, a people of Mongol ancestry, advanced into North China and established a dynasty known to the Chinese as the Liao. Then, from the woodlands of Manchuria in the northeast, a more sedentary race called the Jürchen invaded and conquered the Liao lands, founding in 1122 the Chin, or "Golden," dynasty, and setting up their capital in what is now called Peking. A tenuous frontier stretching along the Yangtze River separated the Chin's newly occupied territory from the lands of the Chinese Sung dynasty in the south. Frequent incursions in both directions occurred throughout the twelfth and early thirteenth centuries, but the Chin maintained the upper hand and actually received tribute from the Sung. This uneasy status quo was shattered by the invasion of Genghis Khan.

Genghis Khan was born in 1162, the son of a clan chief called Yesugei. He was originally given the name Temuchin, after a chief whom his father had recently defeated. He suffered great personal hardships in early life, being driven from his tribe

The Uighur alphabet was adapted to produce a written form of the Mongol language.

were warriors. It is thus remarkable to consider that comparatively small Mongol forces often achieved, by skill and superior tactics, decisive victories over armies four times their size.

Thus organized, Genghis Khan was prepared to conquer the world. His actual motives for doing so were various. It has often been stated that the Mongol expansion of the thirteenth century was the result of the drying-up of their grazing lands—but very little evidence supports such a contention. Rather, a combination of factors made this time propitious for the outward thrust of the Mongol people. To them, war was a profession. To prevent petty feuds and internal divisions in his newly allied nation, Genghis Khan looked outside his own lands for a campaign to occupy the warlike Mongols, to provide them with booty, access to trade routes, prestige and popularity among their own tribes—which in turn would reflect upon him as their Great Khan.

Having united the Mongols, he was not only in control of a mighty warrior people but could now turn toward the West or China, safe in the knowledge that he was leaving no frontier unguarded. It is doubtful whether territorial gain played much part in Genghis Khan's schemes—he had little use for towns or agricultural land, and lacked the political machinery to rule them effectively. On the other hand, the lure of the gold, silver and silks of the cities of China was something neither he nor his generals could resist. It must be remembered, finally, that he considered himself to be embarking on a holy war—he was the instrument of the god Tengri, and he was, in accordance with Mongol custom, out to avenge a blood feud against the Chin who had treacherously murdered his uncles, Okin Barkhak and Ambakai—at least, that was his ostensible justification in embarking on the plunder of North China.

Before turning to China proper, however, he first encircled the Chin's westward approach by defeating the Tangut (a people of Tibetan origins), who occupied the state of Hsi Hsia which lay to the northwest of the Chin lands. After unsuccessful campaigns in 1205 and 1207, he was finally victorious in 1209 when he forced the Tangut king into submission after cutting off his trade links and flooding his capital, Chung-hsing, by building a huge dike and diverting the course of the Yellow River. The daughter of the king was sent to Genghis Khan, with tribute of camels and valuable cloth. At this time, the Chin were aware of the rising threat of the Mongols, but, occupied by their quarrels with the southern Sung and underestimating the extent of the danger, they took no action. Emissaries sent by the Chin emperor to Genghis Khan were rejected. They returned bearing alarming tales of the increasing strength of the Mongol army, but still the Chin took no defensive action. After the conclusion of their war with the Sung, they were occupied with internal problems—economic difficulties, the aftermath of disastrous floods and repeated famines. Although their army

habitants of the towns held back under such circumstances, reluctant to kill their own comrades, and thus were overwhelmed by the onslaught.

Upon vanquishing their enemies, the Mongols seldom concluded formal treaties, relying rather on the loyalty of the conquered people to their new masters. Indeed, Genghis Khan seems often to have been greatly offended when a defeated foe refused to accept him as its new ruler. An important aspect of the Mongol conquests is that, although the entire Mongol nation was mobilized for war, and every able-bodied man was conscripted, the army was not extraordinarily large. The entire Mongol population during the time of Genghis Khan, was perhaps one million, about one quarter of which

was at this time the largest in the world, and they possessed mighty fortified cities, they took no steps against the Mongol threat. With the Great Wall in the west, the Chin clearly felt secure.

The western approaches to the Great Wall were protected by the Chins' allies, the Turkish Ongud people. But by entering into a treaty with them, the Mongol armies were able, after the defeat of Hsi Hsia, to progress right up to the Wall without difficulty. In 1211, Genghis Khan attempted to break through the Great Wall approaches to Peking, but encountered severe resistance from the Chin army. In the fierce battles that followed, so many soldiers on both sides were killed that it was said the battlefields were littered with piles of human bones for years afterward. Their lack of knowledge of siege techniques and inexperience in fighting in hilly terrain held up the Mongol advance, and they were able to take only minor outposts. Eventually, after two years of fighting, the Wall was breached and a number of small fortified towns taken. The provinces of Hopei and Shensi were overrun and Shantung invaded. Genghis Khan had his first sight of the Chin capital, Peking, which he blockaded but made no attempt to besiege.

Dividing his army into three, Genghis Khan took only the less well-fortified towns of the North China plain, steadily shipping the plunder he gathered back to his lands beyond the Wall.

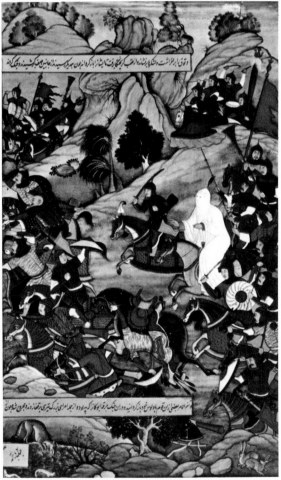

Above left A Mongol encampment. The nomadic Mongols had little material wealth other than their tents and domestic equipment. At the bottom is a fanciful depiction of Mongol ferocity.

Above A Mongol warrior hunting. Their highly disciplined cavalry army never suffered a major defeat.

Left With his mother by his side, the twelve-year-old Genghis Khan pursues rebellious troops. Bred in the saddle, Mongol children grew into the fearsome warriors of the Asian steppes.

Meanwhile, inside Peking, the rebellious minister, Chih-chung, slew the Chin emperor, Wei Shao Wang, raising Prince Utubu to the throne with the title Hsuan Tsung. Chih-chung was himself killed shortly afterward. In 1214, Genghis Khan's armies reassembled outside Peking and offered peace to the new emperor. Utubu sent an enormous treasure consisting of slaves, the daughter of his predecessor, three thousand horses, gold and silks, and with this tribute Genghis Khan withdrew through the Mongol-held Chu-yung pass to his own territory. In the same year, still fearful of the Mongol danger—especially now they had access to his country through the opened passes, the emperor moved his capital south to Kaifeng. After their long sojourn in North China, the Chin ruling classes clearly felt a close affinity with the local culture, and the move south, away from their Manchurian homeland to the northeast, was viewed by many as a desertion. In consequence, a large section of Utubu's army revolted and returned to Peking.

In view of his recent peace agreement with the emperor, Genghis Khan viewed the move south as treachery and dispatched his general, Samukha, to take Peking. The city was well defended. Surrounded by a forty-foot-high wall, about eighteen miles in circumference, with nine hundred towers and three moats, it was connected by subterranean passages with four outside forts, each one a mile square. In the winter of 1214–15, the city was again blockaded. Genghis Khan moved south, but did not travel as far as Peking. The self-exiled emperor sent an army to rescue his magnificent capital; inevitably, under a drunken commander, it was crushed. In the city, cannibalism had broken out, and discord among the remaining generals was rife. In June, 1215, Peking surrendered. The gates were opened and the Mongol army poured in.

Genghis Khan sitting in state. Under his leadership all the Mongol people were united for the first time.

Astonished by the wealth of their prize, the soldiers got completely out of hand, looting and destroying as they went, and killing nearly all the inhabitants. The great palace burned for over a month, and the formerly beautiful city was left a mass of rubble littered with corpses. Messengers were sent to Genghis Khan to tell him of his victory, and the bulk of the city's treasure was forwarded to his camp. Almost simultaneously, all the cities of the province of Hopei surrendered.

The taking of Peking marked the end of Chin rule in North China and the beginning of Mongol domination, for Genghis Khan now had an important hold on China and had driven the emperor to the south. His success sparked off rebellions elsewhere, and although the rest of the Chin empire was not completely annexed until 1234, it was apparent that the Mongols were the new rulers of China. Even before Peking had fallen, Genghis Khan had left for conquests in the West, returning to Mongolia in 1224–25, and after a dispute, renewing his attacks on Hsi Hsia, in 1226. He died the following year, shortly before Hsi Hsia was finally defeated. Genghis Khan left his mighty empire to his four sons. When his grandson, Kublai Khan, conquered the Sung lands in the south, all China was in Mongol hands.

The popular idea that the Mongols were incapable of any action other than looting and killing was proved incorrect by events subsequent to the fall of Peking. From the blazing city came a young Khitan minister called Yeh-lu Ch'u-Ts'ai, who impressed Genghis Khan and became a leading figure in his administration. Acting as a link between the uncouth Mongols and cultured Chinese, he showed Genghis Khan and his successors that an empire won from the saddle could not be ruled from it.

Among the material achievements of the Mongol rule must be included the rebuilding of Peking, which became a center for drama and literature. The Mongols began to appreciate the uses of towns, which had previously meant nothing more to them than the value of their portable contents. Roads and canals were improved and a 200,000-horse postal service was set up. A state-operated grain storage system was inaugurated and trade encouraged. Scientific advances—especially in astronomy and mathematics—which date from the Mongol period, are also noteworthy. The Turkic Uighur people were given prominent positions in the administration, and their alphabet was adapted to produce a written form of the Mongol language. The Mongols showed themselves to be adaptable and willing to learn new skills from conquered peoples.

In time, the Mongol rule grew corrupt and, weakened by economic and administrative problems, it was toppled by the native Chinese Ming dynasty in 1368—but only after a century of profitable rule under the heirs of Genghis Khan.

RUSSELL ASH

Mongol polo players. This was one of the most popular sports of these expert horsemen.

43

King John's chief adversary, and the main cause of his failure, was Philip Augustus, King of France. During his long reign (1180–1223), the kingdom of France doubled in size. When he came to the throne, Philip's royal dominions amounted to little more than five per cent of modern France, while the English king was overlord of more than half the country. Philip conquered both Normandy and Poitou, and the Albigensian Crusade laid the foundations for royal rule in the south.

Philip's internal policy was no less successful. He thoroughly reformed the financial and judicial administration of his realm by employing a corps of professional officials. He was able to reduce the power of the great barons by playing off one great landowner against another. As a result, French feudalism became firmly established, and Philip was able to insist on receiving the military service that his tenants owed him.

The layout of Paris was altered by Philip; indeed it remained almost the same from his time until the reign of Napoleon III in the nineteenth century. Philip built the city walls and paved the streets. He built the Louvre Palace and richly endowed the Cathedral of Notre Dame. Although Philip's fame was overtaken by that of later kings, such as St. Louis, he played a key role in the restoration of France's fortunes as a monarchy.

The Young Henry III

King John's acceptance of Magna Carta did not end his problems. Illness, the civil war, the invasion of England by Philip Augustus' son Louis, and the loss of the royal treasure while John was crossing the Wash in East Anglia, all took their toll. John's death in 1216 was not unexpected. His son, Henry III, was only nine years old, and control of the kingdom was placed in the hands of William Marshal, Earl of Pembroke, who drove the French out of England and gained the tenuous support of the barons by reissuing Magna Carta.

When Marshal died three years later, a triumvirate—consisting of the papal legate, Pandulph; the French bishop of Winchester, Peter des Roches; and the royal justician, Hubert de Burgh—took

An elephant that was presented to Henry III, from Matthew Paris' Chronicles.

power. In 1221 Pandulph was recalled to Rome on the advice of Archbishop Langton and de Burgh. In 1223, Henry came of age, and appointed de Burgh as his chief adviser. Rebel groups, some of which supported des Roches against the justiciar, had to be forced to give up the castles they occupied, and royal rule had to be strengthened. De Burgh was less effective in his dealings with Wales—which was in rebellion—and France—where he sent an ill-equipped army that was easily beaten. As a result, Henry dismissed him and appointed des Roches in his place. This was soon shown to have been a mistake.

Des Roches appointed his kinsmen to high office, showed himself partisan in his attitudes by favoring his fellow-Frenchmen, and alienated the barons. Following in the steps of Stephen Langton, who had died in 1228, the saintly Archbishop Edmund Rich warned the King that his attempt to rule the realm without the cooperation of the barons would end in disaster. Thereupon Henry wisely exiled des Roches and his French supporters.

The period of Henry's personal rule that followed allowed him every opportunity to indulge his highly refined artistic taste. He traveled about the country, rebuilding sixty royal castles and twenty palaces and lodges. But his finest monument is Westminster Abbey, which was rebuilt to be a fitting home for the relics of Edward the Confessor, whom Henry regarded as the model of perfect kingship. It was the first building in England with double piers of flying buttresses and bartraceried windows. "As the rose is to other flowers," runs an inscription on a tile in the chapter-house, "so is this house to other buildings." The nearby palace of Westminster was nearly as

splendid. Its tour de force was the painted chamber, eighty feet long, twenty-six feet wide and over thirty feet high. This richly decorated room was wainscoted throughout, had tiled floors and walls almost covered with paintings. The King was so anxious to see it completed quickly that he told his clerk of the works that it must be ready in time "even though you have to hire 1,000 workmen a day."

Henry was also an efficient dynastic matchmaker: he himself married Eleanor of Provence, who was regarded as the finest match in Europe; his son was married to Eleanor of Castile; his sister was married to William Marshal the younger and then to Simon de Montfort, son of the Albigensian crusader. His brother, Richard, Earl of Cornwall, was elected King of the Romans, an office that carried with it the right of succession to the Holy Roman Empire. His dynastic treaties even brought him the gift of a elephant, which was kept at the Tower of London and amazed the population of the city. Henry's drive did not, however, extend to the activities of government which he found boring. He was terrified by thunderstorms, and even the idea of battle left him feeling weak.

Frederick II and the Holy Roman Empire

The sudden death of Emperor Henry VI in 1197 plunged Germany into fourteen years of civil war. The struggle for the throne was not resolved until 1211, when the German princes deposed the already excommunicated Guelf emperor Otto IV and invited the eighteen-year-old Frederick Hohenstaufen to be their king. Frederick, the son of Henry VI and Constance of Sicily, had been under the guardianship of Pope Innocent III since his mother's death. He soon became the outstanding military and political figure of thirteenth-century Europe. When he came of age in 1216, Frederick recognized the papacy's lordship over Sicily; and in return for the papacy's support in gaining the imperial crown, he promised to go on a crusade.

Frederick was no less determined than his predecessors had been that his empire should be independent of the papacy. Des-

pite his early pledges that he would not attempt to unite the Holy Roman Empire with his inherited kingdoms of Sicily and Naples, Frederick did precisely that—and the resulting confederation hemmed in the Papal States. The imperial title and the power that it confirmed did not mean that Frederick was interested in German affairs. His interests were mainly Italian, and he regarded Germany as little more than a useful source of money and men to further his Italian ambitions. He spent little time in Germany and left it largely in the hands of the nobility. He even thought the situation in Italy more important than his promised crusade; it was only in order to avoid excommunication that he finally set out for the Holy Land in 1227. After a week at sea, he returned saying that he was too ill to fight. Gregory IX, believing that the illness was feigned, immediately excommunicated him.

Frederick II with a hawk.

Ignoring the excommunication, Frederick set out again for Palestine two years later. His military successes and his command of the Arabic language enabled him to extract a ten-year truce from Malik-al-Kamil, the Sultan of Egypt, a truce that granted him control of Jerusalem, Bethlehem and Nazareth. The Pope still refused to lift the excommunication, and on Gregory's orders, the Patriarch of Jerusalem refused to celebrate religious services in Frederick's presence. In defiance the Emperor, who had married the daughter of the late King of Jerusalem four years earlier, crowned himself King in the Church of the Holy Sepulcher.

Frederick's speedy return to Europe was necessitated by an invasion of Naples by allies of the papacy. He quickly dealt with the threat, and Gregory was obliged to withdraw his excommunication by the Treaty of San Germano in 1230. By the Constitution of Melfi (1231) Frederick began to reconstruct and centralize the government of his territories. The policy of centralization was meanwhile being pursued in Germany by his son, Henry, who had been left to govern the country, but this antagonized the nobility and caused a revolt. Frederick deposed Henry in 1235 and at a diet at Mainz promulgated new laws for the Empire.

When Innocent IV replaced the aged Gregory IX in 1243, Frederick's feud with the papacy became even more bitter. Fearful for his life, Innocent fled to Lyons in 1245. There he gathered a synod, demanded Frederick's re-

moval and put forward his own candidate for Emperor. Despite the Emperor's offers of reconciliation, the Pope would not retract his demands and even went so far as to preach a crusade against him. For the last five years of his life Frederick was under constant military pressure.

Known as *Stupor mundi*, the wonder of the world, Frederick II amazed his contemporaries and leaves posterity puzzled. Some have called him "the first modern man to occupy a throne," and certainly his remodeling of his Italian kingdom, with its remarkable code of laws, and his passion for science foreshadow the autocratic princes of the Renaissance. Yet Frederick left Germany much as he found it: a conglomeration of feudal principalities utterly divided on the nature of the Empire and the person of the Emperor.

A brilliant linguist with a real passion for scholarship and the arts, Frederick was as much at home with the philosophy of Aristotle as with the study of

natural science. He wrote a remarkable book on hawking, translated Arabic works and found a niche for the Provençal poets expelled during the Albigensian Crusade. After his own crusade, he installed Saracen garrisons in Italy and his court was exposed to the aesthetic influences of Moslem civilization; the courtyards of his palace were decorated with fountains, the rooms were luxurious with cushions and colorful silk hangings, perfume and exotic fruits. He turned his court into a university, noting that "science must go hand in hand with government, legislation and the pursuit of war." He founded the University of Naples, the first university to owe its origin to royal initiative, and endowed a medical school at Salerno, which admitted women as well as men.

The Teutonic Knights

The thirteenth-century Church proved that it was able to adapt its institutions to changing needs. The primary concern of the great military orders was to protect the Holy Land. The orders of friars were authorized by the papacy as a means of meeting the threat of heresy. The Order of the Teutonic Knights, which was founded in the 1180s, combined the missionary fervor of the friars with the military vigor of the Templars and Hospitallers. Although it had at first operated in Palestine, the Teutonic order was given Prussia in 1226 by Frederick II, in return

Marienburg, headquarters of the Teutonic Knights.

for assistance in purifying and converting the disorderly and heathen Prussians. From the huge fortress of Marienburg, which they built as their headquarters, the knights controlled all aspects of life in their territories. Their power grew steadily in Prussia, Poland and even Russia. It was only broken in the fifteenth century, after their shattering defeat by the Poles at the Battle of Tannenburg (1410). The Teutonic Knights were an important aspect of Europe's expanding frontiers in the thirteenth century. Their attitudes and the brutality of their methods gave a foretaste of the behavior of the European colonists in the sixteenth century in Africa, Asia and America. Meanwhile, beyond the territories of the knights a new power was being created in Russia.

Relief of Frederick with his family, from a cathedral in Apulia.

Fourteenth-century miniature of a Teutonic Knight.

The Russian Giant Stirs

The thaw of 1238 was a particularly heavy one in northeastern Russia and flood waters accompanying it forced the apparently invincible Mongol chieftain Batu to withdraw to the steppes of Central Asia. Batu's retreat saved the city of Novgorod from certain sack and spared its adolescent Grand Prince, Alexander. The significance of Novgorod's escape became apparent two years later when Russian troops led by the young Prince defeated the vast armies of King Erik of Sweden on the banks of the Neva River. In rapid succession, Alexander (who had added Nevski to his name to commemorate his initial victory) routed the Germanic Knights of the Teutonic Order and turned back a Lithuanian invasion. Having secured Russia's frontiers, Alexander devoted the rest of his life to interceding with the Tartars on behalf of his people. His selfless diplomacy led to Alexander's canonization in 1380.

The Archangel Michael; the Orthodox faith alone held Russia together in the thirteenth century, when it was attacked from all sides.

Opposite St. Boris and St. Gleb : these national saints appeared to Nevski's army in battle and scattered the enemy.

Russia began to emerge as a European power shortly after the middle of the ninth century A.D. The Grand Duchy of Kiev, cradle of the Russian empire, was founded during that century by Normans and Slavs—men of Indo-European rather than Asian origin—who built their city along the river route that leads from the Baltic to the Black Sea. Around Kiev arose a great cluster of principalities that were eventually united under the house of Rurik. This powerful dynasty of Scandinavian origin married its daughters to the kings of France, Hungary and Norway, and to the Emperor of Germany, while contracting other family alliances with the Byzantine Emperor and the King of England. Converted under Vladimir the Saint, the Kievian state became a bulwark of Christendom against the nomads of the steppes. Linked with the great European commercial centers by her flourishing trade routes, "the Mother of Cities," as the Russians fondly called Kiev, rapidly became one of the most active and civilized metropolises on the Continent.

A Mongol invasion at the beginning of the thirteenth century put an end to Kiev's promising development, and for the next two hundred years the Russian nation was dominated by Asiatics. After the devastation of Kiev and the banks of the Dnieper by Mongol hordes, or armies, a large part of the population scattered to the north and east, where the virgin forest remained impenetrable to the enemy. The Grand Duke of Kiev, a descendant of Rurik's dynasty, transferred the center of government to the region of the Upper Volga and the Oka rivers, to the principalities of Rostov, Vladimir and Suzdal.

As a result, the whole aspect of national life was transformed. Intermarriage among the colonists and the indigenous Finnish tribes gradually produced a race of Great Russians—bearded, snub-nosed men of sober habits, the hard-working builders of the future empire. With the exception of Novgorod, a great commercial city in northwest Russia that was allied with the German Hanseatic League, the towns of the Suzdal, remote from the stream of commerce, preserved a clearly provincial character. The princes of the Suzdal appeared as nothing more than wealthy landowners, principally concerned with the administration of their large estates. Eschewing the incessant competition for the succession that preoccupied their relations and neighbors, the Suzdal princes transformed their own possessions into hereditary fiefs, a move that greatly strengthened their power.

Nonetheless, these princes were threatened from all sides by the gravest dangers. They had become vassals of the Mongols, and each of them was obliged to appear before the lieutenants of the Great Khan, who were established in the Lower Volga region, to make humble application for their investiture. In addition, the power of the Grand Duke was scarcely recognized over the immense territory—extending from the Gulf of Finland to the approaches to the White Sea—which belonged to the free city of Novgorod. Rich merchants, the real rulers of this patrician republic, chose and dismissed their local princes as they saw fit, with the sole purpose of ensuring the defense of their frontiers—although they generally gave preference to the increasingly powerless descendants of the Grand Duke of Kiev. Only a definite threat from without caused the merchants to request the aid of the younger sons of the house of Suzdal. To all this was added the increasingly strong pressure exerted on Russia by her western neighbors, the Swedes and the Teutonic Knights, who were representatives of more developed civilizations, which were capable of wiping out the last traces of the Russian national idea.

Alexander Nevski stands out in great clarity against the somber background of this tragic period of Russian history. In his spiritual and physical beauty, the clearness of his gaze and the purity of his soul, he represented the archetype of the princely saint as envisioned by Russians in the Middle Ages. In him the themes of patriotism and Christianity

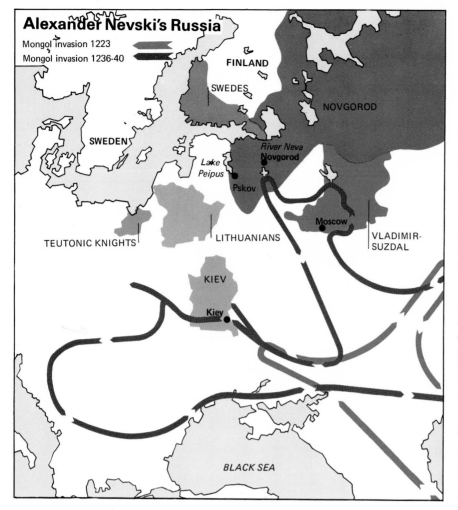

Alexander Nevski's Russia

Mongol invasion 1223
Mongol invasion 1236-40

FINLAND

SWEDES

NOVGOROD

SWEDEN

River Neva
Novgorod

Lake
Peipus

Pskov

TEUTONIC KNIGHTS

LITHUANIANS

Moscow

VLADIMIR-
SUZDAL

KIEV

Kiev

BLACK SEA

A copper cross of
thirteenth-century
Russian origin.

became interwoven and eventually merged into one another.

Alexander was born in May, 1219, at Pereyaslavl, a fief that was owned by his father, who was of the house of the Grand Prince of the Suzdal region. He spent the first years of his life in this small city, which stood on the shores of a lake among trees and meadows and was defended by a simple wooden palisade. He was scarcely three years old when his father was elected Prince of Novgorod and resettled some six miles away from that ever-unruly city in order to preside over its fortunes.

At the age of nine Alexander and his elder brother Theodore were left alone at Novgorod under the guardianship of certain nobles. Their father, who had grown disgusted with his office, rarely returned to Novgorod after 1228, and during a subsequent civil crisis, the children were obliged to flee the city under the leadership of a tutor. Theodore died prematurely some years later, and when his father, in 1236, became Grand Prince of Kiev—that is, the ruler of all Russia—Alexander fell heir to the fief of Novgorod.

The adolescent found himself faced with terrible responsibilities. A great Mongol invasion of the north of Russia occurred the following year. Led by Batu, grandson of Genghis, the invaders swiftly de-

feated the Volga Bulgars and swept into northeastern Russia. By March of 1238, the barbarians had advanced to within sixty miles of Novgorod. Alexander's fief appeared doomed when Batu, fearing that imminent spring thaws would trap his forces in the heavy forests around Novgorod, suddenly withdrew to the steppes.

Alexander's memorable reign at Novgorod lasted for sixteen years. Alexander made it his business to combat the separatist tendencies of the city, to strengthen its links with the central power, and to weaken the economic and political power of the boyars, or local grandees. In 1239 he married the daughter of the Prince of Polotsk, a feudal neighbor. During the next few years Alexander frequently enjoyed the pleasures of the chase, and hunted bear armed only with a sling—but such diversions never swayed him from his administrative duties.

Alexander's first military victory, won in 1240 on the banks of the Neva, had world-wide repercussions and earned him the name of Nevski. In an attempt to conquer those parts of Russia that had not fallen under the dominion of the Tartars—and to cut off Novgorod's sole outlet to the Baltic Sea—King Erik of Sweden gathered together a great army and placed it under the command of his son-in-law Birger. The Swedish sovereign derived some encouragement in this undertaking from a bull issued by Pope Gregory IX in 1237, and addressed to the Bishop of Uppsala. That edict summoned the Swedes to a crusade against the Finns, who had abandoned their Catholic faith under the influence of their neighbors the Russians. King Erik's interpretation of this papal message was clearly somewhat forced, but it appeared to furnish him with some justification for his aggression against Russia.

Alexander had foreseen the danger, and in 1239 he had organized the defense of the routes from Novgorod to the sea, and had placed sentries on both sides of the Gulf of Finland. Pelguse, the chieftain of the local tribe and a convert to Christianity, warned Alexander that a Swedish army was disembarking on the banks of the Neva, and the Prince hastened to meet the enemy. Reviewing his troops before their departure, Alexander uttered the phrase—an allusion to the Psalms—that has remained his most famous: "God is not on the side of force but of the just cause, the Pravda." The word pravda, employed in modern times as the title of the most important Soviet newspaper, is not easy to translate; it means at the same time "truth," "justice," "social equity," and "just cause"—and embodies, even today, the deepest aspirations of the Russian people.

In order to engage the enemy, Alexander's troops were forced to march over marshy land, a region around modern Leningrad that still presents a rather gloomy appearance. Pressing on swiftly, Alexander's army arrived at the mist-shrouded banks of the Neva several hours after dawn. There, according to Russian legend, the local chieftain Pelguse had witnessed a curious vision as the sun rose. He saw a boat bearing several mysterious ghosts coming slowly down the river. As the vessel drew near, the shades

were revealed to be two holy princes, Boris and Gleb, and their heavenly oarsmen, who were coming to the aid of their "brother Alexander."

The battle, which began a short time later, caught the Swedes unawares; they were convinced that the Novgorod forces, deprived of the assistance of a Suzdal army recently destroyed by the Mongols, would be in no position to offer them resistance. Birger, the King's son-in-law, and many of his knights were installed in a gold embroidered tent, but the main body of the Swedish army had not yet disembarked. The Russians carried out their attacks with lightning-like rapidity; while Alexander himself wounded Birger with a blow from a spear, his men-at-arms cut the bridges joining the boats to the river bank. Panic seized the Swedes, who fled in utter disorder. According to legend, archangels swept down from Heaven and wiped out the Swedish knights on the opposite shore of the Neva.

Similar scenes occurred in the following year, when Alexander inflicted total defeat on the Knights of the Teutonic Order, a German crusading force that had acted in concert with the Swedes. The Knights had seized Izborsk, and broken the Truce of Pskov by burning the outskirts of that city before the boyars could open the gates to them. Having crushed the Swedish offensive, Alexander made ready to go to the aid of Pskov. Prevented by the boyars from carrying out this plan, Alexander withdrew to his father's estate at Pereyaslavl. It was not long before he was recalled by his subjects, who had at last realized the true extent of their danger. Alexander returned with regiments raised in the territory of Suzdal, and set off for the western frontier at the head of the combined Russian forces.

Sergei Eisenstein's film classic *Alexander Nevski* has made the public in the West familiar with this battle, in which the steel-clad Teutons initially drove a wedge through the Russian lines, forcing them to retreat out onto the ice of Lake Peipus. There the Russians regrouped, attacked the enemy on two flanks and brought down or put to flight hundreds of German knights. Alexander's victory was complete, and the German advance was arrested for centuries. The battle, which salvaged the very existence of the Russian nation, was supposedly joined by heavenly armies, similar to those that had brought aid to Prince Alexander at the Neva.

Alexander's father, the Grand Prince Yaroslav, died on his way back from the Mongol camp at Karakorum, where he had been summoned by the Great Khan. Russian chroniclers, whose assertions agree with the testimony of Plano Carpini, the famous Italian traveler, suggest that Alexander's

Genghis Khan, the Mongol chief whose death in 1227 saved Russia from annihilation.

Above left Alexander Nevski leads the Russians into battle.

The city of Novgorod in the thirteenth century.

Medieval cathedral of Peroslave with the nineteenth-century statue of St. Alexander Nevski.

Bear hunting : a favored occupation in thirteenth-century Russia.

father was poisoned. The matter of the succession could not be settled without further intervention of the Tartar leaders. For reasons that remain unknown, it was not the deceased prince's eldest son, Yuri, but Alexander who was summoned, together with his brother Andrew, to appear before the Asiatic overlords.

Alexander was now faced with a tragic dilemma. Was the hero of the Neva and Lake Peipus to adopt the attitude of a humble vassal and recognize openly the loss of Russian independence—thus insulting the death-under-torture already suffered by some of Alexander's near relations? A Western knight might not have submitted to such a sacrifice of his honor, but Alexander was a Russian knight—an Orthodox prince—and, thinking solely of the good of his people, he preferred to submit to the Divine Will, and took counsel of the higher clergy. The Metropolitan Cyril—head of the Russian Orthodox Church—gave his approval to Alexander's decision to leave for the Mongol camp on the condition that he worship no idols and not deny his faith in Christ.

Collaboration with the Tartars was, at that moment, a historical necessity. The term "collaborator" has been somewhat discredited in recent times, and has become synonymous with treachery. We consider it a patriot's duty to continue the struggle, as long as the slightest chance of success remains— but there was no chance for Russia in 1246. The nation could count on no help from outside, for the attitude of neighboring countries was entirely hostile.

50

Moreover, Russia's armies, which had been sufficient to confront enemies as courageous as the Swedes or the Teutons in equal numbers, could offer no defense against the nomad hordes, who carried all before them as they advanced by tens, or even hundreds of thousands.

Subsequently, the Russians have recognized the great service that Alexander rendered them by sacrificing his pride for the sake of the Fatherland. The Mongols themselves were profoundly impressed by the conduct of this man, whose reputation had reached them some time beforehand; they granted him the honors due to his rank and spared him both the ordeal by fire and worship of the idols. Nevertheless, they did oblige Alexander to undertake the interminable journey through the deserts of Asia to Karakorum, and only allowed him to return to his native land after three years' absence. In the years that followed, Alexander returned to his masters' camp, situated north of the Azov Sea, on three occasions, to arrange current affairs and to implore the Mongols' mercy for his people.

Alexander's eldest brother was dead, and his second brother, Andrew, had taken to flight after an attempted rising, which ended—as could be foreseen—in terrible reprisals. Alexander thereby became the Grand Prince of Russia. It was his concern now to prevent further invasions, to inspire the Great Khan with confidence, to serve as intermediary between him and the Russian people, and to prevent rash insurrections even at the price of painful concession.

This superhuman task was made no easier by fresh attacks from Sweden, against which, in 1258, Alexander was obliged to conduct a new and similarly victorious campaign. Incessant unrest in Novgorod assumed an especially serious character when, in 1259, the Tartars exacted a tribute from the population of the land.

In 1262, when the exactions of the Tartars provoked another popular uprising, Alexander undertook his fifth journey to the Tartar headquarters, in an effort to ward off a punitive expedition. For a whole year he struggled to pacify the Great Khan and his henchmen, and eventually succeeded in dissuading the Tartars from their plan of raising Russian regiments for a war against Persia. But Alexander had come to the end of his strength. On the return journey, over roads made difficult by the autumn rains, he fell ill, and was taken to a monastery, where he died in November, 1263. Before drawing his last breath, Alexander gave up his princely rank and put on the habit of a monk.

In subsequent years, numerous miracles occurred at Alexander's tomb, which led to his being canonized locally in 1380, and by the whole Russian Church at the Council of 1547. Five centuries after Alexander's death—after the victorious outcome of his successor's war against Sweden—Peter the Great caused the relics of St. Alexander Nevski to be transferred to the new capital of St. Petersburg (Leningrad), where they lie today at the monastery that bears his name. CONSTANTINE DE GRUNWALD

The dormition of the Virgin Mary: an icon of the Novgorod School.

St. George and the Dragon, representing the triumph of good over evil.

Europe's frontiers were also expanding to the far north as well as to the east. Scandinavia had tended to be isolated from the rest of Europe by distance, its small population and its barbaric history. The Norse threat to Europe shrank steadily after the death of King Canute in 1030. Following the centuries-long tradition of southward migration, Norway attempted with brief success, to conquer Denmark. The continuing warfare between the kingdoms of Sweden, Denmark and Norway weakened all three, and European influence spread rapidly throughout Scandinavia. This was in large measure due to the expansion of Christianity. Although the missions were originally mainly run by Englishmen, the whole of Scandinavia was under the jurisdiction of the See of Hamburg and Bremen. As a result of the more settled condition of the twelfth century, the See of Lund was given jurisdiction over the Scandinavian Church in 1104, and in 1152 the Norwegian Church became a separate province under the Bishop of Trondheim. The strengthening of ecclesiastical organization and the increased Europeanization of Scandinavia was accompanied by the beginning of the payment of "Peter's pence," a special tax paid to the papacy. This was organized by the English Pope Hadrian IV, who had been papal legate in Norway.

Magnus Barn-Lock, King of Sweden.

The thirteenth century saw a feudalization of the Scandinavian kingdoms. This was largely due to the need for an effective fighting force in the so-called Wars of the Pretenders, which rent all three countries during the twelfth and thirteenth centuries. More effective armies led to the conquest by Sweden of much of Finland under King Magnus Barn-Lock in the mid-thirteenth century. Norway extended its powers over the Atlantic islands—Greenland and Iceland—in 1261 and 1262. For a few years all the peoples of Norwegian descent were united in one kingdom.

It was only in the early thirteenth century that the Norwegians had been driven from the Scottish mainland, and the islands remained Norwegian until 1266. At the Battle of Largs in 1263 King Alexander III had defeated an army led by Norway's King Haakon, and in 1266 Norway renounced its claims to the Isle of Man and Scotland's western isles. Six years later Scotland seized the Shetland and Orkney islands. The reign of Alexander III was a golden age for Scotland, for not only were the islands absorbed into the kingdom, but the border with England was quiet. It was a rare period of calm in Scotland's troubled history, but Alexander's early death in 1286 marked its end.

The Reconquista

Europe's new self-consciousness was not only apparent in Russia and the north, but also in the south. Spain had never been a wholly Moslem country; groups of small Christian states had survived the eighth-century invasions. With the collapse of the Caliphate in 1031, Moslem Spain lost its unity, and Christian kings such as Alfonso VI of León-Castile (c. 1030–1109) were quick to take advantage of this. Spain remained Moslem only with the aid of further invasions from North Africa during the eleventh and twelfth centuries. It was, however, only from the late twelfth century, when Alfonso VIII (1155–1214) managed to persuade the papacy of the need for a crusade that the reconquista (reconquest) really got underway. Aided by knights from England, France and Italy, Alfonso reestablished the military confidence of the Spanish princi-

Moors and crusaders arrayed for battle.

palities. At a decisive battle in 1212 a Castilian and Navarrese army destroyed a large Moslem army at Navas de Tolosa. The Moorish commander unsuccessfully attempted to defend himself with a human wall of 10,000 Negro slaves, who were chained together. It was in memory of this victory that the coat-of-arms of the Kingdom of Navarre included chains.

Under Alfonso's grandson, Ferdinand (1217–52), who inherited Castile from his mother and León from his father, Cordova and Seville were captured. While Ferdinand subdued the rest of Andalucia, James of Aragon (1213–76) took Valencia and the Balearic Islands. He went on to conquer Sardinia, Sicily and even —briefly—Athens. The Moorish Kingdom of Granada, still able to call on African assistance, was able to survive for a further 200 years; but this was due more to the quarreling of the Christian states —Portugal, Aragon, Navarre and Castile—than to military success. The four kingdoms fought both for territory and political supremacy while their kings seemed mainly concerned with aping the manners and morals of the very Moslem rulers who had been so recently conquered. Moslem influence continued to be felt in other ways. Spanish culture was mainly Moorish in origin, and many Spanish buildings still show Moorish characteristics.

St. Louis

Frenchmen look back upon the reign of Louis IX (1226–70) as one of the golden ages of the French monarchy. Few kings of France were as dearly loved by their subjects or achieved as high a reputation among contemporary monarchs as Louis, who was canonized in 1297. His austere upbringing by his mother, Blanche of Castile (who was queen-regent of France during her son's minority), and his natural piety led Louis to model his life on the ideal of Christian knighthood— and consequently his reign was dominated by crusading ventures against the Infidel. His strategic ability did not match his enthusiasm, however, and his campaigns proved disastrous.

Louis was sickly throughout his life, and his decision to go on a crusade was taken as the result of a recovery—which he regarded as miraculous—from an illness. Actually his illnesses were made worse by his rigid asceticism and fasting.

Louis' political approach was very different from that of his near contemporary Frederick II. Frederick spent much time quarreling with his neighbors, particularly in Italy, but showed great tolerance both toward heretical subjects and toward Moslems. Louis, on the other hand, was determined to stamp out heresy and retain the Holy Land but was always keen to live at peace with neighboring kingdoms. As Christendom's holy knight, Louis had been the chief promoter of peace in Europe. He had, for example, yielded the districts of Limousin and Perigord to Henry III of England on the condition that Henry became his vassal for the attenuated duchies of Aquitaine and Gascony and renounced all English claims to Normandy, Maine, Anjou and Poitou. Unhappily, the Treaty of Paris (1259), which confirmed this arrangement, contained the seeds of the Hundred Years War. Louis ignored many opportunities to expand his territory by military means. The Treaty of Paris (1229), which formally ended the Albigensian Crusade, gave Louis the Duchy of Narbonne, and he bought or inherited a few small counties. However, he made up for those acquisitions by generous grants of land to his children.

Men and nations turned to Louis as the natural arbitrator in their disputes. He advised on the succession to the throne of Flanders and in 1264, by the Mise of Amiens, adjudicated in favor of Henry III against the English barons. Royal power and administration increased in France during his reign, but the country was pushed to the verge of bank-

ruptcy. Louis, who brought tremendous prestige to the French monarchy, was able to follow the Cross only because his grandfather Philip II had established a strong royal administration. France was peaceful enough for him to be able to leave his mother as regent.

The Seventh Crusade

In preparation for his first campaign, the Seventh Crusade (1248–54), Louis IX laid out the port and town of the Rhône in Languedoc. The French army, which sailed from Louis' new port, easily took the Egyptian city of Damietta, but when Louis advanced on Cairo he was captured and his army was massacred. His capture led to a crusade of French peasants known as the Crusade of the Pastoureaux; though unsuccessful in releasing the King, this campaign showed how popular Louis was in France. The French King paid the Sultan of Egypt an enormous sum to ransom himself and many other Christian captives and handed back Damietta. Upon his release, Louis made a prolonged pilgrimage to Jerusalem, postponing his return to France for four years. The objectives of Louis' second crusade—officially, the Eighth Crusade, made in conjunction

St. Louis leaves Damietta and voyages to Acre.

with Edward I of England in 1270—were changed at the last moment, probably at the insistence of Louis' brother Charles of Anjou, and the French monarch found himself leading his followers across the sands of Tunis. The Anglo-French force was struck by dysentery and Louis died, still convinced that he could convert the Amir. Almost at once reports began to circulate of miracles being wrought by means of the King's relics.

Canon Law

The thirteenth century was a creative period for canon law. During the two preceeding centuries huge collections of the laws of the Church had been made, bringing together episcopal and papal letters and decretals and the decisions of Church councils. Many of these were mutually contradictory, and the task of the thirteenth-century canonists was to make sense of these and to provide interpretation, as many of the laws did not go into any detail.

In 1234 Raymond of Pennafort published a collection of papal decretals which he had compiled on the order of Gregory IX. This immediately became the standard canonical collection. Because of

the difficulty of finding the original texts in the huge collections, and of interpreting them, lawyers began to make glosses covering particular points to supplement the text. These lawyers are known as the glossators. The glossators did not merely interpret the law. In many cases they went far further and altered the meaning of the original texts in order to bring them into line with current thought. As a result, it was possible for the law—despite a certain theoretical rigidity—to become a subtle and plastic creative weapon: for instance usury (the lending of money at excessive interest) was theoretically banned, but it came to be widely practised, and lawyers provided argument and justification for its use.

Because of its contradictions, the law could be used to support different aims; papal supporters sought to justify their position by using it, but so also did those who thought that the Church as the body of the faithful should decide its own rules. "Democracy" as well as monarchicalism could find justification in the law. Certainly it was ecclesiastical practice that influenced the growing desire for involvement in secular government that is a noticeable feature of thirteenth-century life and is typified by Simon de Montfort's parliamentary activities.

St. Louis feeding the poor.

Parliament in Evolution

Accused of misgovernment and of mulcting the taxpayers to finance absurd dynastic adventures, Henry III found himself opposed by his own barons, among them Simon de Montfort, brother-in-law to the King. The successful rebellion that Simon led forced Henry to turn over the power of government to a standing council of nine men. Simon, his sons and the Earl of Gloucester became the most powerful men in the realm. Though he was killed, disgraced and repudiated shortly thereafter, the Great Parliament that Simon de Montfort summoned in 1265 remains one of the most important in parliamentary history. He called not only knights from each shire but also, for the first time, representatives from boroughs and towns.

Henry III; his extravagant adventures abroad and failure to consult his barons provoked the rising which led to the calling of the Great Parliament.

On December 13, 1264, writs were issued at Worcester in the name of King Henry III of England summoning a parliament to meet in the chapter house of Westminster Abbey on January 20, 1265. Although the writs were sent out in the King's name, the Parliament was really being called in consequence to a successful rebellion against him, headed by his brother-in-law, Simon de Montfort, Earl of Leicester. Henry agreed to hold the Parliament in order to obtain the release of his eldest son, Prince Edward, who had been surrendered to de Montfort after a decisive battle fought at Lewes in Sussex the previous May. Edward had been kept a close prisoner, for he was the guarantee of the King's good faith in concluding a treaty of peace. Simon, for his part, and the earls and barons who sided with him, intended the Parliament to accept what was virtually a new form of government, but one nonetheless approved as a temporary measure by a previous parliament, meeting some five weeks after the Mise (or peace) of Lewes.

This constitution provided for the appointment of a standing council of nine men who had been selected by Simon and his friends—Gilbert de Clare, Earl of Gloucester, and the Bishop of Chichester. Henry had been accused of misgovernment, of mulcting the taxpayers to finance absurd dynastic adventures. Henry was also blamed for relying too much upon the advice of foreign favorites, notably his French half brothers who came to England from Gascony and had been given lands, titles and offices. An incipient spirit of xenophobia gripped Simon's followers. They no longer shared the King's allegiance to the larger unit of Christendom, under the tutelage of the Pope, but looked inwardly—to England.

The world of the thirteenth century was one of turbulence and conflict. Innocent III and the popes who followed him, claimed that they were the spiritual leaders of Europe, the representatives of God on earth, and that the spirit was mightier than the sword. Therefore their aim was to transform kings into their faithful vassals and to send them as crusaders to conquer or convert the infidels. Henry III's father, King John, had promised that he would go on a crusade and in return Innocent III protected John and John's heir against rebellion by their own subjects. Both Henry and Simon declared themselves to be crusaders. When Henry agreed to dispatch his second son, Edmund, to Sicily to fight against the natural son of Frederick II, who had been an enemy of the papacy, it was in the guise of a crusader, and Pope Alexander IV demanded a tenth of the revenues of the English Church for five years to sustain this holy enterprise.

Henry had not only followed in his father's footsteps as a crusader and papal vassal but had also tried, though in vain, to regain the whole of the Angevin inheritance in France by subduing the unruly Gascons and reconquering Normandy and Brittany from his feudal superior, the King of France. These ambitions pressed hard upon the barons and clergy of England, from whom money and services were constantly demanded. They remembered Runnymede; and on several occasions they compelled Henry III to swear to uphold Magna Carta, which had been reissued in his name when he was a child and had actually, in its shortened version, been approved by a papal legate in England. As a sanction they refused to vote the King funds unless he confirmed the Charter. The barons, however, had additional grievances against Henry III over and above those they had condemned in his father.

Henry's court was filled with foreigners such as the Savoyard relatives of his Queen and his high-spirited Lusignan half brothers, who were generally condemned as greedy, insolent upstarts and alien Frenchmen. Hence a united baronial movement sought to rid the court of foreigners, to compel the King to employ his "natural counsellors," and to curtail his extravagant expeditions abroad. That

An engraving of the window
in Chartres Cathedral which
commemorates Simon de
Montfort. Although he led a
nationalist English reaction
against foreign influence,
Simon was born in France and
his brother was Constable of
France.

Two warlike scenes from a thirteenth-century manuscript: armorers sharpen swords (bottom) and a fallen knight is stripped of his armor (top)

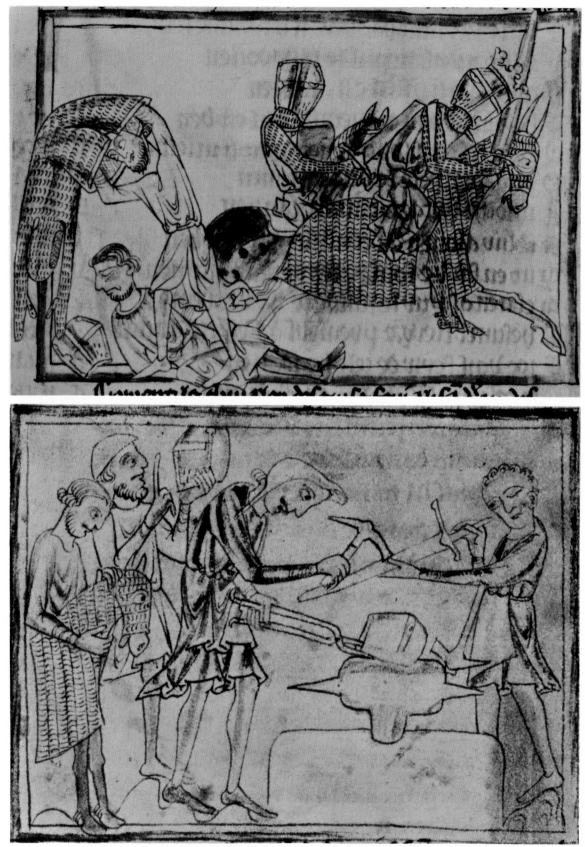

was what contemporary chroniclers recorded, but Simon de Montfort and his followers were also moved by a high sense of purpose which was to maintain genuine harmony between the political community and the royal government. Not only did the barons force the King to swear to abide by the existing charters but they produced in the Provisions of Oxford of 1258, a new charter. It stated that the King's principal ministers should be elected, that the King should be advised by a

A thirteenth-century battle scene showing mounted knights in combat.

standing council, and that parliaments should be held three times a year. When the King reluctantly accepted these provisions (he later repudiated them), along with the new constitution of 1264, his acquiescence was deliberately proclaimed throughout England.

To the Great Parliament at Westminster were called twelve bishops, fifty-five abbots and twenty-two priors—but only five earls and eighteen barons. These were men who, almost without exception, had been friendly to the cause of the rebels. The most remarkable feature of the Parliament, notable for its composition rather than the decisions it made, was that for the first time two representatives (or burgesses) from each borough, together with four men from each of the Cinque Ports in southern England and two knights from each shire, were asked to come to Westminster for consultation on affairs of the realm. Though the knights and burgesses had little power in the Great Parliament—they had been summoned to hear, rather than determine policy—their inclusion was evidence that the barons no longer had complete control over their subjects, nor were they to be the only class with opinions about national affairs.

The gathering in the winter of 1265 might be described as a "packed" parliament. Not only were the bishops and barons there friendly to the rebel cause, but the knights of the shire were also for the most part in sympathy with the reformist aims of Simon de Montfort and his allies. Simon, in fact, constituted himself a Lord Protector or Regent for the King. He nominated the Council of Nine; he chose officials in the royal household; he was determined to prevent the King from exercising arbitrary power by obliging him to rule

The death of Simon de Montfort at the Battle of Evesham and the subsequent decapitation and mutilation of his body.

The official seal of Simon de Montfort showing him hunting. Before leading the revolt against the King, Simon was a senior royal official in Gascony.

from office. The clash of temperaments was complete. The sequel to what was called the Great Parliament of 1265 had indeed an air of fatality about it.

First Simon quarreled with his chief supporter, the Earl of Gloucester. Then Prince Edward escaped. The Marcher Lords, headed by Roger of Mortemer and loyal to the King, failed to depart for Ireland, as they had promised, while Henry's French friends, who had fled the kingdom after the Battle of Lewes, were creeping back into England. Pope Clement IV instructed his legate to work for the reestablishment of King Henry and his family to their former position, and to have no dealings with "the pestilent man," Simon de Montfort. After his escape, Prince Edward acted rapidly; he captured Gloucester and prepared at Worcester to fight Simon, aligning his barons, knights and Welsh infantry along the Severn. Simon forced his way across the Severn and Edward moved to confront him at Evesham, not far from where the Avon joins the Severn. Simon's men were tired, hungry and vastly outnumbered. On August 4, 1265, he was overwhelmed, defeated and killed. His head was cut off and sent as a present to Roger of Mortemer's wife. His mutilated body was buried by the monks in their church at Evesham, where Simon's tomb became a shrine and a place of pilgrimage.

The summoning of the two parliaments in 1264 and 1265, both representative of the political community—the first to frame and approve a treaty of peace; the second to effect a reconciliation between the King and his subjects—was the supreme achievement of Simon de Montfort. Even though soon afterward he was killed, disgraced and repudiated, his leadership was essential to British constitutional advance.

What part did Simon de Montfort play in this movement for constitutional reform? His enemies accused him of overriding ambition, of seeking to create a selfish oligarchy or even to rule as a tyrant. They asserted that he—like the Lusignans—was an alien (his father was French) whose elder brother had been obliged to give up his English earldom in order to serve as Constable in France. Others, like the anonymous author of *The Song of Lewes* (who was probably a Franciscan friar), characterized Simon as a man who rejected a brilliant future at the court of Henry III to champion the cause of downtrodden Englishmen. Simon asserted his right to oppose the King in the general interest of the realm. He felt that "what touches all should be approved by the King's Great Council," strengthened by the middle classes of knights and burgesses.

Simon did not merely concern himself with the complaints of his own baronial class but sought to remedy tenants' grievances concerning property rights and legal procedures. In 1259, Simon was responsible for extending the Provisions of Oxford to cover these grievances in what are generally called the Provisions of Westminster.

in accordance with his coronation oath, with the Magna Carta and with the Provisions of Oxford. The King had deeply resented the Provisions of Oxford and eventually persuaded the Pope as his overlord to absolve him from observing them. But now Henry, beaten on the field of battle in a civil war, was forced to toe the line. On March 14, 1265, Parliament declared that a treaty of peace had been concluded between the King and his rebel barons. The terms were severe; Prince Edward was required to take an oath of loyalty to the new form of government, to invite no aliens into the country, and to stay in England for three years. His household was purged and, although he was released from confinement, he was placed under the supervision of the Council of Nine.

Naturally the King and his eldest son were resolved to shake off the shackles imposed upon them. No love was lost between Henry III and his brother-in-law, though Simon and the King had once been friends. Henry was a dedicated, ambitious king but, like his father, he was suspicious, impulsive and irritable, poor in his judgments and lacking in generosity of mind. Simon de Montfort was a man of passion, determined to have his own way. His shortcoming was his inability to handle people. During his five years (1248–52) as the King's seneschal in Gascony, he had caused such bitter offense that Henry eventually removed him

During Henry III's reign, a community of knights bachelor, who were apprentices to and tenants of the great nobles, was beginning to become vocal. Simon constituted himself their leader; it was chiefly for their benefit that the Provisions of Westminster had been drawn up. The ultimate object of this agreement was to "make everyday life easier for all kinds of freeman" by protecting their lands and liberties from baronial exploitation. Such knights followed Simon into battle and many perished with him on the field of Evesham. The younger barons, the knights who held their lands as fiefs, the bachelors, the Franciscan and Dominican friars and the citizens of London found in Simon a hero whose name was celebrated in song and legend long after he was dead.

The liberal historians of the Victorian age regarded Simon as the founder of parliamentary democracy; he was hardly that, but he can be said to have contributed to the evolution of representative government in England. But it must first be recognized that the institution of parliament was rather different from what it is now. Medieval experts have pointed out that the essence of parliament lay in the presence of the king. Parliament therefore was a special meeting of the king's feudal council (the *Curia Regis*), but generally included a wider membership than that of normal meetings between the king and his courtiers.

Secondly, at these parliaments, "parleys" or "colloquies" would take place in which the king allowed free speech. During the reign of Henry III, they became ordered meetings to discuss public questions and air grievances. A clerk, writing in 1244, described the famous gathering at Runnymede as a parliament, but what was significant in the later part of Henry's reign, and that of his son, was that parliaments were summoned fairly regularly.

It was also during Henry's reign that the nature of parliament was formulated. A distinction was drawn between meetings of the King's court to settle day-to-day affairs, and meetings of parliaments that dealt with major questions and voted funds, as had been foreshadowed in Magna Carta. Knights and burgesses were asked to treat with the King about the common affairs of the realm as well as to give their consent to taxation and the allocation of funds. Thus both the composition and scope of parliaments gradually widened. The kingdom no longer depended upon the sheriffs or itinerant justices for the articulation of its affairs. In order to resolve difficulties, reliance was placed upon selected knights whose duty it became to report to the King about local feelings and the administration of local justice. When these knights

Kenilworth Castle in Warwickshire, the home of Simon de Montfort. The twelfth-century keep which he used is on the right.

Right "The host of Satan." A hostile contemporary manuscript shows the devil leading the barons who revolted against Henry III. The two pennants are those of Simon de Montfort and Gilbert de Clare, while Satan has his own banner with three toads on it!

Below A king sits in judgement on an evil doer. The barons who followed de Montfort sought to limit the arbitrary power of the monarch.

were first called to parliaments is not known with certainty, but representative knights or "lawful and discreet knights" were summoned in 1254. The burgesses, however, first appeared in 1265—hence, its subsequent designation as the Great Parliament.

When Edward succeeded to the throne in 1272, he proved to be more intelligent, adaptable and sympathetic a ruler than his father. He worked with and through parliaments, though he never surrendered executive control by assenting to the introduction of a permanent baronial committee. It was not until 1275 that he summoned the Model Parliament which contained both knights of the shire and burgesses; but the precedents of representation had been established in 1265.

Is there any justification at all for linking the growth of parliaments with democratic ideas? Only this much may be admitted: that between 1258 and 1265 unrest prevailed in England. The winter of 1258 was particularly severe. Incessant rain was succeeded by two months of frost. Crops were ruined, the price of wheat soared, and many people died of starvation. Again in 1264 unrest was widespread. The knights of the shire were summoned to Parliament to report on the social crisis and to suggest remedies.

Henry III's son Edward I presides over a parliament. He called many parliaments during his reign including the Model Parliament of 1275 which contained both knights of the shire and burgesses.

Three other points may be stressed about the importance of this period in political and constitutional history. The first is that the demands put forward by the baronage to appoint the king's ministers and household officials were unique. For no medieval king would readily have surrendered his right to choose his own ministers. Secondly, in the writings of Henry de Bracton and Bishop Grosseteste, as well as in the revolutionary efforts of Simon de Montfort, can be seen the glimmering of the concept of the rule of law. Before then the monarch could declare what the law was, but he was not supposed to make it. It was persuasively argued that the making of law required the agreement at least of the King's council, while the notion that those who paid taxes should consent to their levy came into being. Lastly, one must not forget that the evolution of parliament was a European phenomenon, and it can be contended that earlier parliaments are to be found, say, in Portugal or Spain.

MAURICE ASHLEY

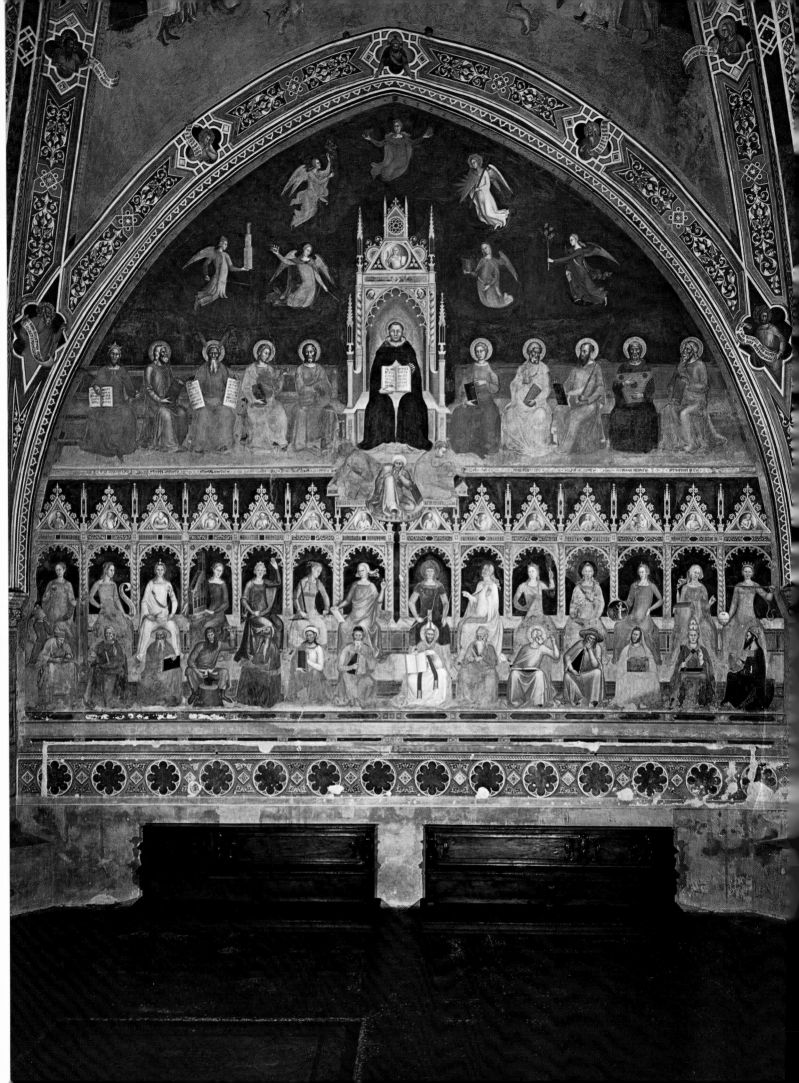

Faith and Reason

Thomas Aquinas joined St. Dominic's recently founded order of friars when he was only in his teens. He was to become one of the principal saints of the Roman Catholic Church and the founder of official Catholic philosophy. Avowedly Aristotelian, he produced a vast body of philosophical work. His most notable contribution, however, is the Summa Theologica. *In it, he denies any conflict between faith and reason. Rather, the two are complementary—reason leads man to many of the great spiritual truths, helping him to understand that which he has accepted on faith.*

St. Thomas Aquinas, the most renowned of medieval philosophers, died on March 7, 1274, on his way to the Second Council of Lyons. In his short life he had transformed Christian theology with an influence that is still felt today. For he had dominated Scholastic philosophy and built an elaborate structure that reconciled pure philosophy with Church dogma by substituting Aristotelianism for Platonism as the most specifically Christian philosophy.

Thomas came from the ruling family of Aquino. He was born in the family castle at Roccasecca, near Naples in 1225. At the age of six, he was sent to the abbey of Monte Cassino to learn his letters, and there he astonished his monastic teachers by suddenly asking one day, "What is God?" Even at that early age Thomas showed an appreciation of the fundamental aim of philosophy, which is to establish the essential nature of a problem by asking "What?" or "Why?" rather than assuming the existence of any particular idea or being by asking "Who?" When he was fifteen, Thomas went to the fledgling University of Naples, founded by Frederick II in the year of Thomas' birth. While there, Thomas encountered a remarkable tutor in the natural sciences, Peter the Irishman. He was dedicated to the newly recovered works of Aristotle and somewhat influenced by Aristotle's Arabic commentator, Averroes. Peter may have been Norman-Irish and have come to Naples via Sicily, where Norman, Arab and Byzantine Greek met at the court of Frederick. One of his surviving works is the account of a disputation, carried on in his presence, as to whether structure in animals is for the sake of function or vice versa. Peter quoted from the writings of Averroes, recently translated into Latin by Michael Scotus. Like Peter, Thomas too was inclined to interpret Aristotle through Averroes' commentary.

Thomas was only in his teens when very much against his family's wishes, he joined the new order of friars founded by St. Dominic. Traveling to

Bologna with some other Dominicans, the boy was kidnapped by his brothers and held prisoner in the castle of Acquapendente. In the same way as was attempted with Abelard, a lovely young maiden was introduced into his chamber to try and rid him of his Dominican ideas. But Thomas, picking up a blazing log from the fireplace, drove her from the room and burned the sign of the cross on the stone wall. After he persuaded his eldest sister to become a Benedictine nun, his brothers gave up their attempts to sway him. He was held captive for nearly two years before his family relented and let him rejoin the friars.

The Dominicans sent Thomas to the University of Paris to take a Bachelor of Theology degree. There his tutor was Albertus Magnus, a Dominican from Germany, on whose work in retrieving the philosophy of the Greeks, Thomas was to base his own monumental system. Three books were given to the Dominican student at Paris: a Bible, a narrative of biblical history (from the creation of the world to the Ascension of Christ) written by Peter Comestor in 1170, and a copy of the *Sentences* of Peter Lombard. This last was a compendium of theology produced about 1152. It is divided into four books: the first deals with the nature of God and the Trinity; the second with creatures, angelic and human, and with original sin; the third with the Incarnation of Christ and the Christian virtues; while the final book covers most of the sacraments of the Church.

It was the practice for an aspiring Bachelor of Theology to prove himself by lecturing for two years on Peter Lombard's book. When Thomas arrived at Paris, Albertus Magnus had just completed this stage of his progress, and Thomas himself would go through it in 1254–56. The inroads made by systematic theology of this kind upon the more pedestrian exposition of the Scriptures were not welcome to all at Paris. Roger Bacon, the English Franciscan friar, complained bitterly: "At Paris the man who lectures on the

St. Thomas at prayer. His work in reconciling traditional theology with reason is the foundation of modern Catholic thought.

Opposite Andrea di Buonaiuto's painting of *The Triumph of St. Thomas*. The great theologian occupies the place of honor in the hierarchy of Christian saints and scholars.

Sentences gets the best hour of the day for his lecture; he has an assistant and rooms with a religious community, while the one who lectures on the Scripture lacks all this and has to beg for lecture-time from his favored rival."

In 1248, Albertus, accompanied by Thomas, left Paris, to help the newly founded university at Cologne. Albertus was captivated by the works of Aristotle, which were just becoming available in abundance from two sources—Arabic and Greek. Grosseteste, Bishop of Lincoln, was translating directly from Greek into Latin and in 1247 pro-

duced a new translation of Aristotle's *Nicomachean Ethics*. Thomas became acquainted with this work during his studies at Cologne. Repeated warnings had been given by the Church that not everything in the philosophy of the pagan Greek was consonant with Christian theology. In 1231, Pope Gregory IX ordered William of Auxerre and two other theologians to "correct" the new Aristotelian material. They never produced any results, either through unwillingness or because they quailed before the enormity of the task. As the accusations against Aristotle's philosophy mounted, it became increasingly necessary to ascertain what he had actually written.

On March 19, 1255, the faculty of Arts at the University of Paris, largely under Dominican influence, issued a syllabus making the study of all the known works of Aristotle compulsory. This caused some rivalry with the faculty of Theology, and the Dominican friars came under attack. Thomas had gained his Master's in Theology and was therefore entitled to hold theological disputes. On these occasions, all theology lectures were suspended and students had to attend the dispute. It was a theological counterpart to the feudal practice of jousting. Over a period of two years, Thomas offered himself twice a week as a challenger. The results of his public debates were compiled (probably by listeners) and have come down to us in the *Quaestiones disputatae de veritate*.

At Paris, Thomas began the first of his two great works, the *Summa contra Gentiles*. This compendium of the Catholic faith, as seen in the light of reason, was not simply a rewrite of Peter Lombard in Aristotelian language. Rather, it was the beginning of Thomas' attempts to reconcile theology with reason. He held that faith and reason constitute two harmonious realms. There is no conflict between the two; rather, the truths of faith complement those of reason. The former was rational and the latter divine—God's gift to man, enabling him to arrive at knowledge of God and salvation. The approach to the subject was new. This was because Thomas felt that whereas one could argue with a Jew on the basis of the Old Testament, or with a heretic on the basis of the New, with a Moslem or a pagan one had to appeal to reason. He showed how Catholic truth was in accordance with reason, while at the same time it excluded particular errors held by the Moslem or the pagan. It is often said that he intended the work as a handbook for friars who went to convert the Saracens, but there was already at that time the prospect that a new power, the Tartars, might be brought into alliance with the crusaders against Islam.

Thomas spent the next three years (1261–64) at the papal court of Urban IV at Orvieto, where a colleague, Friar William of Moerbeke, was translating Aristotle's *Metaphysics* and *Ethics* for the guidance of the Pope. To prove that Aristotle was wrong in certain of his theories some English Franciscans, led by Grosseteste and including

Thomas' tutor Albertus Magnus. On his work in rediscovering Greek philosophy Thomas was to base his system.

A thirteenth-century scribe in his desk chair.

Roger Bacon, conducted a number of experiments in the physical sciences. The results—establishing the Greek philosopher's errors—advanced the scientific study of texts enormously.

In 1265 Thomas moved from Orvieto to Rome to supervise the studies of young Dominicans at Santa Sabina on the Aventine. It was then he wrote the *Summa Theologica*, his greatest work. In it he attempted to create a perfect, all-embracing system, unfolding all that was known of the relationship between God and man. He used a new pedagogical device: each question was first countered by a negative reply; then a text from Scripture, or from an authority such as Augustine or Hilary, was quoted to suggest that the answer should in fact be positive. The subsequent argument showed that the positive answer was correct, and finally the negative reasons were proved wrong. This method has sometimes proved confusing, for incautious modern philosophers have quoted statements from the *Summa* as examples of Thomas' thought, when in fact he was arguing against his own position.

The *Summa Theologica* is divided into three parts, only the first of which Thomas was able to complete in the peace of the Aventine. He began with the existence of God, answering his childhood question, "What is God?" The questions were grouped together under general headings, such as the knowledge of God, or the nature of the Trinity; these were called *quaestiones*, and they number 119. The individual questions, 584 of them, were called *articuli*. By the end of the forty-third *quaestio*, the subject of God and the Trinity had been dealt with thoroughly, and the rest of the book is devoted to God's creations. At the time of the composition of this first part Thomas was also writing a commentary on the psychology of Aristotle, and his treatment of human nature in the *Summa* shows a great advance from his earlier work on the *Sentences* of Peter Lombard.

Work on the *Summa* was first interrupted in 1267–68, when Pope Clement called Thomas to the papal court at Viterbo to appoint him Archbishop of Naples (an office he refused) and again the next year when the outbreak of a crisis at the

67

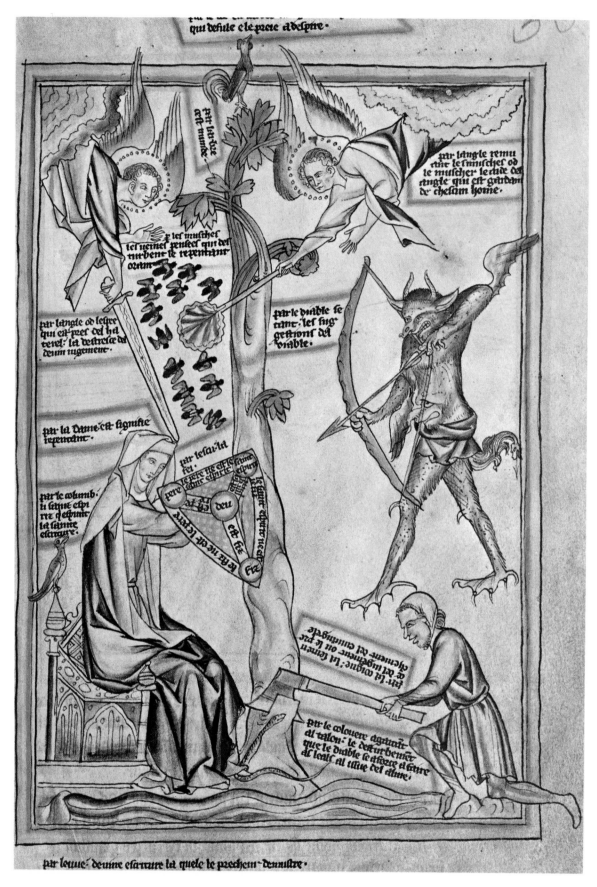

Right The medieval view of the tree of learning. It is protected by the Virgin and angels while Satan and false teachers try to destroy it.

Opposite above Averroes, greatest of the Arab philosophers; through his work the teaching of Aristotle reached Western Europe.

Opposite below An imaginative fourteenth-century impression of Aristotle lecturing to his pupils. The rediscovery of his philosophy made a revision of traditional theology essential.

68

University of Paris necessitated Thomas' return to France. A new hero of the Artists (or members of the Arts faculty) had arrived, Siger of Brabant. He was ten years younger than Thomas, a dedicated Aristotelian, who also interpreted Aristotle with the help of Averroes. Siger advanced such propositions as the world had no beginning, and the soul of man is not immortal, claiming them to be the genuine doctrine of Aristotle. The theologians were profoundly disturbed, there were demonstrations and torchlight processions by the Averroists and their opponents. When Thomas arrived, he announced that he would hold a public debate. He was in a cross fire, considered by some theologians to have gone too far in his esteem of Aristotle, while, for Siger, he had not gone far enough.

This debate is reflected in the second part of the *Summa*, the first half of which, the *Prima secundae*, was dictated in Paris. Its theme is the return of man to God, man's ethical life, virtue and vice, sin and grace. Concurrently with this work Thomas prepared his commentary on the *Ethics* of Aristotle. When he came to the passage where Aristotle encouraged his reader "to play the immortal as best he can," Thomas stoutly maintained that this

A disputed imperial election reverberate

Meanwhile in Germany, Frederick II had died in 1250 leaving the Empire to his son Conrad IV, and Sicily to his illegitimate son Manfred. Both Germany and the Italian kingdom were soon plunged into war. Manfred later succeeded in regaining southern Italy and Sicily, but in 1266 Charles of Anjou, brother of Louis IX, eagerly accepted a papal offer of the Sicilian crown.

Even more disastrous was the "great interregnum" in Germany

Rudolf I, Hapsburg emperor.

(1254–73), for it spelled the doom of the Empire as an effective political organization. During his brief reign, William of Holland (d. 1256) established an electoral system to regulate the imperial succession. Its ineffectiveness was shown by the bizarre "double imperial election" of 1257—which resulted in rival candidates— Richard, Earl of Cornwall (brother of Henry III of England), and Alfonso X of Castile—each claiming a majority of the seven electoral votes. This discredited all concerned; Alfonso never set foot in Germany, while Richard, glorying in his title "King of the Romans," failed to establish his authority even where support was strongest. The problem was exacerbated by Richard's lack of

an heir. After Richard's death in 1272 the electors united in choosing Rudolf I of Hapsburg, a weakling prince who was no threat to them. For the next two hundred years the Emperor was a meaningless figurehead, while the German potentates, lay and spiritual, ruled their districts as they chose.

Guelfs and Ghibellines

During the period after Frederick II's death, politics in northern Italy became polarized along party lines. Names, which probably go back to the twelfth-century war-cries of the Welf and Hohenstaufen families, were taken by each side. The Italian opponents of the Hohenstaufen took the name Guelfs, while its supporters were known as Ghibellines, and the terms soon came to mean "papalist" and "imperialist."

Within two years of Frederick's death, the Guelfs made a treaty at Brescia setting up a league of Guelf towns which supported the papacy. The Ghibellines, under the influence of the rulers of Verona and Cremona, immediately set up a rival Ghibelline league, which supported Conrad. The death in 1268 of Conradin, the last of the Hohenstaufen, might have been expected to end the conflict, but in practice it merely widened it.

Soon most Italian cities had Guelf and Ghibelline factions. The Guelfs for historical reasons

A Guelf knight from the town of Prato.

tended to oppose German influence in Italy, while the Ghibellines tended to be anti-papal; but local issues were often much more important than the papal—imperial struggle. The differences between the two parties came to extend to minor details of daily life. As the historian J. A. Symonds wrote: "Ghibellines wore the feathers in their caps on one side, Guelfs on the other. Ghibellines cut fruit at table crosswise, Guelfs straight down. ... Ghibellines drank out of smooth, Guelfs out of chased goblets. Ghibellines wore white and Guelfs red roses." As late as the sixteenth century the differences persisted, although by then their original meaning had been completely lost.

The Triumph of Gothic

The thirteenth century saw the finest achievements of Gothic architecture. Throughout Europe small parishes sought to glorify God and to impress their neighbors by building huge churches, whose towers and spires would be visible for miles around.

The development of Gothic architecture did not stop after the building of Chartres Cathedral. The main influences in the later development were French, and French masons traveled throughout Europe. Even Rome itself has one Gothic church, the Dominican church of S. Maria sopra Minerva, begun in 1280. Very often the pressure to build came from a bishop who might have studied at Paris, seen the French cathedrals and wanted something similar for his own diocese; for example in 1209, when Magdeburg Cathedral was destroyed by fire, Archbishop Adalbert, who had been a student at Paris, was responsible for a number of Gothic features, and Magdeburg Cathedral is often regarded as the first truly Gothic church in Germany. Gothic architecture was altered in its journey across Europe and most countries produced stylistic adaptations of their own. In Germany, hallchurches (with aisles as high as the nave) became common, while Italian Gothic was characterized by the use of polychrome brickwork. Many Spanish cathedrals suggest an Islamic influence.

Even in France there were regional changes in style. The heavily fortified cathedral of

Westminster Abbey: the nave facing east.

Albi, built by Bishop Bernard de Castanet, formerly a Dominican inquisitor, shows that the dangers of attack for the Albigensians could not be ignored even in 1281 when the cathedral was begun.

While Henry III was lavishing more money than he could readily afford on a shrine for St. Edward the Confessor at Westminster, bishops and priors throughout England were collecting benefactions from the rich and humbler offerings from pilgrims in order to transform the country's Norman cathedrals and churches into truly English edifices. In time, masons and glaziers altered the pointed arches and vaulted roofs of those cathedrals beyond recognition. The west fronts of Peterborough and Wells cathedrals, the transepts of Durham and York, and the chapter houses at Lichfield and Lincoln were erected in this period—demonstrating both the range of craftsmanship and the wealth that could be tapped by finance operations on such a grandiose scale. Salisbury Cathedral, perhaps the finest example of English Gothic architecture, was completely rebuilt in the comparatively short period between 1220 and 1258. In this formative age of religious festivals and mystery plays, pilgrimages—to Becket's shrine at Canterbury, to St. Hugh's tomb at Lincoln, to St. Alban's Bury and Winchester —were commonplace.

Italy

Sandstone church, Ethiopia.

Ethiopia

Although the limits of Christendom could be defined in military and political terms, there were, beyond its boundaries, a few small groups of Christians. In China there were Nestorian heretics and on India's Malabar coast there were many Orthodox Christians who claimed to have been converted by St. Thomas in the first century. In the Islamic lands Christian churches continued to exist though not to flourish. In one African country, however, Christianity was, and remained, the official religion. The Ethiopian kingdom had been converted to Monophysite Christianity in the fourth century. The kingdom had withstood the assaults of Islamic armies, and the faint knowledge of a Christian monarch outside Christendom gave rise to the legend of Prester (or Presbyter) John, which was very popular in the Middle Ages. The reality was vastly different from that legend of a mighty warrior ruling a fabulous land. As the eighteenth-century historian Gibbon wrote: "Encompassed by the enemies of their religion, the Ethiopians slept for near a thousand years, forgetful of the world by whom they were forgotten." The weakness of Ethiopia was not helped by political division. The authority of the emperor was divided from around A.D. 1000, when an unsuccessful attempt had been made to massacre all the legitimate heirs to the throne. For the next 250 years, Ethiopian history was dominated by the struggle between the usurping dynasty, which ruled in the historic capital of Axum, and the legitimate dynasty, whose members claimed descent from the Jewish King Solomon and the Queen of Sheba and which had its capital at Shoa. This civil war was brought to an end in 1268 when the legitimate emperor, Yekīmō Amtak succeeded in reestablishing his authority over the whole country. The reunited empire was able to withstand the renewed attacks of its Islamic neighbors to the north.

Islam in the Thirteenth Century

The first half of the thirteenth century was a period of growth for Islam. The fall of the Fatimid dynasty in Egypt toward the end of the twelfth century left Islam relatively united. The crusader states in Latin Syria were weak, and the fall of Constantinople in 1204 left Latin and Greek at war with each other instead of their common enemy. The danger of Spanish expansion into North Africa was reduced by the rise of the Almohad dynasty which ruled the whole of the western end of North Africa (the Maghreb).

By 1250 it became clear that many opportunities had been missed. The death of the Almohad Yusuf II in 1224 threatened the Maghreb kingdom with disintegration; Granada gained its independence in 1232; and the dynasty was finally overthrown in 1269.

The failure of crusading forces was due more to their weakness and poor leadership than to the strength of Islam. In 1250 the Ayubbid dynasty in Egypt was overthrown and replaced by the Turkish Mameluke dynasty.

A far greater threat came from the east than from the west. The Seljuks had set up a slave dynasty, the Khwarizm-Shahs, to defend the eastern frontiers in the twelfth century. The Shahs, however, were soon at war with the Abbasid Caliph.

As early as 1222 the Mongols had attacked the Shahs, but had not attempted to conquer their land. Further raids frightened the Islamic states, and it was fear of the Mongols that encouraged Sultan Kamil (1218–38) to make peace with Frederick II in 1229, by allowing Frederick to occupy Jerusalem. The recapture of Jerusalem in 1244 by the Khwarizm-Shahs angered the Christians, who now allied themselves with the Mongols against Islam.

In 1255, Hulagu, brother of the Great Khan, invaded Persia. He wiped out the Assassin sect, a drugtaking group of heretical Moslem terrorists. Spurred on by a fanatical hatred of Islam, he attacked the Abbasids. He besieged Baghdad in 1258; then, by breaking dikes, he was able to flood the Caliph's camp. Left defenseless in Baghdad, the Caliph surrendered the city, which was sacked by the Mongols. The Abbasid caliphate, nominal leader of Islam for 500 years, was abolished. The last Abbasid Caliph was rolled up in a carpet and trampled to death by horses. By 1260 all Syria was occupied by the Mongols. It was only the death of

Mongol troops of the Chinese emperor who attempted to invade Japan.

Mangu, the Great Khan, and the succession dispute that followed that saved all Islam from conquest. Hulagu returned to Karakorum, leaving a small army that was defeated in battle by an Egyptian army at Ayn Jalut. This ended all serious hope of Mongol advances to the west.

Afterward there was a slight Moslem recovery. The crusader states were gradually destroyed, and the last Christian stronghold in the Holy Land, Acre, was captured by Egypt in 1291.

The Orient

The death of Iltutmish, Sultan of Delhi in 1236 resulted in near anarchy. A committee of forty noble Turks divided the sultan's power and attempted to impose their own rule. They were ineffective and quarrelsome. The weakness of the system was soon proved when a former slave, Balban, organized an army, seized power and restored order. The new dynasty made energetic attempts to expand the borders of the sultanate. Balban's son reconquered Ghazni, which had been captured by the Mongols in 1221. He smashed Mongol power in India entirely and drove them out of the sub-continent.

Elsewhere in Asia, Mongol power was growing. Korea had become part of their empire. The Burmese refused to pay tribute, and in a devastating raid the Mongols destroyed the capital of Pagan. The Burmese state was so weakened that the whole country split up when it was invaded by the Shan tribes, who had been driven for their Chinese homeland by the Mongols.

Japan, too, was threatened by the Mongols. They demanded tribute and, when it was refused, attempted to invade the country in 1274. Despite some military success, the Mongols withdrew, and for seven years Japan was safe. Kublai Khan attacked with a huge fleet in 1281. This time the Japanese were ready. Assisted by storms that scattered and damaged Kublai's fleet, they were able to beat off the invaders. Although defense precautions continued to be taken until about 1300, the Mongols did not attempt a third invasion. Nevertheless in the late thirteenth century Mongol power was at its height.

When East Met West

Thirteenth-century Europe was only vaguely aware that its imported silks originated in a land to the east called Cathay. China, for its part, knew about the West but was not especially interested in it. Then, in the summer of 1275, three travelers from Venice reached the court of Kublai Khan, China's Great Lord of Lords. The brothers Nicolo and Maffeo Polo and Nicolo's son Marco lingered in the Far East for twenty years, and when Marco returned to Italy he set down his impressions of those years in a book entitled, somewhat grandiosely, **Description of the World.** *Marco Polo's travel narrative fascinated generations of readers; two centuries later it stirred the ambitions of another seeker of Cathay, Christopher Columbus.*

Every year at the beginning of June, Kublai Khan, Great Lord of Lords, "the mightiest man that ever was in the world since Adam our first parent," was accustomed to leave his winter palace in Peking for a three-month-long vacation at his summer palace in Shangtu ("Xanadu"). This princely pile of "marble and other ornamental stones, marvelously embellished and richly adorned, with gilded halls and chambers" stood at the entrance to a spacious game-park which provided food for the imperial falcons. In a pleasant grove, in the midst of the park, stood another large palace—a portable structure of split bamboo poles, held in place by more than two hundred silken cords. This palace was "reared on gilt and lacquered pillars, on each of which stood a dragon entwining the pillar with his tail and supporting the roof on his outstretched limbs."

Here it was that Kublai was visited, one summer day in the year 1275, by three travelers from far to the west—the brothers Nicolo and Maffeo Polo, merchants of Venice, and Nicolo's son Marco. The elder Polos were no strangers to the Khan. Some ten years earlier they had journeyed to his court in the train of an envoy sent by Kublai's brother Hulagu, Il-Khan of Persia. The Polo brothers had been assured that Kublai had never seen a "Latin" and was very anxious to meet one. They had been royally received and plied with questions "about the emperors, the government of their dominions and the maintenance of justice; then about kings, princes and nobles; next about the Lord Pope and all the practices of the Roman Church and the customs of the Latins." Then, because the Great Khan's curiosity was still unsatisfied, the elder Polos had been sent back to Europe on a special mission to the Pope, with a request that "he should send up to a hundred men, well versed in the seven arts and skilled to demonstrate to idolaters and others by clear reasoning that the Christian religion is better than theirs."

Support for a missionary enterprise on such a grandiose scale was scarcely to be expected from any pope. However, after some delay—caused by the two-year electoral deadlock that followed the death of Clement IV in 1269—his successor Gregory X gave the project his blessing and ordered two learned Dominican friars to undertake the task of converting the Mongols. Unfortunately, the friars' resolve failed soon after the expedition set out, and the Polos went on alone. If no attempt was to be made to convert the Great Khan to the Christian faith, at least he would not lack for instructors in the benefits of East-West trade—and if Kublai was disappointed at this imperfect response to his appeal, he was too polite to show it. We are told that, after the ceremonial preliminaries in 1275, Nicolo presented Marco, then a lad of twenty-one, with the words: "Sire, this is my son and your liege man." To which the Khan replied: "He is heartily welcome."

This episode, like all else that we know of the Polos' travels in the East, is described in Marco Polo's ambitiously conceived narrative, *Description of the World.* Marco dictated his account to Rustichello of Pisa, a professional writer of romances, while both men were being held as war prisoners in Genoa in 1298. It is disconcerting but not surprising to discover that the court scene described above reproduces, almost verbatim, an earlier account that Rustichello had written on the presentation of Tristan to King Arthur at Camelot. There are other passages in the book that can be ascribed with some probability to the romance-writer rather than to the traveler, but the work as a whole carries conviction, not only by its wealth of detail, much of it fully supported by contemporary Chinese evidence, but by its sheer matter-of-factness. Much of Polo's narrative is little more than a catalogue—but a catalogue whose items include a dazzling profusion of gold and rubies, silks and sables, perfumes and spices, exotic customs and mysterious arts. Written in French, the traditional language of romance, and extensively copied and translated, *Description of the World* implanted an enticing and indelible image of "the gorgeous East" in the mind of Europe.

By the thirteenth century, Europeans had been vaguely aware for some time that the silks that they

Kublai Khan, Emperor of China and grandson of Genghis Khan; Marco Polo spent twenty years at his court.

Opposite The Venice from which Marco Polo set out on his journey.

The Divine Comedy

Banished from his native Florence during a period of civil turmoil, Dante Alighieri composed his renowned allegory, The Divine Comedy, *to express his resentment and frustration over the enforced exile. The stanzas of his Christian epic contain scornful references to contemporary political figures, well-known clerics and personal acquaintances—but Dante's masterpiece is more than a catalog of grievances. In eschewing classical Latin for colloquial Italian, Dante gave new dignity to the vernacular and made his epic accessible to a vast new audience. And in tracing the Poet's journey through Hell and Purgatory and into Paradise, the Florentine genius provided a synthesis of contemporary political and theological ideologies that is unparalleled in world literature.*

Dante's political enemy, Pope Boniface VIII, consigned to the eighth circle of Hell—although he did not die until 1305, three years after Dante completed the *Inferno.*

Opposite Dante and Virgil, his guide through Hell and Purgatory.

On Good Friday in the year 1300, Dante Alighieri, a citizen of the thriving Italian city-state of Florence, found himself lost in a dark wood. Fleeing from its terrors, he encountered the ghost of his favorite author, the Latin poet Virgil. The poet told Dante that he could escape from the forest only by taking a road that led down into Hell and through it to Purgatory and Paradise. With Virgil as his guide, Dante crossed the river Acheron and began the terrible descent. Hell was a huge, funnel-shaped pit with ledges circling its sides, on which the ghosts of the sinful suffered pains appropriate to their offenses.

As Dante climbed down those tiers, he recognized both unimportant Florentine contemporaries and figures of Christian and classical history, such as Caiaphas—the Jewish High Priest who presided over the council that condemned Jesus to death—and Ulysses, the wandering hero of Homer's epic. At each level of their downward journey, Dante and his ghostly guide encountered sinners of greater guilt. At the lip of the funnel they found those who were merely lustful, but as the two journeyed onward, they passed heretics, seducers, perjurers and traitors—and finally came to Judas, the betrayer of Christ, and Brutus, the betrayer of Julius Caesar, both of whom were being tormented by Satan himself at the cold center of the earth. Virgil led Dante through a tunnel past this final horror, and they emerged at the other side of the world.

The two eventually came to the foot of the mountain of Purgatory, which was in form the exact opposite and complement of Hell: a peak rising up into the skies. Like Hell, the mountain was a series of circles inhabited by those who had succumbed to various classes of sin: those guilty of the more destructive sins, such as Pride, were found near the bottom, those guilty of the more trivial, such as Lust, were at the top. Unlike the lost souls in Hell, the inhabitants of Purgatory were all working, with certainty of ultimate success, for release from the effect of their sins. When Dante emerged at the summit, he could see, across the river Lethe, the Earthly Paradise that

man had enjoyed in his original innocence. The pagan Virgil could not pass into this region, and he was replaced as guide by the shade of Beatrice, a woman whom Dante had known and loved as an adolescent in Florence, and who had remained a symbol of perfection ever since. After rebuking him severely for his life of sin, Beatrice led Dante into Paradise.

Once in the celestial regions, Dante's progress became a weightless ascent through realms of air and light. With Beatrice at his side, he passed through the levels above the earth that contained the planets, the sun and the stars, meeting souls whose earthly lives had embodied a hierarchy of virtues. He was carried before the apostles Peter and John, who examined his understanding of the Christian virtues of Faith, Hope and Charity. Finally the Florentine was admitted to the Empyrean of God and the Saints, where he acquired a new guide, St. Bernard. He was then led before the Virgin Mary, by whose intercession Dante was permitted to look into the light of the Trinity.

Such, briefly, is the story told in Dante Alighieri's *Divine Comedy.* The work itself is one of the most important epic poems and one of the greatest Christian allegories in literary history. Its one hundred cantos are divided into three equal sections: the *Inferno,* which concerns Virgil and Dante's descent into Hell; the *Purgatorio,* which deals with the two poets' ascent of Mount Purgatory; and the *Paradiso,* which describes Dante's voyage through the heavens, culminating in his arrival at the Empyrean of God.

Despite its length and weighty philosophical content, the *Divine Comedy* was an enormously popular work. That success was due in part to the fact that Dante had composed his masterpiece in the vernacular Italian, rather that Latin—a choice that scandalized many of the poet's scholarly contemporaries, but made the epic accessible to a far larger audience. In addition, the *Divine Comedy* was studded with topical references—to members of the papal court, Florentine officials, friends, and

A pictorial version of Dante's Hell by Orcagna.

Dante's Hell

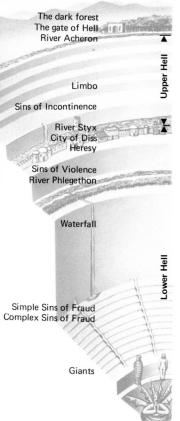

The dark forest
The gate of Hell
River Acheron

Limbo

Sins of Incontinence

River Styx
City of Diss
Heresy

Sins of Violence
River Phlegethon

Waterfall

Simple Sins of Fraud
Complex Sins of Fraud

Giants

Upper Hell

Lower Hell

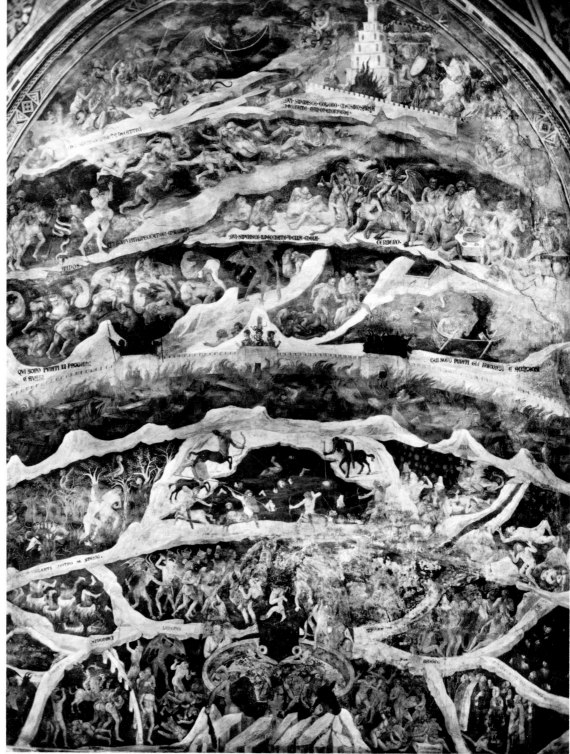

local reprobates—which made the work lively reading. That liveliness was further enhanced by Dante's use of *terza rima* verse form, a rhyme scheme (aba, bcb, cdc, ded, . . . yzy, z) that linked each stanza to the one that followed and gave the *Divine Comedy's* narrative an easy flow.

Stylistic considerations aside, the *Divine Comedy* was, before everything else, the record of the author's own conversion, of his movement from Hell to Heaven. In the *Purgatorio*, Dante portrayed himself as a penitent, shedding the stains of his sins as he climbed through the levels of successful repentence. The Roman poet, Virgil, and Dante's contemporary, Beatrice, were the inspirations of his real life as well as the poetic symbols of Natural Reason and

Divine Grace. Thus Dante was, in one sense, compressing much of the anguish of his earthly career into the few days of his spiritual odyssey. We do not know much about the author's conversion, although, by comparison with his literary equals, Homer and Shakespeare, Dante's public life is rather well documented. The known facts give us some hints of the reasons why Dante fused the account of his own central religious experience with both an elaborate expression of a comprehensive religious and moral outlook and a commentary on the great men and events of his lifetime.

Dante was born into a middle-class Florentine family in 1265. He grew up—and no doubt expected to spend his entire life—in that great city, one of the

most exciting, affluent, colorful and turbulent metropolises of Europe. As a young man he became a good lyric poet, and composed a large number of love poems in the new style of Italian versifying that was becoming fashionable. He also fell in love with a girl named Beatrice, who married somebody else and died when Dante was twenty-five. About that time Dante began to lose interest in love poetry and became more interested in philosophy and theology.

Dante recognized and accepted the responsibilities of his class and, while in his thirties, took a reasonably prominent part in the politics of Florence, which was an independent republic run, for the most part, by its more well-to-do citizens. For anyone with principles, the political world was a dangerous one. Dante's period of political activity, which started in 1295 when he was thirty, was a period of bitter strife between the Black and White factions of the Guelfs, the dominant political power in Florence. It was also the period of the pontificate of Boniface VIII, one of the most aggressive of the medieval popes, who interfered in Florentine affairs on the side of the Blacks. In 1302, while Dante, who was a

White, was absent on a peace mission to the Pope, the Blacks seized control of the city. Dante was one of those banished for life, and he spent the last twenty years of his life—years of increasing fame—condemned, as he said of himself, to "exile and poverty," "a ship without sails or rudder" wandering from one northern Italian patron or court to another.

Most of Dante's important writings were composed during his exile. It is not surprising, therefore, that the political circumstances of his age—circumstances of which Dante was so conspicuously a victim—should figure prominently in his great poem. Florence in his lifetime was at the summit of its material greatness. The thirteenth century had been a prolonged period of spectacular economic expansion all over Europe, and the great Italian commercial centers had played a role in this expansion not unlike the one that England would play in the nineteenth century. They had provided the western world with its textile industry, its great merchants and bankers, and—in 1252—with the florin, the first gold coin to be minted in Western Europe since the fall of the Roman Empire. Dante himself did not belong to a great mercantile clan. In fact, he looked back rather nostalgically to the days of his ancestor, Cacciaguida, who had lived in the simpler Florence of the twelfth century. Beatrice's husband, on the other hand, was one of the Bardi, famous merchants who trafficked with England and France.

The cloth industry and international trade had enabled Florence and several other larger Italian cities to become independent republics and to re-create the city-state spirit of ancient Greece and Rome. By the end of the thirteenth century, the traders, master-craftsmen and shopkeepers of Florence had largely established their freedom from the influence of the local noble families, who still retained a foothold in both the city and the country. This development was confirmed, about the time Dante entered politics, by the Ordinances of Justice (1293), a kind of constitution that based city government on the guilds, or trade associations of ordinary citizens.

Popular government inevitably involved faction. Throughout the thirteenth century, Florence had been torn by the strife between "Guelfs" and "Ghi-

Dante and his poem by Domenico de Michelino, with Florence on the right.

bellines"—broadly speaking, supporters of the Pope and the Emperor, respectively. This feud was traditionally traced back to 1215, when a member of one family mortally offended a member of the other by breaking his engagement to a girl of the latter's house. But for that, as Dante's forebear Cacciaguida said, "many would have been happy who are now sad." Rivalry between the Guelfs and the Ghibellines became an inseparable part of Florentine life. By the end of the century, the Ghibellines had ceased to be a serious threat to civil stability, but feuding between Black and White Guelf elements—which supplanted the original quarrel—led to the catastrophic turning point in Dante's career.

The Italy outside Florence, in which Dante spent his years of exile, was, in his eyes, a political "hostel of woe, a ship without a pilot in a great tempest . . . a brothel." Unlike other parts of Europe, which had been absorbed into such geographically large political units as the monarchies of England and France, northern Italy had no dominant power. The region was a mass of petty states, ruled either by republican cities like Florence or by lords like Can Grande della Scala, the hospitable ruler of Verona to whom Dante dedicated the *Paradiso*. From our perspective, the political chaos of Italy seems one of the preconditions of the Renaissance, necessary to the free and diverse development of life and thought; effective unification of fourteenth-century Italy would probably have been stultifying. But to Dante, who had suffered so much from the effects of that

Dante's house in Florence.

The ideal of *Good Government* in the city by Lorinzetti.

disunity, the vision of a stable order imposed from above was overwhelmingly attractive. There was no power in Italy with the resources or prestige to impose unity, and so Dante, like many of his contemporaries, turned hopefully to the German emperors.

For several centuries the rulers of Germany, claiming to be the successors of the Roman emperors, had been trying intermittently to establish their authority in Italy. In former times several had been partially successful: Frederick Barbarossa, in the twelfth century, and Frederick II, in the thirteenth, had wielded a good deal of power in the peninsula. But the economic expansion of Italy made it increasingly unlikely that a backward German warlord would be anything but a tool of local politicians if he brought his retinue over the Alps. In this hope, as in other things, Dante was a romantic. While he was in exile he wrote a book on monarchy, in which he argued, with references to philosophical and historical matter drawn from his classical reading, that men ought to accept the authority of a single ruler, the divinely ordained Roman Emperor.

The chief opponents of the German imperial claims in Italy were, of course, the popes, particularly Pope Boniface VIII (1295–1303), whose supporters in

Florence were responsible for Dante's exile. In the *Divine Comedy*, which is set in 1300, Boniface is already expected in the eighth circle of Hell, three years before his death. This bit of literary revenge is part of the highly critical view of the papacy as an institution that permeates Dante's work. Earlier medieval popes, although greatly venerated as the successors of St. Peter, had not been very powerful, and the transition from claimed powers to exercised powers took place largely in the century before the *Divine Comedy*, when the fortunes of the papacy were roughly the reverse of those of the Empire.

At the beginning of the thirteenth century, the popes had become the effective rulers of a state in central Italy. More remarkable perhaps, they had acquired control over many aspects of the Christian Church beyond the Alps. The popes played an increasingly substantial part in appointing northern European bishops and rectors, whom they were then able to tax in order to subsidize their political ambitions at home. Boniface VIII was a particularly ambitious pope, who belonged to one of the great Roman families, Gaetani, and was an expert canon lawyer. He asserted the authority of the pope to correct all Christians, including kings, in a Bull published in

The Church Triumphant by Martini : Pope Benedict XI (1303–4) negotiates a peace treaty between Philip IV of France and Edward I of England, with Florence in the background.

1302, which begins with the ringing words "*Unam Sanctam*—One holy, catholic, apostolic Church . . ." Boniface's whole career embodied the conception of the Church as a militant, temporally powerful institution—a conception that Dante denounced.

The papacy was not the only institution that was building up its power at the turn of the century. The most powerful man in Europe at that time was Philip the Fair, King of France, and his ascendancy was indirectly to affect Dante's life.

One of the most significant movements of the poet's lifetime was the developing connection between the papacy and the French monarchy, a compound of attraction and rivalry between the two institutions with the largest claims to real influence over the Christian world. Pope Boniface invited Charles of Valois, brother of King Philip, to bring an army to Italy, and it was while the Pope's supporters in Florence were strengthened by the temporary presence of Charles' army that Dante was exiled. The poet therefore had every reason to hate the royal house of France—and he took the opportunity to denounce it when hè met their remote ancestor, Hugh Capet, in the *Purgatorio*.

More spectacular events were to come. Boniface eventually was forced to devote much of his pontificate to a fierce struggle with Philip the Fair—a contest that became the central theme in the political history of Europe at this period. The Pope's claims to powers of taxation and jurisdiction in northern Europe brought him into conflict with the pretentious and ruthless French King. Boniface issued the famous papal Bull, *Unam Sanctam*—which was plainly

directed against Philip. An exasperated Philip retaliated by sending a small expedition to Anagni, the Pope's birthplace and residence outside Rome. In 1303, the Pope was taken prisoner by the French king's troops—an atrocity that seemed, even to such an enemy of Boniface as Dante, to be the work of a new "Pilate," who was crucifying Christ's vicar.

Before Dante completed the *Divine Comedy*, the power of the French monarchy had led to the election of a French pope, Clement V, and the establishment of the papal court at Avignon, in southern France, where it was to remain until 1377. Whether this was an advantage or a disadvantage for the papacy is a question for debate, but there is no question that the "Babylonian Captivity" left Italy even more destitute of political leadership. The exiled Dante greeted with enthusiasm the election, in 1308, of a German emperor, Henry VII, who was reputedly just and magnanimous, and ambitious to take control of the peninsula. Henry came to Italy in 1310 and remained for three years. His ambitions were ground down by the impossibility of overcoming opposition from various quarters—notably from Florence—and he died of a fever in 1313. It is ironic and rather disconcerting that Dante's political idealism, expressed in his book on monarchy and reaffirmed in the *Paradiso* (where Henry VII was promised a place in the Empyrean), should have attached itself to this last, feeble representative of a barbaric tradition of Germanic power.

Although circumstance drew him into the cockpit of Italian politics, it is not as a politician or political commentator that Dante interests us chiefly, but as the most superb exponent of medieval ideas. Dante had the ideas of the era at his fingertips; he was a superhuman amateur who mastered a dozen disciplines. The *Divine Comedy* is the work of a man driven by a lifelong need to make sense of the world, who has, at great cost, succeeded. For this reason, the *Divine Comedy* is a textbook of medieval attitudes.

The physical world in which the poem is set, for example, is an extremely careful and accurate picture of the universe as it was conceived by medieval man before the Copernican revolution. The earth is at the center; the moon, planets, sun and stars move in fixed orbits around it, and the angelic and celestial regions lie beyond. This attractively unified world picture was not merely of physical importance, for the ascent from earth to heaven was both a physical and a spiritual ascent.

As a young poet and scholar, Dante had already opened himself to the most advanced philosophical influences of his day. The resultant paradox in his intellectual make-up—which was the paradox of contemporary European civilization as well—was that Christian faith was combined with an intense admiration for pagan classical writings. In choosing Virgil as his guide for the journey through Hell and Purgatory, Dante was acknowledging the value of natural reason, unillumined by Christian revelation, as it was used by the noblest pagans. It would be difficult to say whether the general scheme of the *Divine Comedy* owed more to the Christian story of Christ's descent to Hell and ascent to Heaven, or to the descent into Hell that is the central episode in Virgil's *Aeneid*. During the thirteenth century Christian thought had been nearly overwhelmed by the effects of a renewed acquaintance with the writings of Aristotle, which covered, in a masterly fashion, nearly every aspect of natural knowledge—physics, biology, politics, ethics, logic and so on—and made a very deep impression on Europe's foremost scholars. When Dante looked for rational explanations of perennial problems (such as the influence of the stars or the origins of political life), he turned to the writings of the philosophers of Paris, notably Albert Magnus or St. Thomas Aquinas, or to the pagan philosophers themselves, carefully choosing arguments from their works for his own synthesis.

The thirteenth century had also seen astonishing innovations in religious life, chiefly associated with the creation of the new orders of friars. St. Francis and his followers, who founded the Franciscan Order about the time the Magna Carta was sealed, aimed to live a life of utter poverty, in imitation of the life of Christ and his apostles. The Franciscans rejected conventional worldliness, not by retreating to the isolation of a monastery but by living humbly among the common people. In Italy they became as much a part of the texture of life as Wesley's successors were to be in industrial England. In Dante's day, many of the Franciscans were revolutionary critics of the Church, hunted and persecuted by the ecclesiastical authorities. Dante sided with these radicals, who provided him with his vision of an apostolic Church, truly devoted to the original purposes of Christianity,

and set against the Church of Boniface VIII—which, in Dante's view, had "fallen into the mire" in attempting the impossible combination of spiritual functions with political power.

The *Divine Comedy* did not reflect a generally accepted thirteenth-century philosophical, political and religious synthesis—precisely because no such synthesis existed. Its inclusiveness is quite personal, the result of Dante's incomparably wide sympathies. The souls whom the author has placed in the Heaven of the Sun, for example, include not only the great orthodox doctors of the Church, but also Siger of Brabant and Joachim of Fioris—who were commonly regarded as dangerous heretics. Thus, the *Divine Comedy* makes an excellent introduction to thirteenth-century thought, but it does not really reflect the temper of the age.

Unlike the impersonal analyses of contemporary scholastics, the *Divine Comedy* is a highly personal work of art, and—despite Dante's hatred of the Florentines—it is also a product of that city, not of the cloister. It cannot help but remind us of Michelangelo's Sistine ceiling—a similar attempt to make sense out of everything that the Christian and the pagan worlds offered. The desire to achieve such a synthesis was one of the central and recurrent aims of Florentine Renaissance minds. Dante Alighieri's *Divine Comedy* was the first attempt to create that synthesis, and, because every educated Florentine knew Dante's work intimately, it became the constant inspiration for the others.

G. A. HOLMES

Pagan and Christian art contrasted: *Strength* (*left*) by Niccoló Pisano, and *Faith* by Giotto.

The society in which Dante lived was neither static nor rigid. Life in the city-states of Italy encouraged a new approach to political ideas. The ideas of papal and ecclesiastical authority advocated by Boniface VIII and by papal publicists, such as the Augustinian Augustinus Triumphus, who died in 1328, became increasingly unpopular. The doctrine of the two swords, spiritual and temporal, both of which were regarded as subordinate to the pope, was ignored or rejected. This was in part due to imperialist ideas; Dante's political treatises, the *Monarchia* for example, praised the Empire as a divine institution and advocated a universal empire to which all men should be subject. But although Dante rejected the arguments used by papalists, he accepted the kind of argument by analogy on which the papalist position was built. Boniface held that the relationship between papacy and Empire was similar to that between sun and moon. Dante did not deny this, but he attempted to qualify it by asserting the moon's independence of the sun. He even claimed that the moon had a luminosity of its own, and that therefore imperial power could not be regarded as subordinate to the papacy.

Others attacked medieval theocratic ideas on more fundamental grounds. The Franciscan philosopher William of Ockham (c. 1300–50) known as Doctor Invincibilis supported the Empire against the papacy, as did so many Franciscans. He advocated the separation of the Church from the world, and wanted the laity to exercise all temporal authority. Yet another imperial supporter who attacked the logic of papal claims was Marsiglio of Padua (1275–1342). In his *Defensor Pacis* he glorified the temporal state as the only unifying factor in society. He held that the state received its power from the people and that as a result rulers were subordinate to the people and could be deposed by them. According to Marsiglio the Church possessed no rights in society. He accepted that the fourth-century Emperor Constantine had given land, wealth and power to the papacy, but claimed that what one emperor had given another could take away.

Democratic ideas of this kind implied a totally new way of looking at society; instead of power coming from God, it comes from the people, from below instead of from above. Such theories had enormous impact in the Church and provided a basis for conciliar ideas. They may also have been an indirect influence on the leaders of the rebellions that were to become so common a feature in late-fourteenth-century history throughout Europe. Later theologians with revolutionary religious ideas had certainly read Ockham and Marsiglio. It is probable that the ideas of these early-fourteenth-century political philosophers may also have influenced the reformers of the sixteenth century. As so often happened, seminal changes in thought had been called forth by the needs of pamphlet warfare.

The German Succession

The struggle between papacy and Empire continued. The imperial electors had chosen Henry VII as Emperor in 1308 because they thought him too weak to oppose their ambitions. In fact he proved to be ambitious and energetic. This election had caused civil war, because Frederick of Hapsburg felt that he had stronger claims than Henry to the Empire and the papacy supported Frederick. After Henry's death in 1313 the civil war continued. Again the Hapsburg claims were ignored. Again the electors preferred a weak

The Archbishop of Mainz crowning kings

candidate to a strong one and eight more years of civil war followed. Again, however, an emperor elected solely because of his supposed inability to control Germany's princes, showed himself capable both in battle and in government. Ludwig IV of Bavaria, the new Emperor, captured his rival Frederick of Hapsburg at the battle of Mühldorf in 1322. This did not prevent the papacy from continuing to support the Hapsburg claim, largely because of Ludwig's interest in Italian affairs. Using Ludwig's support for the excommunicated Matteo Visconti of Milan as an excuse, Pope John XXII excommunicated the Emperor in 1324, and three years later deposed him.

This led to the pamphlet war between the papacy supporters and Marsiglio of Padua and William of Ockham. It also led Ludwig to a crusade in Italy. Like his predecessor, Ludwig was crowned Emperor in Rome, while the Pope in Avignon could only fulminate and call down God's vengeance on his adversary. There was almost continuous war for the rest of Ludwig's reign, but his position was never seriously threatened. In 1338 the Diet of Rense supported his claims to the Empire by agreeing that a legitimately elected emperor did not need papal confirmation.

During the last few years of his reign, Louis was again troubled by a rival. This time it was Charles of Luxemburg and Moravia. Charles made little progress against Ludwig in battle. It was only Ludwig's unexpected death in 1347 that gave Charles the chance of succession to the Empire.

Edward I and II

In the years after 1320 warfare dominated Europe. Edward I pursued an imperialist policy designed to bring the whole of Britain under his sway, and the success of his Scottish campaigns led to a firm alliance between France and Scotland that persisted until 1560. Wales was for a time quiet. The intervention of Welsh princes in English politics had reached its peak during the Barons' War. Llewelyn the Great had been recognized as Prince of Wales and overlord of the Welsh magnates under the Treaty of Shrewsbury in 1267. But he had

Edward I, the English Justinian, an able ruler and a great legislator.

refused to pledge his fealty to the new King of England and in 1277 Edward had been forced to invade north Wales, in order to subjugate it.

Ireland

In Ireland English rule was threatened. Robert Bruce's brother, Edward, landed in 1315, and in the following year, with the support of local chieftains, he was crowned king. He was, however, unable to maintain himself and was forced to return to Scotland in 1318. But his brief rule showed the chieftains that English rule was not all-powerful and as a result there was increasing discontent. Quarrels among the Anglo-Irish nobility gave the native chieftains

Caricature of an Irish king.

90

an opportunity to recover the land lost to the invaders and English preoccupations in France during the Hundred Years War gave them additional opportunities for success. Edward III was unable to devote any attention to Ireland because of his troubles with Scotland and France and English power gradually declined. By 1349 Ireland had effectively gained its independence.

Scotland's vacant throne

When Alexander III of Scotland died in 1286, his granddaughter, a young Norwegian princess, succeeded to the throne. It was Edward's hope that his son Edward of Carnarvon would marry her and thus unite the two crowns, but the "Maid of Norway" died on her journey to Scotland in 1290. Immediately ten nobles attempted to seize the vacant throne. In order to avert

Robert Bruce, King of Scotland, with his queen.

civil war, the Scots accepted Edward's adjudication that John Balliol, a Scottish nobleman, should succeed the princess. Balliol's nobles soon deprived him of power and formed an alliance with Philip IV of France, with whom England was currently at war over conflicting claims to Gascony, a region in southwestern France.

Edward led an army north in 1296 to subdue the Scots, and at his orders the sacred Stone of Scone, on which Scottish kings were customarily crowned, was

removed to Westminster Abbey. Once Edward's armies withdrew, there was a series of popular risings in Scotland. The rebels, ably led by William Wallace, threw off the English yoke. Scotland's independence was short-lived, however: Wallace was defeated at Falkirk in 1298, and forced to flee to France. In 1304 Edward resumed his Scottish campaign and Wallace was captured and executed.

Robert Bruce, the grandson of one of the claimants of 1290, put spirit into the Scots' revolt and was crowned King of Scotland in 1306. Edward I died shortly thereafter, on the eve of yet another expedition against the rebels, and in the next few years Bruce reconquered most of his kingdom, regaining all the castles garrisoned by the English except Stirling. When Stirling also fell, Edward II at last stirred himself to lead a great army against Bruce. On June 24, 1314, at Bannockburn a few miles south of Stirling, the Scots won a decisive victory, assuring their independence.

The disaster of English arms at Bannockburn left the worthless Edward II at the mercy of his barons, but after the fall of Thomas of Lancaster in 1322, none of them were able to dominate the government. The baronial opposition which had originated with an attack on the King's favorite, Piers Gaveston, concentrated in the later stages of Edward's reign on the removal of the new favorites, Hugh Despenser and his son. Queen Isabella, accompanied by Edward, her eldest son, departed for her native France, where she allied herself with the exiled Roger Mortimer, Earl of March. In 1326 they landed in England to avenge Lancaster's death: the Despensers were slain, Edward II was imprisoned and his son was recognized as King by Parliament. A year later the deposed monarch was cruelly murdered in Berkely Castle and power passed to Isabella and her paramour Mortimer.

Edward III

Edward III was only seventeen when he dismissed Mortimer, excluded his mother from state affairs and became the effective ruler of England. He was a patron

King's College, Cambridge.

of learning, setting up a Cambridge college, King's Hall, for the education of clerks in the royal service. Energetic, and eager to shine on the battlefield as well as on the tournament ground, Edward soon became the most popular of all medieval English kings, a warrior who led his people to national glory. The English monarch's long-range ambition was to enlarge the English duchies in France, but he had first to deal with Scotland.

Edward supported Edward Balliol, John Balliol's son, against Robert Bruce's son, David II. Balliol defeated David at the Battle of Duplin Moor in 1332 and was crowned king. He made a treaty with Edward at Roxburgh in which he recognized the English King as his overlord but this offended Scottish nationalist feeling, and risings forced him to flee to England. His defeat was short-lived for Edward marched north to help his protegé in 1333 and avenged the English humiliation at Bannockburn by defeating David at Halidon Hill, close to the border at Berwick. Balliol was restored to the throne while David fled to France, where he received support from his ally Philip IV.

Edward's main problems were, however, not in Scotland, Wales or Ireland but in his relations with France. His determination not to lose his inherited lands led inevitably to war, as the French crown was no less determined that it should be master of the whole country.

The first of the Valois

The death of Charles IV in 1328 marked the end of the Capetian dynasty in France. It also marked the end of the relative peace between England and France. Edward III of England, the grandson of Philip IV of France, was the most direct heir to the French throne, but he was excluded by the application of a new principle —the Salic Law. An assembly of barons agreed that "no woman or her son can succeed to the monarchy." Since Edward's claim was through his mother it was clear that the Salic Law was solely in order to exclude him.

The closest male heir was Philip of Valois, nephew of Philip IV. His accession ushered in a new period of French history. The Valois kings established a strong centralized monarchy, extended France's rule during the Hundred Years War, and began to involve France in the affairs of Italy. French influence was already great because of the new home of the popes at Avignon.

Isabella was too interested in domestic affairs, and Edward III too young, to concentrate immediately on France. Had Philip been conciliatory toward Edward, war might have been avoided. But the Valois king showed his determination to expand French royal power by purchasing Dauphiné in 1336. The scene was set for a showdown between the King of France and his mightiest subject.

De la bataille qui fut devant poiriers et
de la prinse du roy de france qui plus vailla
ment si mist que nuit autre

Europe's Century of War

The Hundred Years War started as a dynastic struggle between Edward III of England and Philip VI of France. The roots of the conflict, however, went back much further. With the Norman Conquest of 1066, William the Conqueror had set the stage for a cumbersome state lying on both sides of the English Channel, and England's rule of her continental domains was an uneasy one. The Hundred Years War saw the power and prestige of France repeatedly humbled and the European standing of England greatly enhanced. But the greatest casualty of the conflict was chivalry—English longbowmen defeated the flower of French nobility at Crécy in 1346 and again at Poitiers ten years later. It was the beginning of the end for the feudal knight.

During the summer of 1337 Edward III of England and Philip VI of France, both warrior-kings deeply imbued with the medieval ideals of chivalry, drifted, almost casually, into a war that was to embroil their countries for more than a hundred years and cause massive slaughter, pillage and destruction of trade. The hostilities saw the power and prestige of France repeatedly humbled in set battles on French soil and the European standing of England, a comparatively weak and poor country at the start of the conflict, greatly raised. It also witnessed the final flowering and decline of chivalry, embodied by the armored knight on horseback, as first lowly English longbowmen and then French artillerymen began to usurp the knight's decisive role on the battlefield.

If the chivalrous knight, considerate to other members of his class and loyal to his overlord, was a product of feudalism, so was the Hundred Years War which saw his decline. Since the Norman Conquest of 1066, the thrones of France and England had been bound by strong feudal bonds and frequent intermarriage. The ties resulted from the fact that the kings of England possessed lands on the European Continent for which they owed fealty to the French Crown. By 1337 these English domains had been reduced, through wars and treaties, to the small county of Ponthieu, at the mouth of the river Somme, and the large duchy of Aquitaine, centered on Bordeaux and stretching from near La Rochelle in the north to beyond Bayonne in the south. The two thrones were placed in a most delicate position by the homage the King of England owed for Aquitaine, and attempts to apply the relationship in the eighty years prior to 1337 had caused endless and sometimes bloody friction. The King of England, powerful head of a strong administration in his own country, found it galling that the King of France, ultimate feudal lord or suzerain of these continental possessions, was able, if his vassal

failed to fulfill his obligations, to call on his subjects to rise against him.

Relations on the ill-defined border of Aquitaine were constantly tense, with raids and counterraids taking place between the two lines of castles in the adjoining territories. In addition to the uneasy political situation, trade rivalry exacerbated the strain between the two nations. Expanding commerce brought the sailors of Aquitaine into direct conflict with French merchantmen as both looked for fresh outlets in the coastal towns along the English Channel. Piracy, pillaging and brawls were frequent.

Until the 1330s the kings of England, occupied at home with baronial revolts and attempts to conquer Scotland, had neither the time nor the power to challenge the kings of France. But the accession of Edward III dramatically changed the situation. Edward came to the throne in 1327 when his father, Edward II, was forced to abdicate in his favor and was then brutally murdered. But because Edward III was a minor, power remained in the hands of Edward II's unfaithful wife, Isabella, and her lover, Roger Mortimer, murderer of the King. In 1330, however, Edward III led a successful baronial coup d'état against his mother and at the age of eighteen established his control over the country.

The young Edward proved to be a warrior-king, a brilliant military tactician little interested in constitutional, administrative or economic progress, and a man who levied heavy taxes on the country's thriving wool trade with Flanders to finance his continental military campaigns. Although capable of outbursts of anger, he was one of England's most popular medieval kings. Sharing his barons' love of tournaments, he was the first monarch in two hundred years to fire them with grandiose schemes of conquest.

Set against him was Philip VI of France, a man equally dedicated to the chivalric ideal but lacking

Edward III of England pays homage to Philip VI of France for Aquitaine, last continental fief of the English kings.

Opposite English and French knights in battle. Hitherto warfare had been dominated by the feudal nobility, but these campaigns saw the extensive use of yeoman archers. This innovation gave England a military power unique in Europe.

The Hundred Years War: 1337-1360

Map legend:
- Possessions of Edward III
- Possessions of Philip VI
- English gains at the Treaty of Bretigny 1360
- Edward III's campaign of 1339 →
- Edward III's campaign of 1346-49 →
- The campaigns of Edward the Black Prince:
  - To Narbonne 1355 →
  - To Poitiers 1356 →

tactical flair. He was a headstrong ruler, easily angered and thus capable of pursuing an erratic diplomatic course. During the 1330s these two began to plan schemes of military self-glorification: Edward to conquer Scotland and Philip to embark on a crusade. Each saw the other as blocking his aims and mutual suspicion mounted until war broke out.

Edward's ambition to subdue Scotland had been longstanding among his predecessors, but where his father and his grandfather, Edward I, had failed, he thought he could succeed. However, an old alliance existed between France and Scotland, and when Philip started diplomatic machinations with Scottish nobles, Edward feared the possibility of French military intervention. In 1336 an English parliament meeting in Nottingham denounced the French throne's "perfidious maneuvers." Philip, too, had cause for anger: Pope Benedict XII refused to sanction a crusade until peaceful relations were restored with England. Philip, in a fit of pique, ordered his crusading fleet, assembled at Marseilles, to move to the Channel ports and threaten Edward.

The acrimony was further increased when Edward promulgated a decree cutting off wool supplies to the Count of Flanders, who was faithful to the French Crown. English envoys began traveling through the Low Countries and the Rhineland, luring counts and dukes into an alliance against the French monarchy with English gold. Meanwhile, Edward put his country on a war footing—exhorting nobles to learn French and prepare for battle and ordering a nationwide intensification of archery practice.

The final break came in May, 1337, when Philip confiscated Aquitaine. Edward replied with a message of defiance, in which he addressed his adversary as "Philip of Valois, who calls himself King of France." This was but a short step to Edward's later claim that he was rightly King of France, a claim that gave him justification for rebelling against his French suzerain. It also gave support to his Flemish allies, who had revolted against their count but could now argue that they were fighting a just war for the true King of France against a usurper.

Edward's claim had an arguable basis: Philip had come to the French throne in 1328 on the death of his cousin, Charles the Fair, who had sired only daughters. Philip claimed that a woman could not succeed to the throne of France—a ruling first put forward in 1317 to justify the seizure of the thone by another of his cousins, Philip V. But Edward, whose mother, Isabella, was the sister of Philip's two predecessors, argued that the throne could descend through the female line and claimed it as his own.

The war got under way slowly. Edward first planned to invade France through the Low Countries, but this idea was repeatedly frustrated by lack of funds and the failure of his German allies—now joined by the Emperor Ludwig of Bavaria—to provide him with the mercenaries they had promised. But finally, in September, 1339, the English king set out from near Brussels and began to ravage northeast France. Philip's army shadowed him but refused to give battle. As winter set in, a frustrated King of England fell back on the Low Countries, having achieved little.

This was to be the pattern for most of the Hundred Years War, a conflict in which the English offensives generally took the form of systematic raids of destruction, called *chevauchées*. These raids would reward soldiers with booty but did not lead to pitched battles with the massed might of the French nobility or secure any great territorial advantages. The war was frequently interrupted by short-term truces and long-term peace pacts; fighting rarely took place beyond the dry summer months, when rough dirt roads became virtually impassable.

The year 1340 saw Edward return to England with nothing to show for his maneuvers but massive debts. He was even forced to leave his wife and children behind in Ghent as securities to unpaid bankers. Yet the year also saw the first of his great victories, a sea battle at Sluys off northern Flanders. Edward had set sail for Flanders in June with his full fleet, which suddenly came across its much larger rival anchored in Sluys harbor, unable to maneuver rapidly. With the advantage of sun, wind and tide, Edward swooped. His longbowmen loosed a rain of arrows, while men-at-arms grappled with their opponents in vicious hand-to-hand fighting. Within a few hours the French vessels were either captured, sunk or burned, and England had secured a command of the seas that was to last several years. But this auspicious beginning was not followed up on the ground, the pattern of fighting inconclusively following that of 1339. Edward, heavily in debt, his Flemish and German alliances beginning to fall apart and his prestige possibly at its lowest, was forced to conclude a peace pact with Philip and returned ingloriously to England.

It was not until 1342 that Edward again began to make real inroads into France. John, Count of Montfort, and his wife, Joan, turned to Edward after Philip dispossessed them of the dukedom of Brittany. In October, 1342, Edward landed in Brittany with 12,000 men. Although the pope imposed a truce on him, sporadic fighting continued until by the end of 1345 Edward had a firm hold on Breton affairs.

A similar appeal from a dispossessed French noble led to the campaign of 1346, which at last saw the long-awaited set battle between the might of France and England. Philip had confiscated the lands of a powerful Norman baron, Geoffrey of Harcourt, who turned to Edward. On July 12, the King of England and his army landed at Saint-Vaast-la-Hougue in Normandy and proceeded to lay waste the countryside, burning, looting and taking prisoners for ransom. He besieged and sacked Caen and then headed toward Paris—perhaps by design, but possibly because the bridges over the Seine were down, barring his way northward. Panic seized the French capital as Edward marched to within twenty miles of its walls before finally crossing the Seine and turning north toward the coast. Meanwhile, Philip had been gathering a huge army in Paris and finally set out in pursuit of Edward, catching him up at Crécy, not far from Abbeville near the river Somme, on August 26.

Philip had avoided coming face-to-face with Edward for seven years. Now, ignoring the fact that his army was tired while the English were relatively fresh, he decided to join battle. His army was much larger than the English force, and he felt assured of victory. Although contemporary accounts vary widely, the French seem to have numbered about 40,000—nearly three times that of the English band of 15,000. But Edward's pitifully small force had two important advantages —a fine defensive position and superb discipline.

The English rear was protected by a wood and

Archery practise with longbows. With its power, range and accuracy, the longbow was to usurp the knight's decisive role on the battlefield.

Left Mêlée at the Battle of Crécy. Here, using tactics learned in the wars with Wales and Scotland, English longbowmen decimated the French cavalry.

The English attempt to storm Tours, with archers and artillery in action. Note the siege tower and the French troops massed behind the drawbridge for a sortie. From Wavrin's fourteenth-century *Chroniques d'Angleterre*.

that a chivalric battle must involve two opposing armies of knights fighting it out on horseback. Thus, toward evening, they joined battle with a wild, undisciplined dash for the English lines, trampling through their own advancing crossbowmen. They were surprised to find themselves met, not with an equally disorganized charge of English knights, but with a deadly hail of arrows.

Edward had ordered his knights to dismount and stay in fixed positions until he gave the word. He did not do so until his longbowmen, firing three times as fast and with greater range than the Genoese crossbowmen employed by the French, had decimated Philip's unruly host of knights. A contemporary chronicler reported: "The arrows of the English were directed with such marvellous skill at the horsemen that their mounts refused to advance a step; some leapt backward stung to madness, some reared hideously, some turned their rear quarters to the enemy, others merely let themselves fall to the ground." Then Edward unleashed his knights, who waded into their opponents on foot and on horseback and completed the slaughter.

Repeated French assaults, suicidally foolhardy, were beaten back in this way until by nightfall much of the flower of French nobility lay dead on the battlefield and Philip, with a small band of retainers, had fled to a nearby castle. Knights could no longer rush into conflict as a disorganized horde and hope to win the day. That chivalric ideal was killed by the longbowmen at Crécy. But the lesson was not learned, and ten years later the French army suffered a similar fate at the Battle of Poitiers.

Edward, however, did not have the strength to follow up his massive victory. Instead of turning back toward Paris, he continued his march to the coast. At Calais, one of the best fortified towns in France, he began a leisurely siege, building a wooden village for his army, complete with shops,

its front ran down to a small river, ensuring that the French advance would be slow. Edward divided his army into three main units of knights, one of them under his sixteen-year-old son Edward, the Black Prince, who was on his first campaign abroad. Between these blocks of knights were men-at-arms and archers, flexing six-foot longbows of oak or ash. No such organization or coordination between knights and archers was to be seen on the French side. Philip's knights disdained the idea of a unified plan of action, especially in concert with lowly crossbowmen. They remained set on the idea

The effigy of Edward the Black Prince, son of Edward III and victor of Poitiers, in Canterbury Cathedral.

The Battle of Poitiers, at which the heavily outnumbered English routed the French army and took its king captive to London.

near the town walls. The siege lasted throughout the winter and well into the following summer. After almost a year the town's food supplies were exhausted and its people near starvation. Resigning themselves to the fact that King Philip was not going to break the blockade, the townspeople delegated one of their number to go to Edward and plead for mercy. The emissary promised that the gates would be opened if he would spare their lives.

Enraged by the trouble the siege had caused him, Edward at first refused to listen to appeals for clemency. He finally relented and said he would spare Calais if six of its leading citizens dressed in white shirts and with halters around their necks, came to him with the keys of the town. With these men, he added, he would do whatever he pleased. After much debate, six of the town's richest men volunteered for this unenviable task and set out for the English camp, dressed as ordered. When they arrived they pleaded to Edward for mercy. In anger he snapped out an order for their execution.

At this point his wife, Queen Philippa, intervened. Although pregnant, she had joined her husband in Calais to watch the final stages of the siege. She pleaded with Edward to spare the men and he, in accordance with the tenets of chivalry, replied that he had not the heart to refuse her eloquent request, and handed over the six to her for safekeeping. Thus Calais was taken bloodlessly and this important port, guarding one of the narrowest points across the English Channel, remained England's sole possession on the Continent long after other lands were forfeited to the French throne. The town was finally lost some

The coronation of John II of France, a chivalrous knight but a mediocre king. His headstrong attack at Poitiers repeated the tactical errors of Crécy.

two centuries later in the reign of Queen Mary I.

Edward returned home from Calais in triumph. There was a lull in the war as he basked in the glory of his conquests and Philip set about repairing his lost prestige. In 1348, the Black Death swept across Europe, decimating populations and halting any further schemes of military prowess. By the time hostilities resumed in the 1350s, Philip had died and his son, John the Good, was on the French throne. Like his father, John was dedicated to the chivalric ideal, but he too was quickly roused to anger.

Edward receiving the burghers of Calais. At the intervention of Queen Philippa, their lives were spared and Calais taken bloodlessly.

Soldiers looting. The English offensive consisted for the most part of raids of destruction to satisfy the soldiery with booty and plunder.

During the summer of 1355, the King's son Edward, the Black Prince, arrived in Bordeaux to renew the war. With an army of about 6,000 men he set out on a raid across France, returning to the port in November, weighed down with an immense amount of booty. The following summer he set out on a similar campaign, now at the head of a force of about 8,000 men, and marched northward in an attempt to link up with the Duke of Lancaster, who was leading a foray southward from Brittany. The Prince's soldiers left a trail of death and destruction in their wake. In the words of the chronicler Froissart: "They burned and pillaged the whole land; when they entered a town and found it richly stocked with food they refreshed themselves for two or three days and then departed, destroying what remained, staving in

barrels of wine and burning fields of wheat and oats so that the enemy could not have use of them."

When King John heard of the two-pronged English advance he summoned a huge army and set out to drive a wedge between the Duke of Lancaster and the Black Prince. At this, Prince Edward swung round and headed back for Bordeaux. The French army finally caught up with him near the town of Poitiers, about 130 miles northeast of his destination.

Battle was not immediately joined, for two cardinals sent by Pope Innocent VI called a twenty-four-hour truce between the forces. Severely outnumbered by John's army, Prince Edward feared that his troops would either be decimated in battle or else surrounded and starved into submission. In desperation, he offered to withdraw to Bordeaux in peace and not take up arms for seven years. But John, eager to avenge his father's defeat at Crécy, would have none of this. Dismissing the cardinals, he ordered his knights to attack.

The twenty-four-hour delay had enabled Edward to take up a strong defensive position in a vineyard, with his rear protected by a wood and his front by hedgerows and a line of carts and trenches. As at Crécy, an undisciplined French cavalry charge opened the battle, but now the slaughter was even greater because John's knights, slowly attempting to penetrate the hedges and get at the English army, were easy targets for Edward's bowmen.

Then, as the armies finally clashed in hand-to-hand fighting, a small, select band of English bowmen and knights came out of hiding behind a hill on the French army's left flank and charged. John's soldiers were taken quite unawares and began to give ground until a retreat became a rout. But John himself remained in the thick of the

The siege of Calais. After holding out for nearly a year, Calais was starved into surrender, thereafter to become the leading town for the English wool trade.

fighting. He dismounted from his charger and, ordering his knights to do the same, led them forward. It was a brave, desperate attempt to save the day, but the battle was already lost. Finally an English knight turned to him and said "My Lord, my Lord, surrender yourself." John did. A throng of English knights then surrounded him, jostling to get at the King of France and claim him as their hostage, and it was only when two high-ranking barons rode up to take him to the Black Prince that the mêlée subsided.

France was stunned by the Battle of Poitiers and the capture of King John. In the words of a chronicler: "The affairs of the kingdom went from bad to worse." There was a general breakdown of law and order as nobles began feuding, brigands appeared on the roads and the peasants rebelled. "From this day the land of France, hitherto glorious

and honored throughout the world, became the laughing-stock of other nations."

For four years John remained a captive in the Tower of London as King Edward tried to arrange a suitably high ransom and a favorable peace settlement. Finally, in May, 1360, a draft agreement was drawn up at Bretigny. Three million gold crowns were promised in ransom for King John, while Edward was given full suzerainty over Calais, Ponthieu and Aquitaine. He had achieved all his war aims and more. Edward, however, renounced his claim to the French throne. The treaty was a great victory for England, but it was never carried out. Peace lasted only until 1369 and then the war was renewed; for no French king could agree for long to give away so much land and thus undermine his authority.

RICHARD MARTIN

99

The mid-fourteenth century was a time of increasingly nationalist feeling in Eastern Europe. In Poland, for example, the prudent foreign policy of Casimir the Great not only saved his kingdom from partition but also increased its stature. He gained from Bohemia the right to a free hand in Silesia and made a satisfactory peace with the Teutonic Knights—thus providing Poland with defensible frontiers. Casimir codified the law, reformed the administration and encouraged trade (notably by granting the Jews privileges). Having no direct heir, he decreed that his throne should pass to his nephew, Louis I of Hungary, upon his death. This decision, which was supported by the nobility, created future difficulties. The monarchy in Poland became elective, and the nobility used this to increase their power at the crown's expense.

By the time he ascended the Polish throne in 1370, Louis had already built up a reputation as soldier, autocrat and patron of learning. He had avenged the murder of his brother Andrew, consort of Queen Joanna I of Naples, by overruning that kingdom in 1347, but the Pope had refused to sanction his coronation. His long struggle against Venice, which lasted from 1345 to 1358, brought him control of many towns on the Dalmatian coast.

The small Kingdom of Lithuania, on the Baltic coast, was created as a buffer state by the Teutonic Knights, but its subjects quarreled with their overlords. It became an independent kingdom in 1293. Because of the strength of the Teutonic Knights, the Lithuanians were forced to look eastward for expansion, and Russian and Lithuanian history at this period is dominated by the struggle between the two states.

The Serbian monarch, Stephen Dushan (1331–55), also created a strong state. He was helped by the quarrel between the Latin empire of Constantinople and its Greek rivals. He made the town of Skopje his capital in 1346, and in the same year had himself crowned emperor of the Serbs, Greeks, Bulgars and Albanians. He turned the archbishopric of Pec into a separate patriarchate, independent of the Patriarch of Constantinople. His concern was not merely with conquest and elaborate titles. He also drew up an important law code, *Zabonnik*, which was based both on written and on customary law.

In Czechoslovakia, too, national pretensions were advanced by ecclesiastical claims. In 1344 the papacy permitted the creation of an archbishopric at Prague, and in the same year the huge Gothic cathedral of St. Guy was begun. Four years later the University of Prague was founded. The chief intention of the Emperor Charles in beautifying Prague was to create a capital for the Empire. However, the effect was to give added force to Czech nationalism.

Revolt in Rome

The absence of the papacy from Rome left a power vacuum in Italy. The papacy had been the only strong native Italian power and its departure led to increased interest in Italy by the Empire, France, Spain and even Hungary. It also left the Italian cities and states free to expand and develop independently. Venice, for example, was able to make its first mainland conquests in Italy during the Babylonian Captivity. Rome itself was left to the mercy of the local aristocracy: Colonna, Orsini and Gaetani battled for mastery of the papal and imperial city. Anarchy was endemic.

The Roman populace was almost powerless. Its contempt for the nobles was not enough to save it from their rule. The populace several times asked the popes to return, but the popes feared the problems of government in Italy and refused. At last, on Whit-

Cola di Rienzi, the Roman dictator who dreamed of a united Italy.

sunday, 1347, Cola di Rienzi, an innkeeper's son who had become a notary, led a revolution against the nobles of Rome. Marching into the capital, Rienzi summoned a parliament, abolished senatorships and had himself proclaimed tribune and liberator of the Holy Roman Republic. Rienzi, a dictator with extravagant ambitions and a tendency to megalomania, sought to bring the whole of Italy under his sway—not by conquest (as Robert of Sicily had attempted) but through the consent of the people. Representatives of various municipalities assembled at Rome to celebrate the "Feast of Italian Unity" and Rienzi declared that Rome would establish a new "imperium" in the West, giving voice to the dreams of Dante and Petrarch. At first Pope Clement VI supported Rienzi. The innkeeper's son had been a notary in the papal government, and the Pope in any case favored the humiliation of the overpowerful nobles. But as Rienzi's ambitions became more pronounced and exaggerated Clement changed his mind. He urged the exiled Roman patricians at Avignon to depose Rienzi, but the tribune, aided by a Hungarian army, defeated the expatriates' troops.

The papal legate condemned Rienzi as a heretic, and the Colonna family, hoping that the people would desert their tribune, rebelled. They were not disappointed. While Rome returned to its previous anarchy, Rienzi fled. He spent two years in a Franciscan convent, and then asked Emperor Charles IV for protection. Clement was determined that the rebel should be executed, but before the sentence could be carried out, the Pope died. His successor, Innocent VI, was more merciful, and Rienzi was allowed to return to Rome.

Casimir the Great. He provided Poland with defensible frontiers.

Joanna I,
Angevin queen of Naples.

He gathered an army and briefly mastered the city. But his determination for revenge against those who had driven him out made him unpopular with the people. In 1354 they rebelled against him and he was killed by the mob.

Disturbances in Italy

The disturbances in Rome were to some extent paralleled in other Italian cities. More and more often the Republican constitution and ideals of the city-states were set aside as the need for firm government, for expansion in the economy and for military success made speedy decisions necessary. The Italian states, free of most external constraints, made war on each other. Small cities were conquered by larger cities and the number of states in north Italy declined. These "cannibal" wars destroyed the independence of many, and left the map of north Italy dominated by four large city-states: the republics of Genoa, Florence and Venice, and the Duchy of Milan. Among the smaller surviving states there were few republics; Modena, Mantua, Savoy and Ferrara were all duchies.

South of Rome, the Aragonese had established their rule firmly in Sicily in the thirteenth century. King Frederick (1295–37) made a treaty which, if fulfilled, would have led to an Angevin succession in Sicily. But after his death his Aragonese heirs simply ignored the agreement. The Queen of Naples, Joanna, made huge but continually unsuccessful efforts to conquer Sicily and she eventually had to admit defeat; Sicily remained in Aragonese hands, although tribute was paid to the King of Naples.

Economic growth

The thirteenth and early fourteenth centuries were a period of rapid economic growth. Population rose enormously, particularly in the cities. In 1150 no city in Europe had a population as high as 50,000 and there were few with as many as 20,000 inhabitants; by the middle of the fourteenth century there were four cities—Milan, Venice, Genoa and Florence—with populations of over 100,000. Paris and Rome

Cathedral building
in the thirteenth century.

had around 80,000 each, and many cities, particularly in Italy, had around 50,000. This growth in urban life was only made possible by large-scale economic change and expansion. Since it took the labor of about twenty country-dwellers to support a single town-dweller the extent of the economic change was huge.

In part this was due to improvements in technology. Although the Middle Ages were not an age of great technological advance, there was a steady stream of useful inventions. One of the most important was the use of a heavier and more efficient plow, which replaced the old scratch plow. This had a substantial effect on agricultural productivity. Europe's other main industry—wool—was similarly affected by the pedaled loom, which expanded cloth production. Other improvements had an economic effect. Cartography improved, and this saved time on journeys. (One example of the ignorance that had prevailed was that St. Louis of France had allowed himself to be persuaded to attack Tunis in North Africa because he believed that it was on the route from France to Jerusalem!) Improvements in

book-keeping and accounting encouraged the growth of efficient banking houses. The cathedral-building craze of the thirteenth century was made possible by improved building techniques. The gangs of masons responsible for building kept their craft secrets to themselves, but their numbers increased and so did their skill.

The cathedrals and the expansion in education were themselves a result of Europe's economic success. There was surplus money in the economy which could be used for "luxuries." Small towns could only afford large cathedrals because they were wealthy from industry, trade or agriculture.

The main source of this wealth was increasing population and growth in trade. There was no shortage of manpower, whether it was for cathedral-building, agriculture or warfare. Working conditions for laborers were hard as a result: if one laborer refused the terms offered another could quickly be found. In agriculture, particularly, the poor suffered. Many nominally free men were in fact serfs, tied to the land. The expansion of Catholic Europe to the east and the south was made

possible by the rapidly increasing population. The crusades, with the knowledge and wealth they brought back to Europe, depended for their success on land hunger as much as anything else. England's population, for example, doubled or trebled in the two hundred years after the Norman conquest.

One of the main causes of increased trade was the independence of the Italian city-states. Their traders traveled across the whole known world, and Marco Polo was merely the most famous of those traveling merchants. Venice, in particular, owed its prosperity to trade. Venetian ships traveled to the Levant and the Black Sea, to North Africa, into the Atlantic, the North Sea and the Baltic. In the Italian towns a whole trading substructure grew up. The largest single employer in early fourteenth-century Europe was probably the huge shipyard of Venice, the Arsenal. In most of the Italian cities there were warehouses for imports and exports, and banks to supply capital.

The Church disapproved of "usurious" loans, but rates of interest—driven up by shortage of capital and the need for investment—were high just the same. Risks were high, too: piracy, enemy attack and the weather were very real dangers.

The success of the Italian towns is reflected in the wealth of their citizens. In 1292, for example, the two residents of Paris with the highest taxable income were both Italians. Italy's economic dominance can be seen from the success of the florin, the Florentine gold coin. Within a few years of its first minting in 1252 it had become the standard monetary unit of Europe.

There was a slight economic recession in the middle of the fourteenth century. In order to finance his continuous and expensive wars, Edward III had borrowed heavily from two large Florentine banks, the Bardi and the Peruzzi. As he could not easily repay his debts owing to the slow progress of his French campaign, he repudiated both debts. Both banks were forced out of business. The consequent loss of confidence was not helped by a series of bad harvests, which had an effect on the economies of most European countries, for despite the growth of trade Europe's economy was still basically agrarian. Worse was to come.

The Black Death 1348

By 1345 the shipping lanes between Europe and the Levant were regularly plied by merchant vessels carrying cargoes of spices, silks, fine porcelains—and plague. Rats on board those ships harbored fleas on their hides, and those fleas in turn harbored **Pasteurella pestis**, *the bacillus that causes bubonic plague, in their stomachs. Within a decade after the first outbreak of plague in Europe, some 33,000,000 people—roughly one-third of the Continent's population—had succumbed to the dread disease. Medieval physicians were powerless to check the plague's spread, and clerics convinced their followers that the disease was divine retribution for unnamed sins. By the time the plague had run its course, it had decimated Europe and doomed its feudal social structure.*

The sailing vessels that plied the trade routes linking fourteenth-century Europe and the Levant were invariably rat-infested—and those rats were usually flea-infested. As a result, sailors, dockworkers and port dwellers of the era frequently developed severe skin infections, worms and typhus. Flea-borne diseases rode the caravan routes and shipping lanes in the early 1300s, and minor epidemics were common.

Within the stomach of each flea lurked *Pasteurella pestis*, the bacillus that causes bubonic plague. Infection followed these host rats westward: by 1346 the plague was rampant in Asia Minor and by early 1348 it had reached Sicily and the mainland of Europe.

To fourteenth-century Europeans, the Black Death—as the first great epidemic was later called—was a God-sent punishment for their sins. The plague itself was occasionally said to be visible—as a cloud of mist or a pall of black smoke—but it remained mysterious in its origins and its workings. Doctors were powerless to control it. They prescribed a variety of arcane treatments for its prevention and cure, but most physicians had as little confidence in the efficacy of their prescriptions as did their patients. That mutual lack of confidence was more than justified; it would have required powers of diagnosis far beyond the range of the medieval doctor for him to identify the three lethal strands of pure plague—bubonic, pulmonary and septicemic. Indeed it is only within the last few decades that techniques have been evolved to check and stamp out such an epidemic.

Once launched on the mainland, the plague spread with awesome speed. It must have seemed to contemporary Europeans that nothing would stop the disease until the last man had died. Indeed, the only medical mystery that remains today is why the bubonic plague did *not* consume the whole population of Europe.

Villages which avoided infection were all but impossible to find in Italy, the first country on the Continent to be overwhelmed by the Black Death. Florence, one of the greatest cities of Europe, possessed somewhere between ninety and a hundred thousand inhabitants in 1348. Of these, according to one contemporary chronicler, "not one in ten was left alive" when the plague had run its course. In a memorable description of the plague contained in the prologue to the *Decameron*, Boccaccio claims that a hundred thousand Florentines died during the epidemic. Such statements were not intended to be taken as precise estimates; rather they were hyperbolic expressions by eye witnesses of the enormity of their experience—as meaningless statistically as an assertion made by the Pope's advisers that the Black Death cost the lives of 42,836,486 people throughout the world.

From Italy, the plague spread both overland and, on shipboard, along the European coastline. On land, where the advance of the disease was governed by the motion of rats or infected men, the progress was laborious. It is noteworthy, for instance, that the Black Death reached Moscow from the Crimea by way of Italy, France, England, and the Hanseatic ports—not by moving overland. Germany, on the other hand, was assailed principally by land, as the plague moved up the Mosel valley, through Bavaria and through the Balkans.

The fearful suffering was made worse by the ferocious persecution of the Jews that accompanied it. Medieval man felt a desperate need to blame his tribulations on some scapegoat, and the Jews were a convenient minority group, already unpopular for economic and social reasons. A few unfortunates were tortured into confessing that they had poisoned local wells, and instantly the whole race was inculpated. In Germany the Black Death also produced the Flagellant Crusades. In an attempt to take upon themselves the sins of the world, long processions of penitents literally whipped themselves into a frenzy at services held in every town they visited.

Marseille seems to have been the first French town to be infected. The plague soon reached Avignon,

Boccaccio, whose *Decameron* describes the horror which the Black Death aroused, by Andrea del Castagno.

Opposite Death Riding Triumphant, from Palermo Cathedral.

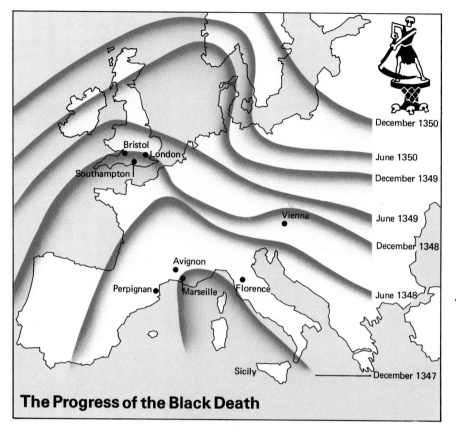

The Progress of the Black Death

December 1350
June 1350
December 1349
June 1349
December 1348
June 1348
December 1347

Bristol
London
Southampton
Vienna
Avignon
Perpignan
Marseille
Florence
Sicily

where it spared Pope Clement VI—who retreated to his chamber and took refuge between two enormous fires—but treated the populace with particular severity. The Pope's immunity was not exceptional, however. Although many men of importance perished throughout Europe, the rich—who could flee the cities and take shelter in their spacious and relatively hygienic manors—suffered conspicuously less than their poorer contemporaries.

In France, as elsewhere in Europe, little pinpoints of reliable data about the plague's course stand out from the mists of uncertainty and vagueness. In Perpignan, for instance, records show that, out of 125 scribes and legists active before the Black Death, only 44 survived; seven of the town's eight doctors and sixteen of its eighteen barbers and surgeons also disappeared.

The first case of bubonic plague in England almost certainly occurred at Melcombe Regis in Dorset in June or July of 1348. Other ports, however, vie for the doubtful honor of being the first victim, and Bristol and Southampton must certainly have been infected within a few weeks of the outbreak of the epidemic. It is possible to visualize the plague's spread, in the first months, as a kind of military operation: the initial attack on the Dorset ports, followed by a bold thrust across the country to the north coast, seaborne landings at scattered ports to outflank the defense, slow mopping-up operations in Devon and

View of a city by Ambrogio Lorinzetti; the plague, brought by boat from the East, spread rapidly due to crowded and unhygenic living conditions.

104

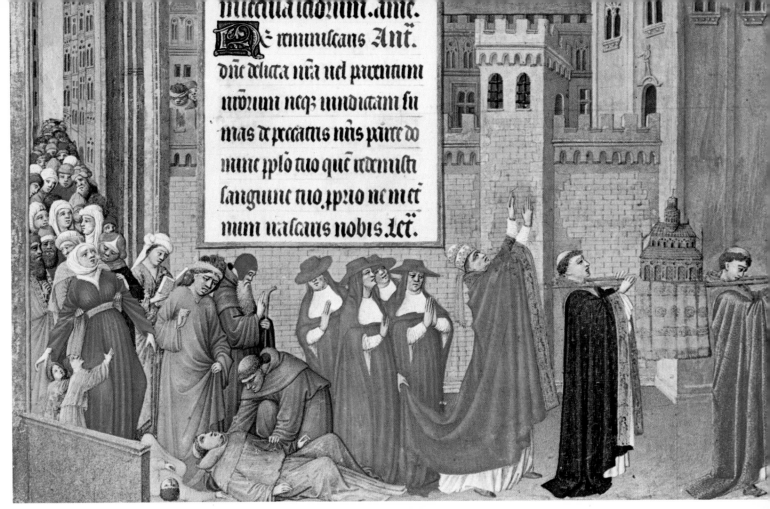

Cornwall, and then a final thrust up the Thames valley towards London. After March, 1349, the campaign analogy can no longer be pursued; the disease poured forward in a hundred different directions and sprang up simultaneously in a hundred different spots. By the end of 1350, virtually every village in England, Scotland, and Wales had suffered casualties.

It is possible to chart the progress of the Black Death in England with greater accuracy than elsewhere because of a wealth of manorial and ecclesiastical records. It is, of course, dangerous to argue that because only twenty-five per cent of the beneficed clergy died in the deanery of Henley, while forty-three per cent died in the deanery of Oxford, the same ratio applied to the general population in those areas. There is, however, enough evidence to establish a general pattern: East Anglia and the West Country were probably the worst afflicted areas; London, where the Black Death raged throughout the whole of 1349, seems to have lost between twenty and thirty thousand people out of a total population of some seventy thousand—a stark figure, although modest in comparison with the lurid estimates of contemporary chroniclers and some nineteenth-century historians.

By December, 1350, the epidemic had blanketed the whole of Europe—and by December of the following year it was virtually at an end. Certain areas—Bohemia, large sections of Poland, a mysterious pocket between France, Germany and the Low Countries, and tracts in the Pyrenees—had largely escaped the effects of the plague.

Attempting to establish any overall estimate of mortality is hazardous and speculative. There is a better chance of doing so in England than elsewhere, yet even in England's case calculations differ widely and must be hedged around with a multitude of qualifications. Reliable sources have estimated that England's mid-century population of 2,500,000 to 4,000,000 persons had been reduced by 50 per cent by 1400. As a rule of thumb, the statement that "roughly 33 per cent of the population of Europe died of the plague before it had run its course" is reasonably reliable. That figure could conceivably have been as high as 45 per cent or as low as 23 per

The Church's pleas for forgiveness and an end for the plague are ignored as Death strikes a friar during a papal procession; from the *Tres Riches Heures du Duc de Berry*.

Medical knowledge was as powerless as religion to help victims of the Black Death.

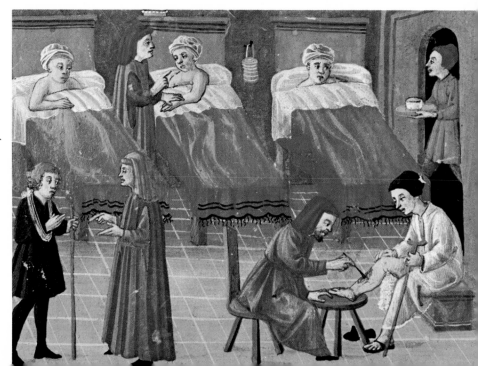

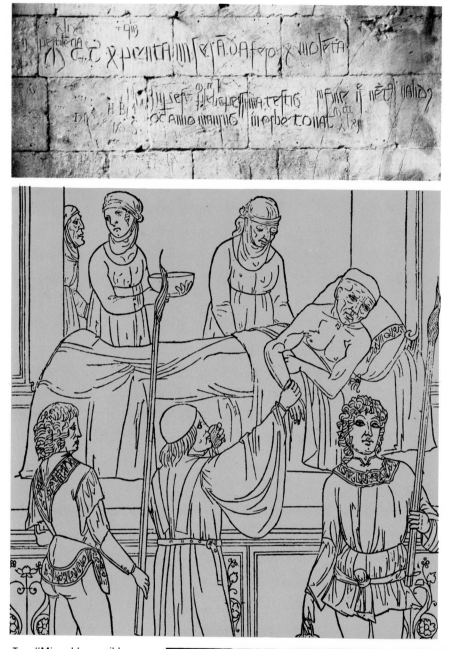

cent—but those are certainly the outside limits.

It is impossible to eliminate one-third of a continent's population over a period of some four years without desperately dislocating that continent's economy and social structure. In Europe in the mid-fourteenth century, that blow was buffered by the fact that the Continent was suffering from over-population—or rather from a surplus population that current agricultural techniques could neither feed nor employ. Vast economic expansion in the thirteenth century had already given way to mild recession, and the population of Europe in 1345 was probably only slightly above what it had been in 1300—that is, in the neighborhood of 100 million persons.

Chronic underemployment remained widespread, however, until the plague struck. The sudden disappearance of roughly one-third of the labor force inevitably altered the relationship between employer and employee, and radically modified the relationship between landlord and tenant. To maintain his available labor supply, or to bribe reinforcements away from neighboring employers, the manorial lord was now frequently forced to pay greatly increased wages. To ensure that his cottages were occupied, he had to accept reduced rents or modified labor services.

In theory, the movement of labor was controlled; tenants should not have been able to dictate terms to their masters. But in the chaos produced by the plague, such regulations could not be enforced. Economic realities asserted themselves within this feudal framework: prices of manufactured products soared in England, as canvas, iron and salt all more than doubled in cost between 1347 and 1350. At the same time, livestock—such as cows, sheep and oxen —fell disastrously in value. The result was that the typical landlord was paying more for his purchases, getting less for his farm-produce, and less as rent for his cottages, and was at the same time being forced to give higher wages for whatever labor he could secure. Most found themselves in grave economic straits. A common remedy was to reduce the extent of the land that a landlord farmed himself, and to

Top "Miserable ... wild ... distracted, the dregs of a people alone survive to witness." Graffiti on the walls of England's Ashwell Church, dating back to 1350, show the horror that the living continued to feel when the plague was over.

A doctor protects himself with a pomander and by burning herbs as he takes the pulse of a plague victim.

Burying plague victims at Tournai, Belgium.

rent vacant tenements, and this profoundly affected the structure of rural society.

Thus the Black Death created striking modifications in the social structure of the European countryside. Its influence upon the Church was perhaps even more dramatic, however. Among the lower ranks of the clerical hierarchy particularly it is almost literally true to say that anyone who did his duty conscientiously had barely one chance in ten of survival. Where the most infectious, pulmonary form of the disease was in question, continued contact with the sick was almost sure to prove fatal. In such circumstances, only a priest who shirked his responsibilities could reasonably hope to see out the epidemic; in England and Germany—and probably in the other countries of Europe as well—roughly half the clergy proved that they knew how to do their duty. But even though the clerics suffered more severely than the laity, they somehow contrived to leave their contemporaries with the impression that they were behaving with something less than nobility. The reputation of the Church fell almost as rapidly as the death roll of priests mounted. By 1351 the Catholic Church in Europe had been stripped of its ablest members.

G. M. Trevelyan has claimed that the Black Death was as significant a phenomenon as the Industrial Revolution, and that the latter was actually less striking in its effect because it was not, like the plague, "a fortuitous obstruction fallen across the river of life and temporarily diverting it." "The year of the Black Death" wrote Friedell, even more emphatically, "was . . . the year of the conception of modern man."

Today one feels less certain that the years of the Black Death were in fact so marked a watershed. For one thing, it should never be forgotten that the plague of 1348 was only the first of a series of epidemics that sputtered throughout Europe until the beginning of the eighteenth century. Bubonic plague returned to England in 1361, 1368–69, 1371, 1375, 1390 and 1405.

In addition, it is hard to identify with precision any major trend that was initiated by the Black Death, rather than simply reinforced by it. The substitution of wages and cash rent for labor services was certainly given striking impetus by the depredations of the plague, but this was a process that was already far advanced in some areas before 1347—and the next half century by no means witnessed continued and uninterrupted progress toward the

disappearance of the feudal relationship. It was unquestionably easier for a tenant to desert his manor during the immediate aftermath of the Black Death, but that right had already been tacitly conceded by many landlords during the years of surplus labor that preceded the plague. The dearth of available manpower that followed the plague often made it more, not less difficult for the peasant to choose his place of work and move his home. Even in such fields as architecture—where it has often been accepted as dogma that the shortage of skilled workmen after the

Above left Flagellants try to drive off the plague by whipping themselves.

Above Our Lady of Mercy protects the faithful while plague strikes down its victims with arrows.

plague led to the substitution of the Perpendicular for the Decorated architectural style—the seeds of change had actually been sown long before the first workman died. The transept and choir of Gloucester Cathedral—the very cradle of the Perpendicular style—were completed as early as 1332.

The Black Death may not have been a conspicuous innovator of new trends, but its influence on the second half of the fourteenth century was nonetheless considerable. For one thing, the position of the tenant was permanently strengthened in relation both to his landlord and to the wage scale, which never fell back to the rates prevailing before the plague. The Black Death was the most significant among the factors contributing to the turmoil that marked the end of the fourteenth century. The insurrections of the Jacquerie in 1358 and of Tuchins in 1381, the rising of the weavers in Ghent in 1379, the Peasants' Revolt in England in 1381, all arose from social and economic conditions that would have existed even if *Pasteurella pestis* had never left its home in Central Asia. But it is highly unlikely that conditions in Europe would have reached a point of desperation as rapidly as they did if the plague had not occurred. The Peasants' Revolt, for example, was at least in part a reaction to the Black Death. Attempts by labor-hungry landlords to wrest from their tenants many of the rights that the latter had won over the preceding decades did much to create a climate of discontent in England.

The real "contribution" made by the Black Death was far less precise. By the second half of the fourteenth century, the disintegration of the manorial system was already far advanced. The Black Death aided the process immeasurably by exacerbating

existing grievances, heightening contradictions and making economic nonsense of a situation that previously had seemed outmoded but still viable. It is not even absolutely certain that the plague "caused" the Peasants' Revolt or the similar uprisings in other countries. It cannot even be said that, but for the epidemic, the Revolt would have taken a substantially different form. What can be asserted is that

if there had been no Black Death, bitterness would never have risen by 1381 to the level that it did.

In the same way, it can be argued that although the Black Death did not "cause" the Reformation, it did create the circumstances that made such ecclesiastical reform possible. "The plague not only depopulates and kills," wrote Neibuhr, "it gnaws [at] the moral stamina and frequently destroys it entirely." Paradoxically, the decades that followed the plague saw not only a decline in the prestige and spiritual authority of the Church, but also the growth of a new, radical, questioning religious fervor, based upon disillusion and even despair. In Italy, those decades marked the great period of the Fraticelli, Franciscan rebels who once had been denounced as heretics by the Pope and now deemed the Pope himself a heretic. In England that era was the age of Wycliffe and of Lollardy, a period of new and aggressive anti-clericalism that drew its strength from the discontent and doubts of the people at large. The age was one of spiritual unrest, or pertinent questioning of the value and conduct of the Church, and of disrespect for established idols.

Such a spirit would have been abroad even if bubonic plague had never visited the shores of Europe. The Black Death can hardly be made responsible for the growth of doubts about the doctrine of the Transubstantiation—but it did create a state of mind in which doctrines and dogmas were more easily doubted. Wycliffe was a child of the Black Death in the sense that he belonged to a generation that had suffered terribly and learned through its sufferings to question the premises on which the Church and society were based. The Church itself became a victim of the Black Death; large numbers

St. Roch, the plague saint.

of its dedicated ministers perished, and its reputation and authority began to decay. The Reformation was inevitable, but it might not have come so quickly and so violently if the walls of establishment religion had not first been undermined and outflanked by the visitation of the plague.

Can it truthfully be said, then, that "the year of the Black Death was the year of the conception of modern man?" Such colorful generalizations must be viewed with suspicion; eras seldom end and new generations rarely begin with such convenient tidiness. However, the Black Death—especially when considered as a series of epidemics rather than an isolated phenomenon—did unquestionably hasten the decline of values and the breaking down of behavior patterns that had stood firm over many centuries. It opened men's minds, dispelled their illusions and awoke their doubts. It played a crucial role in the phenomenon that can be most conveniently described as "the ending of the Middle Ages."

PHILIP ZIEGLER

A German *Pestblätte* for protection against the Black Death.

A New Dynasty for China 1368

The Mongol Yuan dynasty ruled China for more than a century, and it was during that time that the bellicose "barbarians" abandoned martial skills for the pleasures of the palace. Shortsighted, discriminatory policies only increased the hatred that the Chinese felt for their alien overlords, while a succession of weak, dissolute emperors and increased factionalism within the royal family made the Yuan dynasty even more vulnerable. In the age-old tradition of patriotic resistance to foreign oppression, the Chinese under Chu Yuan-chang at last rose against their Mongol masters. The vanquished Yuan dynasty was replaced by the native Chinese Ming dynasty, and Chu (later known as Hung-wu) became its first emperor.

Following the invasion of North China by Genghis Khan at the beginning of the thirteenth century, and the subsequent conquest of the south by his grandson Kublai Khan, all China was for the first time under alien rule. The Mongol "barbarians" cherished many of the traditions of their steppe homeland, but they rapidly fell under the spell of Chinese culture, especially after the foundation of their Yuan dynasty in 1271. Their wars over, and a rich and exciting new country at their feet, the Yuan Mongols settled into the complacent urban and court life of their Chinese predecessors.

Within a century or so of their arrival in China, the former vigor of the Mongols was beginning to wane. A rapid succession of weak, pleasure-seeking emperors, almost without exception totally lacking in ruling ability and influenced by cunning ministers and Buddhist lamas, characterized the declining years of the Yuan dynasty during the first half of the fourteenth century. Petty squabbles and fratricidal rivalries split the imperial clan. Involved in court intrigues, the Yuan were oblivious to the growing clamor of peasant revolt outside the palace walls.

By their shortsighted, discriminating policies, the Mongols had aroused much ill-feeling among the Chinese. Their conquered enemies were more slaves than subjects. The Chinese had very low status and effectively no rights whatsoever. The Chinese were forbidden to intermarry with Mongols, to carry weapons, or to learn foreign languages—including Mongol. Particularly as a result of the latter measure, there was little communication between the Chinese and the Mongols, and the Chinese were excluded from trading activities and from all spheres of political life, which became the exclusive provinces of foreign bureaucrats, one of whom was Marco Polo, and of the Mongol ruling class itself.

After destroying the resplendent city of Peking, the Mongols became aware of the advantages of its position. Close to their homeland and well served

by roads, they could retreat from the oppressive Chinese summers to their old territory beyond the Great Wall, and remain in close contact with events in their northern dominions. The Mongols therefore conscripted Chinese labor—a technique that they used extensively in other public building projects—to rebuild Peking yet more magnificently than before. In their new imperial capital, they installed the machinery of government—a large bureaucracy, highly dependent on the rice-growing lands of South China for its food supply, and hence connected to the southern provinces by a complex network of roads, canals and sea links. The flow of food and other resources northward to Peking was expected to continue even during famine and flood, and placed an additional burden on the already heavily taxed and brutally exploited southern peasantry. A large disparity thus existed between the sumptuous cities and rich court life described by foreign travelers of this time, and the miserable existence of the majority of the population of China. In the late Yuan period, however, the wealth that outsiders saw was largely illusory because the economic situation was critical. Wealthy merchants—ironically, under Mongol protection—were rapidly draining away China's metal currency. It was replaced with worthless paper money as the inflationary situation grew progressively worse. Weak and improverished emperors were thus ruling over an alienated and oppressed peasantry. In this ground the seeds of revolt quickly germinated.

As the revolutionary movements gathered speed, however, their avowed enemies were not at first the Mongol overlords, but the landowners and Buddhist monasteries which enjoyed considerable social and economic privileges denied to the masses. This confrontation was inevitable in the former Sung territory of the south. Long-established Mongol and other forms of alien rule in the north had undermined the old landlord-peasant relationship there, and the country and its resources

Chu Yuan-chang, the peasant farmer who became in turn Buddhist monk, rebel leader and eventually founder of the Ming dynasty, the Emperor Hung-wu.

Opposite Guests arriving at the imperial palace. Hung-wu's court revived the traditional forms and precedents of the T'ang dynasty, even adopting T'ang dress.

A drafting document issued by Chu, bearing his reign title "Dragon and Phoenix."

Below A contemporary portrait of Chu showing the ugliness that earned him the nickname of "pig."

were very firmly in Mongol hands. In the south, however, Mongol rule was relatively new. Their remoteness from the territory meant that in order to control and exploit the country the Mongols sought the alliance of the landowners, granting them rights that their northern counterparts had long since relinquished. The landowners in turn looked to the Mongols for military support when anarchy swept through their villages.

In fact, the Mongols were now ill-equipped to provide this support. Like so many other aspects of Mongol life, the martial arts were in decline. Once believed invincible, the Mongol army had, after years of city life without any real function, fallen from its formerly high military standards and strong morale. It was even said that some soldiers were incapable of using their weapons, and sad cases of incompetence began to appear. Where once a small Mongol contingent might have wiped out a much larger enemy army, now a force of 1,000 was proved to be incapable of crushing a band of a mere fifty Chinese brigands. When revolt came, therefore, the landowners had little protection against the peasant armies, and were thus quite often compelled to submit to rebel demands. Once committed in this way, they were obliged to maintain their ostensible support for the rebel cause. As the revolt, which began in about 1325, gathered impetus, the change in allegiance of the landowners contributed toward a shift in the very aim of the struggle. It gradually acquired intellectual and popular appeal as a movement to overthrow the Mongol regime by force of arms. The groups of rebels that emerged have been regarded by Chinese historians as heroes in the true tradition of patriotic resistance to foreign oppression.

In common with the situation in certain other countries where power was usurped by invaders, the rebels often adopted the roles of followers of a messianic cause. They believed (or found it pragmatic to believe) in prophets and soothsayers who asserted that the day of reckoning was at hand when the Mongol tyrants would be expelled, and China would again be in the hands of the Chinese who would thereby win back their rightful prestige and place in the world. Because the Chinese considered themselves culturally superior to the "barbarian" Mongols, and because they were a genuinely oppressed majority, these movements gained considerable support.

The messianic cults followed various themes. Some leaders pretended descent from Chinese Sung emperors; their followers would thus be restoring the old order. Some were more closely based on religious ideals—particularly the coming of the Buddha Maitreya who would set all to right again. Often the movements took the form of underground resistance groups organized along the lines of secret societies—a long-standing tradition in Chinese society. Of these, the most prominent was the Pai Lien Hu, or White Lotus Society. Unlike the uncoordinated bands of rebels in some

which underwent harsh treatment at the hands of their Mongol masters—and on the farms from which they had been conscripted and where their absence caused great hardship. While this enforced work was being undertaken, a curious event occurred. A stone image of a one-eyed man was unearthed, apparently fulfilling part of a prophecy that the Yuan dynasty would be toppled when a "one-eyed man of stone" appeared. As a result of this superstitious belief, many malcontent workers rallied to the red banner of the White Lotus Society, adopting the Society's red headband as a badge of allegiance. A number of new leaders emerged, largely drawn from the ranks of the oppressed poor, and even including a famous Chinese pirate, Fang Kuo-chen. The movement also attracted many thieves and bandits, eager for the opportunity to loot and destroy—regardless of the political motives of the Society—and much quarreling and infighting thus occurred. However, during the subsequent period of strife, one figure in particular rose to power. His name was Chu Yuan-chang.

Chu was born in 1328 at Chung-li in the Huai Valley province of Anhui, the son of a poor peasant farmer. Little is known of him personally—other than that he was extremely ugly, and the name "pig" was often used in connection with his own, partly for that reason, and partly because the Chinese word for pig has the same sound as his first name. So poverty-stricken was his family that

of the former Sung strongholds, the revolutionary policies of the White Lotus were coherent and the Society well organized, and thus it attracted a large following.

The Society claimed that it had been founded in the fourth century, but in reality it dated back only as far as the twelfth century. Dedicated to the Amitabha Buddha, or the Buddha of the Pure Land (which adherents believed they would enter by following its tenets), the Society soon had a wide following. It was even said that an important sect in Japan had been based upon it. Under a strong central government, the White Lotus failed to thrive; and thus during the T'ang period it had been severely persecuted. But in the new troubles it rose again with renewed vigor, creating disturbances in parts of South China, but at first achieving no notable military successes.

At this time, the Mongols were causing further discontent by continuing to recruit slave labor for various public building projects. In 1351, they took more than 170,000 men from the provinces of Honan, Kiangsi and Shantung to repair the broken dikes of the Yellow River, which had recently flooded with disastrous results. Vociferous objections arose in the ranks of this slave army,

Above Planting rice in the paddy-fields of the south where Mongol rule had left the landlord-peasant relationship undisturbed.

Above left Yuan Mongols hunting. Time and the pleasures of the palace were to sap them of their native vigor.

A Ming ewer with red underglaze. Some of China's finest artifacts date from this period.

Right A coin from the "between" period, minted during the upheavals between the two dynasties.

when both his parents and his eldest brother died of starvation in 1344, he could afford neither proper coffins for their bodies nor sacrifices for their souls. It is said that the ghosts of his parents appeared to him in a dream, urging him to become a Buddhist monk—in China often a last refuge of the very poor. He accordingly enrolled at the Huang-chueh monastery near Fengyang. The monastery was itself impoverished, and in 1348 the monks were compelled to leave it temporarily to become wandering beggars. Chu's travels took him westward along the Huai valley during the next three years, after which he returned to the monastery.

Shortly after his arrival, during the disturbances of 1352 which resulted from the Yellow River incident, a band of White Lotus supporters under Kuo Tzu-hsing raided and burned the monastery. The other monks fled, but Chu remained and offered his services to Kuo. A Mongol force was close at hand and Chu was at first throught to be a spy and almost executed. But when he finally managed to meet Kuo, he so impressed him that the latter made him an officer in the rebel army. In China it was by no means unusual for monks to become peasant leaders, for they were held to be in close contact with supernatural powers and were usually better educated than the rabble they led. Through his proven military skill in raids—and by marrying Kuo's adopted daughter—Chu rose rapidly to a position of power.

When Kuo died in 1355, Chu was able to usurp his brother-in-law's authority and, taking a large force, crossed the Yangtze toward Nanking (then called Ying-tien). The following year, his army took this strategically important town, thereby creating a rallying point for rebels and cutting off food supplies to the north. Thus reinforcing his power, Chu proclaimed himself Duke of Wu—the ancient name for the region. In 1363 he defeated the only other significant rebel leader, Ch'en Yu-liang, seizing his territory in the provinces of Hopei, Hunan and Kiangsi after only relatively minor battles, and adopting the more grandoise title of Prince of Wu. By 1364 Chu had crushed all opposition in the provinces of the southeast—both Yuan and other rebel factions—in most cases by winning the inhabitants over to his side, rather than by defeating them by force. Having subdued most of southern China by 1367, Chu turned toward the Mongol-held north.

Theoretically, the north could hold out against the rebels by importing Mongol reinforcements from their homeland. However, at this time the Mongol imperial clan was feuding with a rival group and was quite unprepared for war. Thus on September 10, 1368, Chu's army of some 250,000 was able to march into Peking virtually unopposed. The last Yuan emperor, the debauched Toghan Temur, and his court fled farther north.

Chu proclaimed a new dynasty called the Ming, or "Brilliant," taking for himself as its first emperor the title Hung-wu, or "Boundless Valor." The capture of Peking marks the effective end of

Mongol rule in China. Minor skirmishes took place in subsequent years, but without significant Mongol gains—in fact, the Ming army was even able to march beyond the Great Wall, attacking the Mongol capital of Karakorum, and extending Chinese influence far into Mongolia, Manchuria and Korea.

The Ming capital was established at Nanking, which means "Southern Capital." It was important to have a capital there because it was the center of Chu's popular support, geographically well-located, and far enough removed from the lingering Mongol influences in the north. Peking was, for the present, ignored.

In the same year as the fall of Peking, the remaining provinces of China began to ally with the rebels—first Fukien, Kuangtung, Kuangsi and Shansi, and then Shensi. In 1371, Szechuan fell, and in 1382, Yunnan, by which time the whole of China was under Ming rule.

The success of the new emperor was not in the first instance that of a liberator. Rather, in the anarchy and civil war that took place, particularly in the 1350s, Chu rose as one leader among many who fought primarily against Chinese landowners. His advantage was secured by turning his campaign into a unifying nationalist movement, and thereby enlisting even the support of those Chinese whom he had first opposed. While other rebel bands killed and looted, he concentrated on winning important areas by diplomacy. Having gained preeminence in this way, he reconquered China for the Chinese. Now began the task of reestablishing a firm government.

The Ming administrative code which Hung-wu founded in the early years of his reign persisted, with modifications, until this century. Its complex structure involved the abolition of the premiership and its replacement with a cabinet, or Nei Ko. A census was taken for taxation purposes, and the country was divided into provinces under the rule of nine of the Emperor's sons (he had twenty-six sons)—an action that is often regarded as his greatest mistake, since much subdivision and dispute occurred under his heirs. In devising the new system, as in many other areas of activity, Hung-wu and his advisers looked back to the traditional forms and precedents of the great T'ang dynasty—even to the extent of adopting T'ang dress. In doing so, they undoubtedly created a spirit of conservatism which made later innovation difficult.

An important contribution of Hung-wu's reign was the reintroduction of the civil service examinations. To Westerners, such a move does not sound very sweeping—but it was one way to ensure the essential homogeneity of Chinese society. It meant that even the poorest could rise by merit and attain important administrative rank—the same sort of attitude that had made possible the rise and acceptance of the peasant Chu as the Emperor Hung-wu. (He was not the first peasant to found a dynasty—the Han and the first of the Five Dynasties had been so founded.) This practice also encouraged conformity in the ruling class. The bureaucracy under the Ming rose, by 1469, to 100,000 civil officials as the government became more and more complicated (and, of course, as the

River travel: the Ming improved the commercially important Grand Canal, as well as introducing flood controls and irrigation systems.

Bronze figure of a lion in the grounds of the Forbidden City. The Ming transferred their capital to Peking in 1421.

118

population grew—from 65 million at the beginning of the Ming dynasty to 150 million by its fall in 1643). Symptomatic of the traditionalism of Hung-wu's rule was the emphasis placed on the worship of the sage Confucius, and in the Emperor's surrounding himself with Buddhist monks—a reminder of his former way of life. Also reminiscent of his early poverty (he was sometimes known as the "Beggar King"), were Hung-wu's attempts to check the power of the landowners. To this end he induced 45,000 members of wealthy families from the lower Yangtze to move to Nanking where they were placed under imperial surveillance. Aware too of the disruptive force of the secret societies, he took great pains to crush them, even denying officially that he had ever had any connection with the White Lotus Society.

Many historians regard Hung-wu as the cruelest despot China has ever known. Certainly, life at his court was precarious. Ministers summoned to his presence would bid a last farewell to their families because they knew that they might be executed on the slightest pretext. In poetry, allusions to violence were taboo in case the Emperor read into them some reference to his own tyranny. Toward the end of his life he became even more distrustful— with some cause, as several attempts were made to depose him. In 1380, his premier, Hu Wei-yung, made an unsuccessful bid for the throne. Hung-wu had him executed, along with thousands of people even remotely connected with the former premier

and his family. Another abortive coup in 1393 resulted in a similar purge.

However, under Hung-wu and his successors, Chinese military power eclipsed even that of the T'ang, and under its protection, the Chinese empire expanded and prospered, regaining much of its former prestige in Asia. Among the material achievements of the Ming must be included such public works as the improvements to the commercially important Grand Canal, the Great Wall and other defenses, shrines, flood controls and irrigation systems. Craftsmanship excelled throughout the period, and some of China's finest paintings, pottery, textiles and books date from the Ming. Drama, literature and education also flourished. Contacts were made with the outside world, and China received many important influences and new products—such crops from the New World as the sweet potato, peanuts, maize and tobacco, cotton, which became a major crop throughout the empire, spectacles from Italy, and a new disease: syphilis.

Chinese historians of the Ming largely wrote under the subsequent alien Manchu dynasty, and therefore had little good to say of it. In recent years, however, the achievements of the Ming have been more fully appraised, and despite Hung-wu's cruel and despotic methods, we can now see that the dynasty he founded in 1368 was of immense benefit to China and to the world.

RUSSELL ASH

The Five Dragons Pavilions in Pei Hai Park, Peking; a fine example of late Ming architecture.

The Provençal city of Avignon was independent but surrounded by papal property. Thus, when Clement v had set up the papal administration there in 1305, he could claim to be independent of King Philip iv of France. Yet, in truth, all seven Avignon popes were politically pro-French, all were largely dependent on the French monarchy, and all were Frenchmen. This caused considerable difficulty for England in the coming Hundred Years War, and was one of the reasons for France's ultimate success in that war. Frenchmen also dominated the college of cardinals (113 out of 134 Avignon cardinals were French).

The papacy's dependence on France is illustrated by the Council of Vienne (1311–12) which was entirely dominated by Philip iv, who forced the pope to call it in order to get the Order of the Temple suppressed. The power and wealth of the Templars in Europe caused envy even among princes. At first the council refused to accept the trumped-up charges of witchcraft put forward by the French. But Philip simply besieged Vienne until the council accepted the bull, *Vox Clamantis*, which abolished the order.

The fact that Rome, "the Eternal City" and Western Christendom's traditional center, was left without a pope while the Bishop of Rome set up court in Avignon, struck many contemporaries as a contradiction in terms, and they roundly denounced the "Babylonian Captivity." Others attempted to justify it more theologically; since the pope was seen as the head of Christendom, he could not be limited to one city. A few papal theologians even tried to separate the pope's functions as Bishop of Rome from those of the Church's earthly head.

Contemporary rulers as well as theologians urged the popes to return to Rome. Emperor Charles iv, for example, tried to persuade Gregory xi to go back. The influential Italian mystic, St. Catherine of Siena, encouraged Gregory to consider all aspects of the matter and reminded him that "it is more needful for you to win back souls than to recover your earthly possessions." But it was not until 1377 that Gregory summoned up courage to exchange the dominion of the King of France for that of the Roman people.

The move to Avignon did not save the papacy any money. Its income from Italy was reduced, while at the same time expenditures rose: a whole series of Italian wars was necessary to protect the remnants of papal territorial possessions there. As a result a far-reaching reform of papal finances and administration was necessary.

Papal finances

Apart from its income from its Italian possessions, the papacy was able to rely on fees from newly appointed bishops and abbots, which could amount to the whole of the first two years' income. The income from vacant sees was also often available for papal use. The papal tax collectors were willing to use almost any methods to get their money. Excommunication was frequent, and at least one recalcitrant bishop was refused burial until his heirs paid his debts.

Extraordinary taxes could also sometimes be levied. Usually they were paid, albeit reluctantly. Occasionally, however, clerical anger led to a revolt. The clergy of the dioceses of Mainz and Cologne refused to pay a tax of a tenth in 1372. Papal tax collectors were sometimes attacked, imprisoned or killed. All the Avignon popes had continuous financial difficulties. For example the papal treasury had 1,117,000 florins in 1342; by 1352 it had only 312,000 florins—and most of this sum had been borrowed. Part of the reason for the decline can be found in the drain of expenditure caused by the Italian wars, part by the expenses of the papal court at Avignon. The pope paid 80,000 florins to purchase Avignon itself in 1348; the papal palace needed extending and the walls of the city had to be strengthened against possible attack.

The administration of papal government became a pattern for secular governments. The Avignon papacy was largely responsible for the administrative improvements in the fourteenth-century papal government. It reorganized the four main departments (the *camera apostolica*, chancery, penitentiary and justiciary) and improved their workings. Despite their personal defects, which were mercilessly exposed by their enemies, all the Avignon popes were men of considerable ability and the improved machinery of government that they left was to be of great value to their successors.

Mysticism

The increasing institutionalism of ecclesiastical government and the horrors of the Black Death produced varying reactions. One was the growth of mysticism. There had been men and women in the early medieval Church who had found an unusual knowledge of God through contemplation, but mysticism became a particular characteristic of the late medieval Church. The teaching of a

A woodcut of the German mystic Henry Suso with a psalter.

German Dominican friar named Eckhart (1260–1327) was very influential in the spread of mysticism. The Church was deeply suspicious of the independence of his ideas from ecclesiastical teaching and he was to be posthumously condemned as an heretic. Because of his influence, mystics continued to be suspect. Among Eckhart's pupils, the two most important were Henry Suso (1295–1366) and Johann Tauler (1300–61), both of whom were also Dominicans. A more orthodox mystical school grew up in Holland. This was started by a canon regular of St. Augustine, Jan van Ruysbroeck (1293–1381), from whose influence much later Dutch spirituality sprang. It was not only in Germany and Holland that mysticism became popular: an Italian, Catherine of Siena, had an immense influence in her short life; while in England there was a flourishing local tradition.

Although mysticism was not necessarily heretical, it was often mixed up with heretical movements. It was deeply suspicious of the pomp and wealth that the Avignon popes appeared to encourage, and implied dissatisfaction with the spiritual life of the Church. This gave it some links with a wider movement for reform.

Christ delegating spiritual and temporal authority.

mysticism and reform

Reformism

The financial needs of the Avignon papacy were unpopular among the clergy, who were obliged to bear the costs of the expensive Italian wars and of the luxurious papal court. But it was not merely for selfish reasons that the clergy opposed the huge financial demands that were made on them. Many—of whom the spiritual Franciscans were merely the most extreme—felt that the teaching of the Gospels was opposed to such emphasis on material possessions.

Some of the pressures for change came from the newly conscious national monarchies. In England the papacy's dependence on France, the national enemy, led to a feeling of hostility toward it. This was expressed in a series of laws typified by the statutes of *praemunire* and provisors. The former (originally passed in 1353 and renewed in 1365 and 1393) was designed to prevent the papacy from infringing rights claimed by the Crown; the latter (passed in 1351 and renewed in 1353, 1365 and 1389) attempted to restrict the practice, which grew rapidly under the Avignon popes, of papal provision (appointment) to vacant church offices. In Germany too there were attempts to limit papal power by statute.

The growing popularity of the political ideas of Ockham and Marsiglio of Padua also had an effect. Theologians increasingly asked how an heretical or schismatic pope could be deposed. The whole relationship between the Church and the pope was beginning to be called into question.

In addition, many specific practices were attacked as corrupt: the papal court was increasingly condemned for simony and bribery. Even devoted admirers of the papacy such as Catherine of Siena were vigorous in their attacks on corruption. Papal provisions were often a cause of pluralism and non-residence as they were seen as a cheap way of paying officials at the pope's court. The Church in Italy was faced with a flourishing native "purified" tradition, the reformed Waldensian Church, which had its main support in the north.

Wycliffe and Church reform

An extreme reformer was John Wycliffe (1329–84). While studying at Oxford he gained a considerable reputation from his attacks on established ideas. He was able to rely on the patronage of John of Gaunt, who, in 1374, made him rector of Lutterworth, although he did not reside there. He found the prosperous Church out of touch with the changes taking place in the structure of society: on all sides men were crying out for Church reform, yet the smallest change was prevented by the institution itself. The Oxford don provided his own remedy for a decaying faith by gathering together a band of "poor preachers," scholars who spent their free time preaching the Gospel in market places and on village greens, as the friars had in their heyday. Wycliffe studied the era of primitive Christianity in the Acts of the Apostles and in Paul's epistles. By contrast, the fourteenth-century Church, with its rival popes living in great splendor at Avignon and Rome and its English bishops too occupied with state affairs for pastoral work, seemed to have over-reached itself. Wycliffe preached a return to Biblical simplicity with an enthusiasm that was to prove infectious.

Wycliffe became known to a wider audience by the publication in the 1370s of *De Dominio Divino*. He held that divine grace was the key not merely to salvation, but also to worldly power. He believed that the Church was no longer in a state of grace and that it should therefore be disendowed. His ideas had dangerous political implications; some of the leaders of the 1381 Peasants' Revolt had similar ideas.

In *De Potestate Papae* (1379), Wycliffe argued that since the pope's salvation was uncertain, papal supremacy was unacceptable. His ideas later became more extreme: he attacked the pope as Antichrist, regarded transubstantiation as a false doctrine, auricular confession as unnecessary, and condemned nonresidence and pluralism.

His greatest achievement was to inspire the translation of the Bible into English. He thought that the believer should be able to read the scriptures. Two Wycliffite versions are in existence: one by the Carthusian monk, Nicholas of Hereford; the other, by a John Purvey (of whom nothing is known), was a revision of Nicholas' work. Despite official condemnation, both versions remained popular until the sixteenth century, when they were replaced by Tyndale's translation.

Social and religious discontent were connected in Wycliffe's lifetime. This connection continued after his death. Wycliffe's followers, who came to be known as Lollards ("Mumblers of prayers") were often accused of causing political dissension. In 1417, Sir John Oldcastle, a wealthy English knight, was burned as a Wycliffite after leading an unsuccessful rebellion. Oldcastle, a former friend of Henry v, has sometimes been taken as the model for Shakespeare's Falstaff, but, unlike Falstaff, he was certainly no coward.

Wycliffe's works along with those of John Huss were condemned at the Council of Constance (1415) and in 1428 Wycliffe's body was disinterred. The sixteenth-century reformers regarded Wycliffe as the "morning star of the Reformation," but his exact influence on them is uncertain.

While most fourteenth-century reformers were more moderate than Wycliffe, the demand for "reform in head and members" began to be heard. Fuel was added to the demand by the outbreak of the Great Schism.

The reformer John Wycliffe.

A comical allusion to clerical impropriety.

Rival Popes

Faith and dogma played little part in the Great Schism; it was instead a matter of personalities and politics. Pope Urban VI's offensive actions had estranged him from the majority of his cardinals, and they met at Anagni to declare his election null and void. What followed was a struggle between rival popes, with all the countries of Western Christendom lining up on either one side or the other. The forty years of anarchy were a clear warning of what could happen if all power and responsibility in the Church were entrusted to individuals who put their own interests and ambitions first.

In the autumn of 1376, thirty ships set sail from the French Mediterranean coast, bound for Italian shores. The French pope, Gregory XI, had decided, against the advice of all his cardinals, to leave Avignon and return to Rome. Stormy weather caused considerable delays, and it was not until four months later that the ships put in at Genoa. They remained there until the city governors agreed to let the Pope and his party into Rome. The papal city was ablaze with lights when Pope Gregory entered it in January, 1377. It was an important occasion. Not only was the head of the Church returning to the ancient city of the apostles and martyrs, the traditional center of Christianity in the West, an earthly ruler was also returning to his dominions. For the Pope was the civil governor of Rome and ruler of much of the surrounding territory.

It was high time the popes took an interest in their homeland. For the last seventy years, while the popes had made their home in a fortresslike palace at Avignon, Italy had been ravaged by war, rebellion and plague. The pope's own lands had been overrun by ambitious neighboring rulers, and cities had rebelled against his authority. The popes at Avignon had had to spend almost two-thirds of their revenue hiring mercenary soldiers to win back a foothold in their own lands. Church property throughout Italy had been allowed to decay and Church revenues were almost nonexistent. The city of Rome itself was in ruins—its once splendid buildings, churches, monasteries and palaces crumbling into dust. The Roman people blamed the popes for this situation, arguing that their long absence proved how little they cared for their own lands and subjects. Another cause of complaint was that the last four popes had all been Frenchmen, and had appeared to act in the interests of the French king.

It was not long before Pope Gregory began to doubt the wisdom of remaining in Rome. His cardinals urged him to return to Avignon. They were anxious to leave the war-torn city where they had to forgo the luxuries of France. Eleven of the sixteen cardinals were French, and they were aware of the hatred of the Romans for a "foreign" pope and his "foreign" friends. They feared for their possessions and their lives, and it did not take them long to persuade Pope Gregory to leave Rome. But before he could do so, he fell ill and died on March 27, 1378. It was said his death was divine retribution for his decision to go back to Avignon after spending only fourteen months in Rome.

Thus in April, 1378, for the first time in decades, the Roman people were to witness the election of a new pope. Normally this was a straightforward affair. It was the responsibility of all the cardinals, or as many as could easily be assembled in one place, to choose a new pope. They were locked into the conclave, a special room in the papal palace, cut off from all contact with the outside world until at least two-thirds of them had cast their votes for one man. He was then proclaimed pope.

Obviously a great deal of "electioneering" went on behind the scenes before a formal election, and the election of 1378 was no exception. As soon as it was obvious that Pope Gregory would not recover, the cardinals began to discuss possible successors. They were not simply looking for a man whose spiritual understanding and leadership would benefit the Church. By the fourteenth century, the Church had become a highly organized, bureaucratic institution, which had all the legal, financial and diplomatic machinery of a secular government. It needed a politician and administrator at its head. The pope's relationship to his cardinals was that of a monarch to his trusted counsellors and civil servants, and there were many privileges to be gained by a cardinal who was in favor with his pope.

The discussions reached an impasse. The eleven French cardinals had split into two opposing factions: the Limousins (who came from the area near Avignon) and the Gallic group (who came from northern France). The latter had also won support of the Spanish cardinal, and one of the

The death of Urban VI. His blunt manner and reforming zeal caused the split in the curia that led to the Great Schism.

Opposite The papal court, from a fourteenth-century manuscript.

Top Gregory XI returns to Rome, thus ending the "Babylonian captivity." His death precipitated the riots that led to Urban's election.

Above Sarcophagus of Urban VI showing St. Peter handing him the keys which are the symbol of papal authority.

Italians. The three other Italians formed a separate group. Although each faction wanted to elect its own candidate, the Gallic group suggested a compromise nominee who was acceptable to all. The Italian Bartolomeo Prignano, Archbishop of Bari, was not even a member of the college of cardinals. He was from Naples, but the Limousin group was prepared to support him as they were convinced he was Limousin in outlook, having lived for a long time at Avignon. The Gallic group were also prepared to support him to prevent the possibility of another Limousin pope. Prignano had already proved himself an able administrator under Gregory XI. He was from a humbler background than many of the rich and aristocratic cardinals, and they probably thought he would be easy to manipulate.

There was nothing unusual about a struggle for power among the cardinals. This was a normal part of fourteenth-century Church life. But it is obvious from accounts written at the time—eyewitness reports, letters and official records—that the atmosphere in Rome at the time of the election was unusually turbulent. The leading officials of the city had already put pressure on the cardinals to choose a "suitable" candidate, by which they meant an Italian, preferably a Roman, who would be concerned with the welfare of Rome and the surrounding areas. The cardinals declared that they would not be influenced by such pressure, but they were obviously aware of the possibility of riots and disorder—as soon as Gregory died they ordered all their goods and valuables to be taken to the Castle of St. Angelo for safety.

Ten days were allowed to lapse after Gregory's death before, on the evening of Wednesday, April 7, 1378, the sixteen cardinals gathered in their separate cells in the conclave of the Lateran palace. Guards had been carefully posted at the door of the conclave, around the palace and on the bridges that led to it. Crowds of excited Romans surrounded the palace shouting, "We want a Roman." One guard later testified that the mob seized his key and prevented him from locking the door to the conclave. The milling crowds made it impossible for the guards to brick up the entrance to the conclave in the traditional way.

Months after the election, the cardinals tried to give the impression that this crowd included a band of 6,000 armed and violent men, brought in from the surrounding countryside to intimidate them. They claimed that this hostile mob occupied the palace throughout the election and coerced them into voting as they did. But other witnesses give a very different picture of the events. An excited crowd certainly accompanied the cardinals to the palace, and probably surged in with them through the door of the conclave. But they dispersed fairly rapidly and spent most of the night drinking in the taverns near St. Peter's. Here lies the reason for their riotous behavior the next day; they were *vinolentia*, "drunk," not *violentia*, "violent," when they returned to the palace for news of the election.

Meanwhile, in the conclave, the cardinals had reached a decision, but were reluctant to announce it. They were afraid of what the crowd's reaction to the news would be, for the new pope, Archbishop Prignano, was a Neapolitan, not a Roman. While the cardinals delayed, the crowd broke open the papal cellars to quench its thirst. The city officials twice tried to enter the conclave. When they were finally allowed to address the cardinals, they urged them to choose a Roman swiftly, if they valued their lives.

Rumors began to spread through the crowd that a new pope had already been chosen. The cardinals were still reluctant to announce their decision, but the crowd forced their hand by breaking into the conclave. The frightened cardinals persuaded the aged cardinal of St. Peter's (a Roman) to pose as the newly elected pope, hoping that he could pacify the crowd. While the other cardinals fled to their quarters or to the castle of St. Angelo he explained to the crowd that in fact the Archbishop of Bari had been elected. The new Pope was forced to hide in the palace until the disappointed crowd dispersed.

The result of the election was officially announced to the civic dignitaries the next morning. Contrary to the cardinals' fears, they were satisfied with the result, and there was no violent reaction on the part of the crowd. No protests were made about the circumstances of the election, and on Easter Sunday, the new Pope was crowned as Urban VI. The next day, the cardinals wrote to their colleagues at Avignon explaining their choice, and papal bulls were sent out to every European country announcing Urban's election.

The city officials may have been satisfied with the election, and the crowd easily pacified, but the cardinals themselves soon began to realize that they made a serious error. Instead of rewarding those who had raised him to St. Peter's throne, Urban did his best to humiliate them. He paid no attention to their advice, and announced his intention of reforming the Church. He began with the cardinals. He attacked them both as individuals and as a group, in private and in public meetings, using insulting and abusive language. His temper was so uncontrollable that on one occasion he physically attacked a cardinal. He criticized their love of the "yellow money" and their luxurious life-styles. No doubt some cardinals deserved criticism, but Urban's tactics were greatly undermining their dignity and position as leaders in the Church. They decided to retaliate.

At first they tried to persuade Pope Urban to return to Avignon, thinking that they could put more effective pressure on him there. When Urban refused to leave Rome, the rebellious cardinals gathered at Anagni. By the end of June, 1378, only the four Italian cardinals remained with the Pope.

A pope and his cardinals at loggerheads made Church administration impossible, and obviously the sooner the conflict was resolved, the better. Any reconciliation would require a degree of tolerance on both sides. But Urban had already ignored countless pleas from St. Catherine of Siena that he restrain his temper. And he was certainly not prepared to resign his position. The cardinals' attitudes were also hardening, for they were finding supporters in their quarrel with Urban. What had started as an ecclesiastical squabble was turning into a political struggle. The Duke of Fondi, for example, was prepared to give military and financial aid to the cardinals. They also looked to Charles V of France, hoping that he would support French cardinals against an Italian pope, but the French king was not anxious to commit himself. When Urban learned of this support, he was afraid to join the cardinals at Anagni, thinking he might be captured or even murdered.

The cardinals' confidence received another boost when mercenaries the Duke of Fondi had

sent to attack Rome won a decisive victory. They were now strong enough to dictate their demands. Toward the end of July they ordered the remaining Italian cardinals to come to Anagni and declared the Holy See vacant. Urban thought it was still possible to negotiate and sent them with instructions to press for a general Church council to resolve the dispute. The cardinals refused this suggestion out of hand, persuaded their colleagues not to return to Urban, and on August 9, published their declaration. It stated that the election of Urban VI was null and void, and that the Holy See was vacant. Urban was excommunicated and Christians were ordered to withhold their allegiance from him. A new election was held shortly thereafter, and Robert of Geneva was elected Pope. He was hastily crowned as Clement VII.

This action on the part of the cardinals was quite illegal. According to canon law, the cardinals had no right to declare that a man was not the rightful pope, nor could they start an inquiry into his election, let alone declare it null and void. They argued that they had been compelled to elect Urban by the Roman mob, hence invalidating the election. It was a weak argument, especially as they had made no protest at the time. Even when they first arrived at Anagni, where they were certainly not under compulsion, they still treated Urban as Pope.

But who was empowered to inquire into the circumstances of the election and pronounce judgment? The French lawyers, commissioned by Charles V to look into the matter, said that the dispute should be referred to a Church council. Others agreed, but it was not certain who had the authority to summon a council in this particular situation. Urban had suggested it, but the cardinals were not prepared to submit their case to the judgment of a council, and they argued that there was no pope to call one.

No other practical suggestions for a reconcilia-

The coronation of Boniface IX, successor to Urban in the Roman line of popes.

Below Charles V of France. After consulting with his clergy, he supported the Avignonese pope, Clement VII.

The Division of Europe during the Great Schism

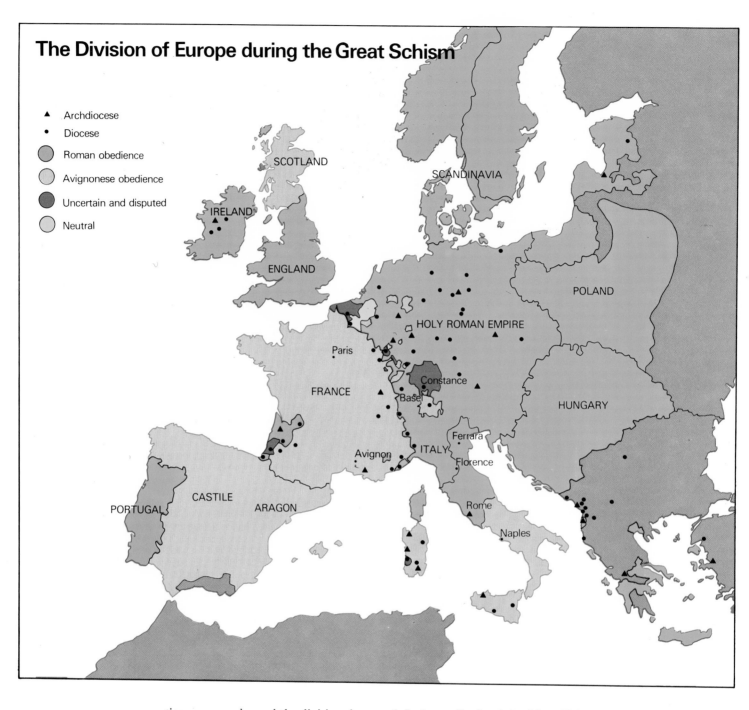

tion were made, and the division deepened. In late November, 1378, Urban retaliated by excommunicating Clement, and appointed a new college of cardinals. Rival envoys were sent to every European kingdom to fight for the recognition of their master as the only true pope.

The rulers who received these envoys were more concerned for their own political advantage than for the welfare of the Church. They knew that they could exact concessions from a weak pope as the price of their support. Some saw that they could use this division within the Church as a weapon in their struggles with other nations. England and France, who were sporadically at war throughout this period, took up opposite sides. Charles v of France supporting Clement, and Richard II of England backing Urban. The German emperor supported Urban, but was unable to enforce obedience to him throughout his dominions. In many German cities public worship was nearly impossible as rival bishops railed at each other, and excommunicated their opponent and his followers. Some rulers tried to remain neutral—Castile and Aragon for example—but found it impossible. After much hesitation they gave their support to Clement. Scotland followed her old ally France and gave her allegiance to Clement. Hungary followed the German emperor's lead and supported Urban.

By 1380, what had started as a quarrel between a pope and his cardinals had split the whole of Western Christendom. Every country in Western

Europe was lined up on one side or the other. In some places, countries, regions, even cities were divided against themselves. Monastic orders split into two factions. Most of the laity never knew the cause of the schism. All they heard from the pulpit were the bulls of excommunication issued against both popes. Popes and clergy had come in for much criticism before this schism split the Church, but the cry for reform was to become much louder in the forty years before it was brought to an end. The successors to the rival popes and their cardinals evaded all attempts to resolve the crisis, for they had a vested interest in the situation. More and more leading churchmen pressed for a general council to end the schism for the sake of the Church.

Eventually a number of cardinals deserted both popes and called a council at Pisa in 1409. They deposed both rivals and elected Pope Alexander V. This meant there were now three rival popes, until the Emperor Sigismund forced Alexander's successor, John XXII, to call a fresh council at Constance in 1414. After many disputes and difficulties, Martin V was elected Pope and the Western Church was united once more.

The Great Schism constituted a major exposure of the weaknesses in the Catholic Church of the late Middle Ages. The forty years of anarchy were a clear warning of what could happen if all power and responsibility in the Church were entrusted to individuals who put their own interests and ambitions first. The schism had shown up the papacy in its true colors: how deeply embroiled it was in secular politics; how it was prepared to use any means—even murder—to further its own ends; how all its financial and administrative resources could be put to political ends. Disrespect for the papacy and for the clergy in general grew and even reached the level of heresy in some European countries, notably Bohemia. The schism had another important lesson to teach European rulers, many of whom were extending their control over their lands at this time. They saw the advantages of a firm royal control of the Church in their own dominions and the possibility of forcing concessions from a weak pope.

The Council of Constance provided the Church with an outstanding opportunity to implement the necessary reforms: to limit the power of the papacy, to check administrative corruption, to improve the morality of popes and clergy, and thereby to win back the alienated and the heretical into the Catholic fold. The tragedy for the Catholic Church was that it did not succeed in doing any of these things. The council did claim that it had absolute authority over the pope in matters of faith and reform, but it could find no way of limiting the pope's actions. The conciliar system only lasted until the middle of the fifteenth century. Attempts were also made to restrict the financial resources of the papacy, but these met with little success as the council had no administrative machinery to deal with such matters itself.

In short, the fifteenth-century popes found that they quickly recovered their power if not their prestige. But there was no attempt to deal with moral corruption in the Church and there was no improvement in the caliber of Church leaders at all levels. Thus instead of being given a sympathetic hearing, the Hussite heretics were condemned out of hand. Secular princes negotiated their own terms with the papacy during the fifteenth century and gradually came to control their national churches more and more. Because it failed to seize this opportunity to reform its ways, the papacy earned the violent criticisms of Luther and others which in the next century finally destroyed the unity of Western Christendom.

HEATHER SCEATS

Clement VII, antipope. His election at Anagni split Western Christendom into rival obediences.

Avignon, from the Rhône. Seat of the papacy from 1305–78, it housed the line of antipopes during the Great Schism.

Wat Tyler "Captures" London

For decades English peasants had been forced to contend with residual feudalism, intermittent warfare, spiraling taxes and recurrent plague. In late May of 1381, the oppressed peasants of Kent and Essex rose in simultaneous, spontaneous rebellion against the Crown. An army of incensed tenant farmers marched on London in early June of that year, and King Richard II's helpless ministers took refuge in the Tower. The apparently doomed government was saved by the fourteen-year-old King's bravura: crying "Sirs, will you shoot your King?", Richard rode out to meet his assembled subjects. And by the time the Lord Mayor of London had rallied a force to "rescue" the King, Richard had made peace with the peasants. His actions averted civil war but they could not stem the popular tide; similar risings erupted across Europe in the next decade as peasants everywhere demanded a voice in their government.

Domestic scene from *The Occupations of the Months*.

Opposite Richard II, whose courage destroyed the Peasants' Revolt.

At the end of May, 1381, some villagers at Brentwood in Essex roughhoused a tax collector. There was nothing unusual in their action: the age was a turbulent one in which disputes led readily to violence, even among respectable members of the community. A visit from some awe-inspiring officer of the law was usually sufficient to quell any local disorder. But in the early summer of 1381 the usual did not happen.

No less a person than the chief justice of the King's Bench went down to Essex to hold an inquiry and punish the Brentwood rowdies. The justice found himself surrounded by an armed multitude who drove him off after making him swear on the Bible never to come their way again. Manhandling a tax collector was one thing; mishandling a royal justice was quite another—and infinitely more serious. However, instead of taking to the woods as outlaws or fleeing the country, the villagers appealed for the support of their neighbors, and insurrection spread rapidly throughout the county.

These events appear to have taken the government by surprise, although they were simply the sudden boiling over of an already seething mass of discontent that had been brewing in the countryside for several months. Now that some had openly defied authority, countless peasants left their homesteads and took to the roads. Dissidents in Kent made their way to Maidstone, and there chose as their leader Wat Tyler.

Nothing is known for certain of Tyler's origins or background. Some said that he was a highway robber, others that he was an artisan from Deptford who had slain a tax collector for insulting his daughter. It was reported at various times that he was a disbanded soldier from the war in France, and that he was the wayward younger son of a respectable Kentish family. It is clear from the way Tyler impressed himself upon contemporaries and chroniclers—and hence on posterity—that he had a strong personality and a gift for leadership. Yet Wat Tyler was never anything more than the leader of the rebels of Kent. There was no single "Peasants' Revolt" with a single leader, but rather a number of uprisings, each with a separate identity and separate leader (if it had any leader at all). What gave Tyler prominence, and turned his share in the revolt into a dramatic political event, was the decision made by the men of Kent to combine with those of Essex, on the other side of the Thames, and march on London. On June 11, these two great peasant armies began to converge on the capital.

When the news filtered through to the King's ministers at London, disbelief gave way to despair. The revolt was the culmination of a decade of troubles. The war against France had faltered ever since the Black Prince, heir to the throne, had contracted a recurrent fever. The Prince died in 1376. His aged father, King Edward III, followed him the next year and was succeeded on the throne by a ten-year-old grandson, Richard II. Aristocratic factions competed for control of the government and for the spoils of office.

When the war had begun back in 1337, the English economy was booming, with a rising population that made even the cultivation of marginal land profitable. But the boom was already weakening when, in 1348, the bottom was knocked out of the economy by the arrival of the Black Death. Competition for increasingly scarce labor pushed up wages. Landless laborers, hitherto the lowest stratum of the village community, were suddenly quite well off, for they could offer their services to the highest bidder. Some of those who had steady jobs on a yearly contract gave them up to work for higher daily wage rates somewhere else.

Above A bullock-drawn plough from the Lutrell Psalter.

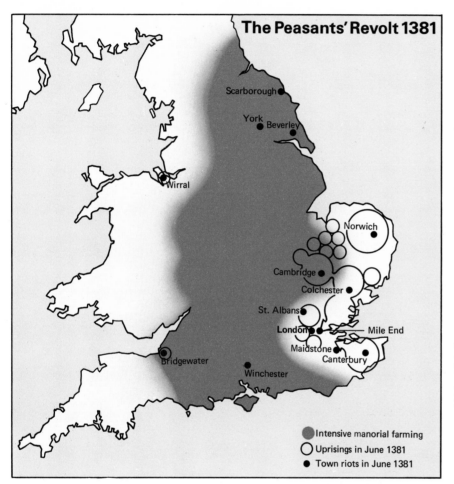

The Peasants' Revolt 1381

Scarborough
York Beverley
Wirral
Norwich
Cambridge
Colchester
St. Albans
London — Mile End
Maidstone
Bridgewater Canterbury
Winchester

⬤ Intensive manorial farming
◯ Uprisings in June 1381
● Town riots in June 1381

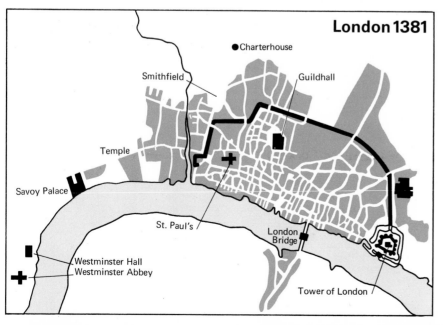

London 1381

● Charterhouse
Smithfield Guildhall
Temple
Savoy Palace
St. Paul's
London Bridge
Westminster Hall
Westminster Abbey
Tower of London

The more established peasants on the other hand —those who held land and paid for it in rents and labor services to their landlord—found themselves in an invidious position. Caught in an economic squeeze, the landlords raised rents while exacting every ounce of old-fashioned labor services (which did not have to be paid for, and were hence much more valuable than they had been when labor was cheap).

It was this economic crisis that made Parliament all the more reluctant to grant taxes—and all the more ready to believe that the men who controlled the government in the King's name were incompetent and spend-thrift. The situation was becoming desperate and the Commons very truculent, when, in January, 1380, the Archbishop of Canterbury, Simon Sudbury, a fair-minded man and a sound administrator, offered to take over as Chancellor. With another prominent churchman, Robert Hales, the prior of the Knights Hospitaler, acting as treasurer, there was a fair prospect that the country would at least be governed honestly.

Unfortunately, Parliament failed to provide Sudbury and Hales with a proper revenue; instead of a tax graduated according to people's ability to pay, the Commons would agree only to the levy of a flat-rate poll tax—of one shilling per head of the population over sixteen years of age. This was both inadequate and iniquitous.

For some reason, the government did not attempt to disperse the rebels who gathered outside London on June 11. It probably hoped that the peasant armies would break up of their own accord when they became weary and short of food—but the rebels proved to be much better organized and better disciplined than anyone had anticipated. By the evening of Wednesday, June 12, the men of Essex had reached the outskirts of London and had camped at Mile End. The main body of the Kentishmen encamped at Blackheath, while an advance guard pushed on to the south suburbs. The only bridge across the Thames was closed against them, but many sympathizers from London crossed over by boat to join the rebels, who broke open two prisons at Southwark and sacked the Archbishop's palace at Lambeth. The King and his ministers, gathered at the Tower of London, caught sight of flames in the distance and knew for certain that the uprising was serious. They could not make much sense of it, however, and sent envoys to ask the rebels' purpose; the peasants replied that they were loyal subjects of the King who wished to ask him to take action about the misgovernment of the realm by John of Gaunt.

That night at Blackheath, a priest named John Ball preached a now famous sermon to the assembled multitudes. In the beginning, he said, all men were created equal, and it was only the contrivances of the wicked that had reduced some men to servitude. Englishmen now had the chance, if they would seize it, of casting off the yoke that they had borne so long, and winning the freedom they had always desired.

Early the next morning, the fourteen-year-old King attempted to speak to the rebels from a boat lying on the river at Gravesend, while his listeners crowded the banks. They clamored for him to come ashore, but his ministers took fright when the rebels abused them as "traitors," and made the rowers pull away. As the royal party retreated to the Tower, the rebels poured into the city. It proved impossible to defend the gates against the insurgents, who had many supporters among the urban proletariat, and the houses and property of unpopular ministers, foreigners, and lawyers (against whom the rebels showed a special animosity) went up in flames.

That night the young King held council in the Tower. Opinions were divided: some were for an immediate show of force; others said that attempts should first be made to calm the mob down by negotiation. Siding with the latter, King Richard had it proclaimed throughout the city that everyone should come to meet him the following morning, June 14, beyond the city boundary at Mile End. Part of the plan was to draw the rebels away from the Tower, allowing unpopular ministers a chance to escape, but the plan misfired when some of the rebels remained on watch.

The Mile End meeting went well. The rebels were courteous and the King conciliatory. He agreed to free everyone from the burdens of serfdom, and set his clerks to work preparing charters. As to the alleged traitors, he said that the rebels could do as they wished with them—but only after their guilt had been proved by due process of law. (Meanwhile, some of the rebels had decided to settle this matter for themselves. While the King was at Mile End,

they broke into the ill-guarded Tower, dragged out Archbishop Sudbury and Robert Hales, and beheaded them on Tower Hill.)

Some of the rebels were satisfied with the Mile End meeting and the execution of "traitors" and began to disperse; but many remained, including the more militant leaders of the Essexmen and the Kentishmen who followed Tyler. Later on that Friday, June 14, the rebellion degenerated into a reign of terror, and attacks on property gave way to the slaughter of anyone the mob disliked. In an effort to regain control of the situation—by dividing peasant protest from the passions of the London mob—King Richard called another meeting for Saturday at the Smithfield cattle market, just outside the city wall.

Riding up to the King at Smithfield, Tyler added several new and impossible demands to those made at Mile End. He insisted that all men should be equal, and admit no lordship save that of the King, that the estates of the Church should be confiscated and distributed to the laity, and that all bishoprics should be abolished save one. The King kept up a show of sympathy, but Tyler's studied insolence provoked a member of the royal party to denounce him as a notorious highwayman and thief. Tyler drew a dagger and lunged at the enraged noble. The mayor of London, William Walworth, intercepted Tyler and struck him down from his horse, and one of the King's squires ran a sword through the rebel leader.

The peasants let out a great cry and strung their bows, but Richard rode toward them crying, "Sirs, will you shoot your King? I will be your leader, follow me." For one perilous moment the peasants hesitated—and then followed Richard out to the field of Clerkenwell. Mayor Walworth hurried back into the city to raise every armed man who could be trusted—but when he and his party returned to rescue the King, they found him talking at ease with the rebels. Richard would not allow force to be used, but granted the peasants his pardon and sent them away to their homes.

Events in London provided the most dramatic story, but risings elsewhere were no less important. There were disturbances at York, Scarborough, Beverley and Winchester—although whether these were anything more than town riots of a kind familiar in the fourteenth century is difficult to say. At towns in eastern England, however, there was clear evidence of opposition to merchant oligarchies and monastic landlords. At St. Albans the townsmen forced the abbot to grant them the sort of municipal self-government that towns of comparable size elsewhere had long before achieved, and at Bury St. Edmunds there was a violent assault on the abbey that owned the town lands.

Meanwhile, the royal government had taken the offensive. Proclamations announced the death of Tyler, repudiated concessions extorted by force, and called on local officials to establish order. Dismay among the peasants in Essex revived insurrection—but this time the government was prepared, and the rebel forces were cut down by troops at Billericay.

A thief at work.

Feeding the barnyard cock—and sparrows.

133

Peasants reap wheat under the direction of a reeve.

Rebel leader John Ball leads his "army" into London. The banners are those of England and St. George.

Judicial commissions were set up to search out and punish offenders, and a hundred or more were executed before the government relented and banned capital punishment. In the Parliament of November, 1381, a general amnesty was granted to all except 287 named offenders who had committed serious crimes.

Any account of the peasant uprisings of 1381 must attempt to explain why they were concentrated in eastern England. If peasant misery, provoked to rebellion by an iniquitous tax, were the only cause, it is surprising that there were no risings in midland England, where the manorial economy was most strictly organized and the burdens of serfdom most severe. Peculiarly, Kent, the center of rebellion, was the one part of England where there was little if any servile tenure; it was a county inhabited by both peasant smallholders and numerous wage laborers, and it was one of the few places where the Statute of Laborers was enforced effectively. Freeholders were common in East Anglia, but there were also many serfs—tied to the soil and obliged to render services and special payments to a landlord. Unlike the great estates of midland England, the manors there tended to be small—too small to be economic-

ally viable agricultural units—and most lords allowed the peasants to farm the tenements in their own way. Some landlords had freed their serfs, relying instead on rents, but others retained their legal hold over the peasants in order to exploit their labor as well as their prosperity.

It was this contrast between free and unfree, between the good fortune of some and the ill luck of others, that apparently lay behind the discontent in East Anglia. Moreover, both there and in Kent there was a distinctive social custom; when a peasant died, his holding was divided equally among all his sons. This policy had subdivided and ultimately impoverished peasant holdings. The Black Death was therefore a blessing in disguise, for it gave the survivors new opportunities for prosperity, provided they were prepared to work hard and build up a little capital to invest in vacant holdings. Too often, however, those opportunities were whittled away by exacting landlords; savings were reduced by rising rents, and hard-won capital drained away in unfair taxes. Thus, the basic cause of the Peasants' Revolt was mounting frustration—the poll tax was simply the last straw. England's peasantry resorted to evasion, and rebelled against pertinacious attempts to collect the infamous head-tax.

On the whole, the rebels were remarkably moderate in their demands. They were simply seeking a fair deal—all they asked for at Mile End was abolishment of the remaining burdens of serfdom. Instead of demanding an end to rents, they merely asked for the reasonable rent of fourpence an acre. And instead of seeking an end to taxation, they asked only for the sort of taxes "which our forefathers knew and accepted."

Fearful monastic chroniclers made much of the element of communistic equality revealed by Wat Tyler at Smithfield, but there is little evidence that such sentiments were widespread. The peasants were rebels against the iniquities of an economic system, not revolutionaries attempting to overthrow it. Indeed, nothing is more remarkable in the English rebellion of 1381—in contrast to contemporary peasant uprisings on the Continent—than the infrequency of attacks upon landlords themselves. There was astonishingly little bloodshed during the English rising—until the rebellion began to degenerate into anarchy. Even then, most of the bloodletting was in the towns, where personal animosities were sharper. The houses of the gentry were invaded and plundered (probably for food as much as for anything else), and their manorial accounts and legal records destroyed, but the gentry and their families were unharmed. Those individuals who suffered did so because they were the agents of central or local government, or because they were lawyers. The hostility shown toward lawyers is particularly significant—it was they who were taken as the chief symbols of obstruction to free enterprise and self-help, rather than the landlords, who were considered victims of economic circumstance.

The nobles and gentry could voice their discontent in Parliament, but rebellion was the only pos-

sible resort for the unenfranchised. The rebels voiced no demand—at least no articulate demand—for a share in Parliament or government, but the political consciousness of the rebellion was strikingly manifest. Admittedly, that consciousness was crude and shallow: the rebels demanded the heads of supposed traitors—but in murdering Sudbury and Hales, they murdered men who were honestly, if feebly, trying to improve the situation. Sudbury and Hales became the scapegoats for a decade of political ineptitude. Many of the gentry would have sympathized with the rebels' disdain for the ruling clique. But in the rebels' unswerving loyalty to King Richard and their insistent claim that they were "his true Commons," they were criticizing the failure of the knights and burgesses, as well as the magnates in Parliament, to serve the country properly. It was a forcible reminder that the upper classes could no longer treat political affairs as if they alone were concerned.

In their distrust of central government, and in their hankering after what they fondly imagined were the good old days in matters of rents and taxes, the rebels were manifesting a very conservative form of discontent—a discontent that fastened upon mismanagement rather than upon the structure of society. In demanding the abolition of restraints upon peasant free enterprise, the rebels were, of course, asking for economic change—but their actions do not indicate that they wanted social re-

volution. Thus, John Ball's famous sermon concentrated more on democratic freedom than on socialist equality, and in this way may be said fairly to reflect the aspirations of his listeners.

Those who rose in rebellion achieved little for themselves, but they did for the first time reveal the power and determination of the lower orders. The story, garbled and simplified in the telling, of how Wat Tyler "captured" London remained to fortify the courage of individual peasants and frighten the ruling classes. Some of the consequences were unfortunate: upper-class fears manifested themselves in a renewed insistence on order and conformity, new ideas were made synonymous with subversion, and criticism—such as Wycliffe's criticism of the Church—was driven underground. But beneath that show of upper-class solidarity, change went on nevertheless. There was a tacit understanding that the clock could not be put back, or the lower classes disregarded, and as economic developments made peasant free enterprise seem good sense, landlords relaxed their insistence on ancient customs and found more acceptable ways of exploiting their tenants' prosperity. English peasants eventually gained their freedom—without having to resort again to armed rebellion. Perhaps this was because they had not made the mistake of asking for too much or waging a class war. On the Continent of Europe, the story was a different and far more bitter one.

W. L. WARREN

A double view of the Revolt: on the left Wat Tyler is killed while Richard II looks on; on the right Richard addresses the mob.

135

The Peasants Revolt was not the only sign of agrarian discontent in late-fourteenth-century Europe. The changes brought about by the Black Death had a decisive effect on the economy, but this effect was not always immediately translated into social change. Peasants no longer had to accept the conditions of landowners in order to get work. Throughout Europe there was enormous demand for labor. The Bishop of Winchester, for example, one of England's richest and most powerful landowners, unable to find enough laborers to work his many farms, was forced to sell off thousands of acres to peasants and small landowners. The economic changes affected society throughout Europe and not merely in England. The impact was not only on country society but was also felt in the towns.

In France there was a whole series of risings. The first occurred in 1358. There were at least six armies in France—English, French and Burgundian—and the peasants suffered from their foraging. A group known as the "Jacquerie" emerged on the French political scene. The movement took its name from the derisive nickname, Jacques Bonhomme, which the French nobility had given to the peasants because of their patience in enduring all oppressions, such as crippling feudal wars.

The Jacqueries could rely on support in a few towns such as Beauvais and Senlis. Etienne Marcel, provost of the Paris

merchants, who dominated the meetings of the Estates-General that were called in 1357 to stabilize the country's finances, was the most powerful individual in France. He tried to use the Jacqueries to assist him in reducing the power and prestige of the nobles, only to be murdered on July 31, 1358.

As in England attempts at taxation in France were often the excuse for risings. In 1382 this was the justification for troubles in Paris and Rouen, where the townspeople used metal mallets to attack property (and were therefore called Maillotins). At the same time bands of peasants, known as *tuchins*, spread terror in the country. There was also a rising in Languedoc, in protest against the rapacious Duke of Anjou, who quashed an insurrection at Montpellier and then sent two hundred men to the stake, two hundred to the gallows and two hundred to the block, while depriving 1,800 others of their property.

No country in Europe was entirely free from troubles of this kind during the late thirteenth and much of the fourteenth centuries, although the exact form of the troubles differed.

France after Charles V

The outbreaks and the manner of their suppression in France owed much to the early death of Charles v. One of the major problems was the independence of Burgundy.

The Battle of Roosebeke.

The territory of Burgundy had a long tradition of independent rule. The duchy had been united with the kingdom of France in the eleventh century, but this brief interlude had not brought Burgundy into the main stream of French politics. The dukes of Burgundy were a cadet branch of the French royal house. In 1361 Duke Philip died without leaving a male heir, and the duchy was reunited with France. Two years later King John II gave it to his younger son Philip. Philip extended his territory by purchase, marriage and inheritance, while his valor in battle led men to call him Philip the Bold. The monarch's death in 1380 left his young son Charles VI (1380–1422) and his kingdom at the mercy of "The Princes of the Lilies," as the royal dukes of Anjou, Berry and Burgundy were called. The princes, who had intervened in the rebellion in Flanders, defeated the Flemings in a pitched battle at Roosebeke on November 27, 1382, and crushed resistance in Ghent.

The weakness of the French government after Charles' death was evident in the speedy recognition of John de Montfort as Duke of Brittany. This was the only way in the government's power of stopping de Montfort's rebellion, which was supported by the English army led by the Duke of Buckingham.

When the Count of Flanders died in 1384, his son-in-law, Philip the Bold of Burgundy, inherited his lands. The death of the Duke of Anjou later that same year left Philip in a position of enormous power in France. In 1388 however, Charles VI reached

his majority. He restored his father's councilors and turned to his brother Louis of Orléans for support.

In 1392 Charles had an attack of insanity and as his malady became gradually permanent the government passed again to the royal dukes, who quarreled about its administration.

The war of Chioggia

In 1378 war between Venice and Genoa broke out again. The Byzantine emperor, John V Paleologus, had granted the Venetians the island of Tenedos, which held a key position in the Dardanelles, in 1376. In the same year his son, who claimed the Byzantine throne, granted it to the Genoese. The Venetian navy seized the island in 1378. In retaliation, in 1380 the Genoese admiral, Luciano Doria, sailed into the Adriatic, defeated the Venetian Vittorio Pisano at Pola in Istria, seized Chioggia, which controlled Venice's harbor, and blockaded the city. Venice, which was largely dependent on imported food, was threatened with starvation. With the Genoese fleet already inside the lagoons that protected the city, Venice's days as a great seapower seemed numbered. Suddenly Pisano seized the channel leading from the lagoons to the sea. His masterly stroke turned the tables on the Genoese, who were now in their turn faced with starvation. In June 1380, Doria surrendered. Genoa never recovered, and Venice became undisputed master of the Levantine trade. The treaty of Turin in 1381 limited Genoa's trading role.

The Italian Town Bosses

The fourteenth century saw a continuation in the rise of tyrants in the Italian city-states. In Milan, for example, the Visconti were able to rule the city almost continuously from 1278 when the archbishop, Otto Visconti, drove out the della Torre. The della Scala family ruled Verona from about 1315 until 1404 when the Paduans invaded the city but were driven out by Venice who annexed the territory. From 1318 until its conquest by Venice Padua was ruled by the Canova

Defeat of the Jacquerie at Meaux in Brie.

nenfranchised peasantry

Equestrian statue of Cane I della Scala ("Cangrande") podestà of Verona.

family. The rise of many of the dynasties was due to the decreasing power of the German emperors, who were willing to give away certain of their powers in return for survival support. Milan, Verona and Padua are merely three examples of what was happening throughout northern Italy.

During the first half of the fourteenth century domestic issues had been the chief concern of most of the cities; in the second half of the century two of the city-states, Venice and Milan, attempted to dominate the whole of northern Italy. This, combined with the social problems caused by

the Black Death and the power vacuum caused by the decreasing interest of the papacy and the Empire, led to a period of continuous local warfare.

Portuguese independence

In Portugal John I, illegitimate son of Pedro I, succeeded to the throne in 1385 after leading a popular revolt to drive the queen, who had become regent in 1383, and her daughter Beatrice from the country. At the time of the coup, Beatrice was betrothed to John II, Prince of Castile—and the Castilians promptly invaded Portugal and besieged Lisbon, only to be decisively defeated at the Battle of Aljubarrota in August, 1385. After centuries of insecurity, the independence of Portugal from Castile was finally assured. As a further guarantee, John I signed the Treaty of Windsor in 1386. That agreement, by which Portugal and England became permanent allies, was secured when John married the daughter of John of Gaunt (Portugal is still regarded as England's oldest ally). In 1411, Castile accepted the inevitable and recognized Portugal's independence. During John's reign the policy of *reconquista* was modified; instead of merely reconquering "lost" territory in the Iberian peninsula, the Portuguese adopted a more aggressive policy. They invaded North Africa and captured Ceuta from the Moors.

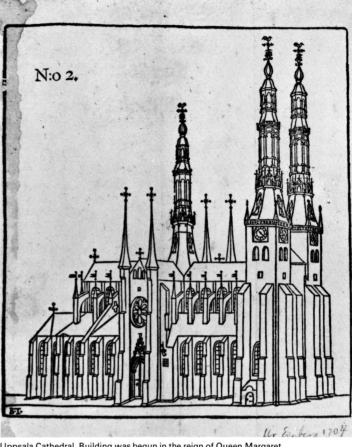

Uppsala Cathedral. Building was begun in the reign of Queen Margaret.

Scandinavia united

Denmark's period of stability in the early fourteenth century ended in anarchy in the 1320s. The next sixty years were a time of civil war and of determined efforts by the Hanseatic league to establish a stranglehold on trade. The Treaty of Stralsand, signed in 1370 after the Second Hansa War, even allowed the League a say in the royal succession. After the death of Waldemar IV in 1375, the male line died out, and his daughter Margaret became regent for her son Olaf V.

Because of the intermarrying among Scandinavia's royal families, Margaret soon found her power further expanded. Royal power in Sweden had been weakened as a result of the ineffectual rule of Magnus VII, who was King of Norway (1319–43) and King of Sweden (1319–65). He had abdicated the Norwegian crown in favor of his son, Haakon VI, who was Margaret's husband, in 1343 and had been deposed from the Swedish crown by the nobles in 1365. His successor, his nephew

Albert, proved no more capable and was deposed in 1387. The nobles elected Margaret as queen. She gathered an army in Denmark and defeated Albert.

Haakon VI of Norway died in 1380. Olaf V became king, but his early death in 1387 left Margaret as ruler of all three kingdoms, although her power base and the center of her government remained Denmark. Her energy was more like that of a king than a queen, and earned her the title "Lady King" among her subjects. The Swedish nobles soon found that the royal power was again increasing at the expense of their own.

Margaret believed that Scandinavia should again be one kingdom, and in 1397 the Union of Calmar stipulated that the three kingdoms should be united for defense and rule although their internal affairs would be unaffected. The union was not formally accepted by any of the three kingdoms, but Margaret arranged for the coronation of her great-nephew, Eric of Pomerania as King, although she remained the power behind the throne until her death in 1412.

The Battle of Aljubarrota, which assured Portuguese independence.

Father of English Poetry

Geoffrey Chaucer was a well-known court figure and the composer of several works on the theme of courtly love. At a time when poets used Latin or French to reach a large audience, Chaucer deliberately chose to write in the vernacular London dialect—and thus earned the title "father of English poetry." About 1387 he assembled a collection of entertaining, often bawdy tales as he imagined them to be told to one another by pilgrims en route from London to the shrine of St. Thomas à Becket at Canterbury. Although it is only a fragment of his projected grand scheme, **The Canterbury Tales** *remains as Chaucer's masterpiece; it is impossible to imagine English poetry without this enduring work.*

Courtly love—the romantic code of the feudal aristocracy. This was the dominant theme of Chaucer's earlier poetry, for which he was most praised in his own lifetime.

Opposite Chaucer reciting *Troilus and Criseyde* before a court gathering. The palaces of Richard II were the English centers of a dazzling international court culture.

Geoffrey Chaucer is often called "the father of English poetry." To what extent is this designation justified? Poetry had been written in England for several hundred years before his birth, in fact for about as many years as now separate us from Chaucer himself. But poetry written in England and English poetry are not necessarily the same thing. The Anglo-Saxon verse composed in England before the Norman Conquest is English only in the sense that it is not French or German. There is little continuity between this poetry and the poetry written in England following the Conquest. Alliterative verse was soon abandoned (except in some provincial outposts) in favor of the rhymed, syllabic verse brought to England by the Normans.

English poetry then, if one may judge from surviving manuscripts, properly begins in the early twelfth century. But this still leaves more than two centuries until the time of Chaucer. It is important to note that most pre-Chaucerian verse had one of two aims: to entertain or to instruct. Poetry fulfilled many of the functions that now belong to prose. History, philosophy and practical information were put into verse, as well as adventure and mystery stories. None of these set very high standards for writing in verse. Chaucer was the first English poet whose verse was didactic and entertaining, while at the same time revealing conscious craftsmanship. If not exactly the father of English verse, Chaucer, surely stands at the beginning of English poetry as we now know it.

Chaucer was an innovator in another important respect. In his time there were several dialects of English that a poet might write in. Some of these differed so greatly as to be mutually unintelligible to their respective speakers; there was no standard dialect such as we now have on each side of the Atlantic. If a writer wanted to reach a large audience, it was best to write in Latin or French. With an eye to posterity, Chaucer's friend and fellow-poet John Gower wrote his three major poems in Latin, French and the Kentish dialect respectively. But Chaucer chose consistently to use the London dialect. By so doing he gave to London speech a prestige enjoyed by that of no other English region. It became the standard literary dialect for all subsequent poets to use.

Geoffrey Chaucer was born about 1343, the son of a prosperous London wine merchant. Apart from a score of impersonal entries preserved in official documents, there is comparatively little material with which to construct the poet's life. What we do have gives in outline the career of a successful courtier and civil servant. As a boy, Chaucer probably attended St. Paul's Cathedral School, but beyond this conjecture we know nothing about his education. The earliest record of Chaucer that survives (1357) indicates that he served the Countess of Ulster, probably as a page. Two years later he was with the English army in France, where he was captured and later ransomed for £16 by King Edward III. We do not hear of Chaucer again until 1367, when he is mentioned as being in the king's service. About 1366 he married Philippa Roet, one of Queen Philippa's ladies-in-waiting and sister to the third wife of John of Gaunt, Chaucer's patron.

From this time on, the record of Chaucer's life is a series of appointments to diplomatic missions abroad and to official duties at home, all of which brought him into contact with a wide variety of people. He went to France several times in the service of the king, and to Italy at least twice. In 1374 Chaucer obtained a house above Aldgate and later in the year was made Controller of Customs and Subsidy on Wools, Skins and Hides for the port of London. But his career was not always smooth.

The year 1386 in particular seems to have been a bad one for Chaucer. Perhaps for political reasons, he quit not only his post as Controller of Customs on Wools, but also the controllership of Petty Customs. Yet, when King Richard II came of age in 1389 and asserted his authority, Chaucer seems to have come back into royal favor. He was at

Geoffrey Chaucer, successful courtier and civil servant. He was the first poet to write a large body of verse in English, and he constantly strove to master a variety of styles.

he is so interested in his books that he fails to observe the world around him. We know, of course, that this is not true. Why did Chaucer feel it necessary to adopt such a guise?

The answer lies partly in his being a court poet with a middle-class background. We must remember, too, that in Chaucer's time it was normal practice for the poet to read his poems aloud. When Chaucer recited his poetry before a court gathering, the members of the audience would see before them Geoffrey Chaucer the courtier and civil servant. Under the circumstances, he could pretend to be an incompetent bourgeois versifier, thus establishing a close rapport with his audience. The same bond between poet and audience exists for the modern reader of Chaucer.

The court of Richard II was an ideal place for a man with Chaucer's abilities to advance himself. Richard's palaces at Eltham, Windsor and Sheen were the English centers of an elegant international court culture and thus provided the poet a dazzling contact with the art and literature of continental Europe. It was there that Chaucer met the contemporary French poets Froissart and Deschamps. As part of the court circle, but also as a man with a middle-class background, Chaucer was in an excellent position to absorb the best features of this culture and to hold a mirror to the lords and ladies who gathered to hear him read his poetry.

The taste of the court ran to the refined literature of love and chivalry, and it looked to French poetry for the expression of those ideals. Today we retain only vestiges of the conception of love held by educated men and women of the late Middle Ages.

What is now known as courtly love was a feudal development. The castle, the center of feudal life, was often left in charge of the lord's wife while he was away fighting, and the young men remaining there obeyed and worshiped the lady. Gradually a code of behavior evolved whereby such men alternately languished and attempted various feats to prove their love and so secure the lady's pity. The essential features of the courtly code were humility, courtesy and secrecy. What seems to have begun as an amusement in twelfth-century France (perhaps as a parody of the worship of the Virgin Mary) became the accepted code of behavior, at least in polite society, in later medieval Europe.

Although most courtly love literature was in French or Latin, Chaucer nonetheless chose to write in English. His native poetic inheritance was fairly substantial. He had certainly read some of the many rhyming romances written in the preceding 150 years; he is even thought to have owned an important anthology of this sort of verse. The early English romances deal with love, betrayal, separation, fighting and reunion; their basic pattern is that of the quest. The love celebrated is not exactly courtly love. The knight fights for his lady, but his actions are not necessarily marked by humility or courtesy. Love is simply an excuse for

once made Clerk of the King's Works. In this capacity he supervised the maintenance and construction of buildings, managed payrolls and was the custodian of various royal valuables. Although this was the most distinguished position that Chaucer attained in his long career as a civil servant, he resigned from it after only two years in order to become the deputy forester of the royal forest of North Petherton, Somerset. From 1391 on he continued to receive signs of royal favor, and in 1399 he leased a house in Westminster Abbey garden. He was not to live in it for very long. Chaucer died, according to the inscription on his tomb in the Abbey, on October 25, 1400.

It is extraordinary that in his busy official life Chaucer found time to read widely and to write prolifically. But we do not need to imagine that he smuggled writing materials into the Customs House, or that beneath the accounts on his desk there was always a copy of his favorite author. While we know little about his life from external evidence, we know Chaucer the man better through reading his verse than we do any other English poet. He is frequently a character in his own poems and always a spectator.

In *The House of Fame* Chaucer suggests how he managed to fit his literary life into a successful official career. The Eagle in this poem says to Geoffrey that he is a dull, unobservant fellow who does not know even his own neighbors:

> For when thy labor done all is,
> And hast made all thy reckonings,
> Instead of rest or some new thing
> Thou goest home to thy house anon
> And, as dumb as any stone,
> Thou sittest at another book. . . .

Some truth may be found in this picture of the poet going home from work at the end of a day and reading in his study. But there is also humor. The poet makes fun of his dogged pursuit of learning:

adventure, as in the early thirteenth-century *King Horn*:

Today, so Christ me bless,
I shall show my prowess
For thy love in the field
With spear and with shield.
If I come back alive
I shall take thee for my bride.

The world of the romances is fairly elementary, with plenty of action. But there seems little motivation for much of this action, a fault that Chaucer was later to burlesque in his *Tale of Sir Thopas*. What Chaucer undoubtedly did learn from the romances was the art of telling stories in verse, something that French love poetry, with its elaborate digressions, could not provide.

Love is the dominant theme of most of Chaucer's poetry before *The Canterbury Tales*, and it was on this poetry that Chaucer's fame rested in his own lifetime and for nearly two centuries after his death. His French contemporary Deschamps paid tribute to him as the English God of Love, primarily for his translation of the French love allegory *Le Roman de la Rose*. Only the first part of the existing translation, entitled *The Romance of the Rose*, is now thought to be by Chaucer. In it the poet tells of a dream in which he enters a beautiful garden inhabited by personifications of the qualities that the successful lover must possess. Here the dreamer is to learn the art of love, enabling him to win the Rose (representing a young girl) on which his heart is set. In a fairly literal yet accomplished rendering of the French, Chaucer paints a picture of an idealized dreamworld that was in many ways the real world of the court for which he wrote.

Chaucer's first original work is *The Book of the Duchess*. It is an elegy written, probably in 1369, as a consolatory offering to John of Gaunt, whose first wife, the Duchess of Lancaster, had died of the plague. Cast in the form of a dream, the poem tells of the poet's encounter with a man in black, whose lady has also died. Here we see Chaucer for the first time posing as the naïve narrator. Unlike the audience, he does not learn of the death until the end of the poem. Thus Chaucer is humorous at his own expense and at the same time, by creating a measure of suspense, adds poignancy to the knight's eventual statement of loss. Though full of borrowings from French love poetry, *The Book of the Duchess* is not an allegory. We listen to and hear about real people.

Chaucer continued to use the dream convention in later poems, such as the unfinished *House of Fame* (1374) and the exquisite *Parliament of Fowls* (1382), the latter probably written for court celebrations on St. Valentine's Day. In both these poems Chaucer develops his guise as the incompetent but good-hearted narrator and, especially in the *Parliament*, reveals a keen observation of various human traits. Love is the subject of Chaucer's last experiment with the dream convention, the prologue to *The Legend of Good Women*, written after *Troilus and Criseyde* and just before he began *The Canterbury Tales*. In the prologue the poet-dreamer is arraigned by the God of Love for having written poems that show the love of women in a poor light. The Queen, Alcestis, defends Chaucer with the unflattering (but not surprising) suggestion that perhaps the poet did not fully understand what he was writing! The upshot is that Chaucer must do penance by writing of virtuous women. He probably grew tired of straightforward virtue, since the legends themselves, like several of Chaucer's poems, were left unfinished.

Part of the evidence for the charge brought against Chaucer by the God of Love is the book telling of the betrayal of Troilus by his lady, Criseyde. Written about 1385, *Troilus and Criseyde* is Chaucer's longest single poem and has been called the first English novel. Certainly it is Chaucer's finest attempt at sustained narrative. The central figure in the poem is not so much Troilus, Chaucer's fullest portrait of the medieval courtly lover, as it is Criseyde. Criseyde has tragic stature: her betrayal of Troilus and her taking of a lover in the opposing Greek camp is presented as the inevitable outcome of her fear of being cast adrift in a hostile world. But Chaucer knew the value of humor in tragic writing, and in Pandarus, the lovers' go-between, he has given us the first and one of the most delightful comic figures in English literature.

Although in his own lifetime, and for some time after, Chaucer was most highly praised for his love poetry, we now see *The Canterbury Tales* as his greatest achievement. The collection stands beside *The Faerie Queene* and *Paradise Lost* as one of the finest long poems in English. It is here that Chaucer sums up and interprets for us the ideals, follies and commonplaces of life in the late Middle Ages. The *Tales* are a canvas of life as it was, and also of life as it is, for most of Chaucer's observations of men and women have enduring value. It is possible to imagine English literature without *Troilus and Criseyde*, great though that is in many respects, but not without *The Canterbury Tales*.

We do not know precisely when and how Chaucer first came upon the idea of assembling this collection of tales, though the work as a whole is a product of his later years (1386–1400). Some of the tales had been written previously to stand on their own, but most were composed after the device of the pilgrimage had taken shape. The plan of the work is fairly simple. The poet meets a group of pilgrims at the Tabard Inn in Southwark, from which they are about to travel to the shrine of St. Thomas à Becket at Canterbury. The host of the inn, a jovial and forceful fellow, proposes that everyone should tell a tale on the way to the shrine and another on the return journey, the winner receiving a dinner at the inn at the expense of the whole company. This ambitious scheme demanded 120 tales in all and Chaucer obviously

Chaucer's greatest achievement, *The Canterbury Tales*, presents a witty, sympathetic and realistic picture of the times. *Top* The pilgrims meet at the Tabard Inn, Southwark. *Middle* The Knight. *Bottom* The Wife of Bath.

The manuscript page contains Middle English text from the Prologue to the Canterbury Tales, written in medieval script within an illuminated border.

realized that he would never live to complete it. There are in fact only twenty-four tales, one of which (the Cook's) is fragmentary. The collection is headed by a general prologue in which Chaucer, in a series of masterly portraits, describes the various pilgrims, a company consisting of all manner of men and women.

"Here," as Dryden justly remarked, "is God's plenty." In passing from the earlier poems to *The Canterbury Tales* we realize how much fuller Chaucer's world has become. The world of dreams and classical tales gives way to a vast panorama of good and evil, humor and seriousness, joy and sorrow, the sublime and the ridiculous. Chaucer's powers of observation are given full rein. But for all that, he remains the shy, in-

The Prologue to the *Canterbury Tales*, from a fourteenth-century manuscript. The Prologue contains a masterly series of word-portraits of the various pilgrims.

competent, good-hearted narrator. Chaucer does not look on the human comedy from a distance: he is himself one of the pilgrims, willing to observe and to accept life for what it is. Unlike his contemporary, William Langland, the author of *The Vision of Piers Plowman*, Chaucer is never reduced to savage indignation by the follies and injustices of this world.

The variety and quality of *The Canterbury Tales* can be suggested in a general way by reference to aspects of Chaucer's personality as a poet: his humor, sympathy, resourcefulness and seriousness. The humor will at once be obvious to all who open the *Tales* for the first time. Chaucer has the genuine gift of making people laugh, and often his desire to do so brings out the best in him as a narrative poet. Consider, for example, the ingenious *Miller's Tale*, with its complicated double plot. Just enough detail is given to set the plot in action and to give us a clear picture of the characters involved. The humor is not simply a matter of indelicate incidents and coarse vocabulary, but of seeing credulousness exposed. The silly carpenter's downfall ends with all his neighbors laughing at his plight, and the reader is led to join in the chorus of laughter. Chaucer is also willing to raise a smile at his own expense. As a pilgrim, he tells the feeblest tale of all, the *Tale of Sir Thopas*, a patchwork romance that he says he learned long ago. Having been interrupted by the indignant host, Chaucer complains that it is unfair to let others complete their tales and not him.

Humor can easily shade into satire, if the author's purpose is to ridicule rather than simply to expose. But Chaucer's pointed observations are seldom a matter of ridicule. As an observer, he is sympathetic even when he sees hypocrisy or other vices. The prioress, described in the general prologue, is a target for criticism, being more concerned with manners and the health of small animals than with religious life and duties. Yet Chaucer does not condemn her; he observes and has a measure of sympathy even for the misguided.

A piece of advice occurring more than once in the *Tales* is "make virtue of necessity," and as a poet Chaucer heeded it. *The Squire's Tale* is unfinished, having taken us temporarily into the world of romance where rings have magic powers and birds can talk. Chaucer may have begun this story with the intention of completing it and then found it would not do. His solution is to give it to the youthful squire, from whose mouth it is very appropriate, and then to have it courteously interrupted by the older franklin. In this way Chaucer kills three birds with one stone. We can enjoy the fantastic tale for itself, its suitability to the narrator, and the dramatic moment of the interruption. Chaucer's resourcefulness often manifests itself in translations from other poets as well, in which he works an almost magical transformation of the old material.

Behind the humor and sympathy, the genial acceptance of life as it is, there is also seriousness,

English travelers setting forth. As a medieval Christian, Chaucer saw man's life on earth as a constant pilgrimage.

though never righteous solemnity. While Chaucer looked with a keen and sympathetic eye at the world around him, he remembered always that earth was part of a divinely ordered universe. As a medieval Christian poet, he believed all below the moon to be subject to change and decay, and that man's lasting joy came only when he passed from this world. Man's life on earth is a pilgrimage, as the final tale in the collection reminds us. *The Parson's Tale* is a prose sermon on the seven deadly sins. While perhaps not to the taste of modern readers, it testifies to the serious side of Chaucer as a poet of mirth and morality.

In conclusion, Chaucer's poetry is the first great landmark in English literature; the title "the father of English poetry" justly is his. *The Canterbury Tales* present a splendid pageant of life in which we see all forms of medieval writing perfected. On the pilgrimage we travel from the world of chivalric romance into that of ordinary men and women, from the saint's legend to the bawdy tale. *The Canterbury Tales* are also a landmark in European literary history. There had been other collections of tales, notably Boccaccio's *Decameron*, but none so various as Chaucer's. There had been more profound visions of human life—one thinks at once of Dante—but none with the same healthy and cheerful spirit that informs *The Canterbury Tales*. Chaucer's crowning achievement remains unsurpassed in Western literature.

GREGORY ROSCOW

Opposite above The Miller, whose tale in the cycle is one of ribaldry and credulity.

Opposite below The Clerk of Oxford. His is a moral tale of virtue rewarded.

A near contemporary of Chaucer was John Gower (c. 1325–1408). His most important works were the lost *Speculum Meditantis*, which was written in the 1370s; the *Vox Clamantis* and its later continuation the *Chronica Tripartita*, which was begun in 1381 and completed in around 1400; and the *Confessio Amantis*, which was begun in 1383 and completed ten years later. The *Vox* and *Chronica*, although masquerading as a defense of King Richard II against the rebels of 1381, who are described as wild beasts, is in fact a savage attack on Richard's conduct of affairs.

The *Confessio Amantis* is more interesting. Despite its Latin title it was written in English. Its 3,000 lines are in the form of a dialogue between a lover (Gower himself) and a confessor sent by Venus and Cupid to cure him of his love. Like

The English poet John Gower.

Boccaccio, Petrarch and Chaucer, Gower used the basic structure as an excuse for telling stories taken from the Bible and from classical and medieval literature.

Chaucer and Gower were friends for many years, although it is possible that they quarreled toward the end of Chaucer's life. Chaucer dedicated *Troylus and Criseyde* to "moral Gower," and in the *Confessio Amantis* the goddess Venus praises Chaucer as her own poet. Although not of Chaucer's stature as a writer (Chaucer praised his moral not his literary qualities), Gower has an important place in the development of English literature.

The trend toward vernacular literature was not confined to England: in Scotland, John Barbour's *The Brus*, a twenty-book poem on the achievements of Robert Bruce published in about 1370, became very popular.

The foundation of New College

Within five years of Wycliffe's death, Oxford University entered on a new phase of its existence: William of Wykeham's scholars moved from their temporary quarters to the new buildings of St. Mary College of Winchester familiarly known as New College. Wykeham, Bishop of Winchester and Lord Chancellor, designed his college to house a warden, seventy poor scholars, ten chaplains and sixteen choristers—and to ensure that his benefaction was not wasted, he established a grammar school at Winchester where boys were given instruction in Latin (an essential preliminary to the university course). After a two-year probation at New College, those students qualified as perpetual fellows. Statutes minutely regulated the lives of Wykeham's scholars, who were the first in Europe to have study rooms to themselves. The buildings, no less than the statutes, were planned with great care by Wykeham and set the standard for collegiate buildings in England for centuries to come.

Richard II and Henry IV

Richard II's government became increasingly unpopular as his reign continued. At first the King himself was not blamed; those around him were considered to be at fault. Richard attempted to take over the government himself in 1385, but the Duke of Gloucester was able to win the support of Parliament for keeping power in the hands of the council. Five of Richard's supporters were executed in 1388 by order of Parliament.

In 1389, Richard seized power. For the first eight years of his

Henry IV, in the tall, black hat, claims the throne before Parliament.

Wadham College and New College, Oxford, with doctors and scholars.

personal rule, the government managed to recover some of its lost popularity. But in 1396 he married the six-year-old daughter of Charles VI of France. The marriage was unpopular and Richard's attempts at this time to introduce new ways of government into the country were even more unpopular.

Parliament opposed his requests for money and asked the King to present accounts. Richard attacked the peers whom he thought responsible for the opposition: two, Arundel and Gloucester, were executed; the Archbishop of Canterbury, the dukes of Norfolk and Hereford and the Earl of Warwick were banished.

The Duke of Hereford, Henry (surnamed Bolingbroke from his birthplace), son of John of Gaunt,

quickly became the leader of the party opposed to Richard; after John of Gaunt's death, Bolingbroke succeeded him as Duke of Lancaster. In 1398 while Richard was in Ireland, Bolingbroke landed in England and it soon became clear that not only did he have military support, but that the populace was also keen that he should become King. Richard returned to England and surrendered to Bolingbroke at Flint. He abdicated and was imprisoned in the Tower of London. In 1400 the ex-king was moved to Pontefract castle, where he was probably murdered.

Bolingbroke became King as Henry IV. Because of the weakness of his claim to the throne, he was very dependent on parliamentary support and had to give way to parliamentary demands for accounts. Henry's reign was punctuated by frequent rebellions, the most serious of which was led by a wealthy Welsh landowner, Owen Glyn Dower (1350–1416). In 1400, unable to get what he regarded as justice against an English neighbor who had encroached on his property, he simply invaded his land. Many Welshmen saw this as the signal for rebellion against the English. A general uprising followed in many parts of Wales. Glyn Dower was proclaimed Prince of Wales. He could rely on support from Charles VI of France and a small English army was defeated in 1402. Henry IV was too busy suppressing another rebellion led by the powerful Percy family in the north of England to devote much attention to Wales, although he made two short expeditions against Glyn Dower in 1402 and 1403. The Welsh captured Harlech Castle, the key fortress for the English occupation of Wales. In 1405, with temporary peace in the north, Henry could turn his undivided attention to Wales. Despite the support of French troops, Glyn Dower was twice defeated. Hoping to distract Henry's attention, he made an alliance with malcontent English nobles, and a partition of England was proposed. The success of the English Prince of Wales (the future Henry V) made this impossible. In 1405 the important town of Aberystwyth was recaptured by the English, and in 1409 Harlech fell. Support for Glyn Dower quickly faded away. Despite his fairly continuous victory against rebels, Henry IV was never entirely secure on the throne: the words that Shakespeare put into Henry's mouth, "Uneasy lies the head that wears the crown," were apt. Henry's early death was, however, caused by epilepsy not rebellion. His son Henry V succeeded him.

The chief importance of Henry IV's reign lay in the expansion of the power of Parliament. Although the principle of taxation by consent had always been accepted, Parliament had never had any right to question the expenditure of the royal income. Henry was forced to acknowledge the principle of accountability. The reign of Richard had already led to an expansion of parliamentary rights—the reenactment of such anti-clerical legislation as *mortmain* (which attempted to control the passing of real-estate into the "deadhand" of the Church), *praemunire* and provisors was largely due to parliamentary pressure. But Henry's claim to the throne was itself dependent on parliamentary support: the future kings of England could never again entirely ignore Parliament.

Early fifteenth-century China

On the death of Hung-wu in 1400, his grandson succeeded to the dragon throne and took the name Chien-wen. However, his uncle refused to accept him as emperor and civil war broke out. This was to some extent a struggle between the south, which supported Chien-wen, and the north. In 1402, Chien-wen was defeated and disappeared, probably killed in a fire. But his uncle, who took the name Yung-lo, never felt entirely secure and made elaborate enquiries throughout China to find him. The new emperor moved the seat of government to Peking, although Nanking remained the official capital until 1421. Yung-lo rebuilt Peking, and the general plan of the city has remained unchanged since his time.

Despite some territorial losses, Yung-lo's reign ushered in a period of wealth and cultural progress. The botanical interests that had flourished in Hung-wu's reign continued and several books on the subject were published. Far more important was the attempt to produce a compendium of all knowledge. In 1403, 2,000 scholars were set to work to copy and gather information for this project. In three years they produced the *Yung-lo ta tien*, an encyclopedia of 11,095 volumes. It had origin-

Murad I, Sultan of Turkey.

ally been planned to print the work, but because of the cost and difficulty of printing so large a work, this was not done. Two manuscript copies were made, both of which were destroyed during the fall of the Ming in 1644. Most of the original was burned in 1901 during the Boxer Rising, although a few hundred volumes were saved.

Yung-lo's reign was a great age for architecture. Buildings such as the nine-storey Porcelain Pagoda at Nanking (built in about 1420) and the emperor's tomb at Peking (1424) were regarded as wonders. Other arts, particularly poetry and porcelain manufacture, also flourished.

The early fifteenth century saw energetic Chinese exploration of the lands around her. Desire for conquest, geographical interest and the need for new trade routes to replace those damaged by Timur were probably among Yung-lo's motives for sending long expeditions into the "Western Ocean." They were led by the chief eunuch, Cheng Ho, and were highly successful: foreign kings were even brought back as prisoners to Peking, foreign nations were impressed by China's might, trade flourished and maps of far-distant places were published. Places as far afield as Mecca and East Africa were visited. A description of these voyages by Ma Huan, *Ying-yai Sheng-lan*, quickly became a travel classic. After Yung-lo's death the exploration stopped, probably as a result of domestic difficulties.

A porcelain cup of Yung-lo's reign.

The Rise of the Ottomans

An increasingly serious threat both to Christian and to other Moslem states was posed by the rise of the Ottoman Turks. Under the founder of their dynasty, Osman (c. 1270–1326), a small new Anatolian principality had been created. His successor, Orkhan I, extended the Ottoman Empire to cover most of modern Turkey, including such important Byzantine cities as Iznik (Nicaea) and Brusa. Under Murad I, who ruled from 1361 to 1389 the European city of Adrianople was taken from the Byzantine Empire, and became the capital of the Ottoman domains in 1402. The Balkan states and the Byzantine Empire had to acknowledge Murad as their overlord. This did not prevent Murad from continuing to expand his territory into the Balkans. Important towns such as Sofia (1385), Nis (1386) and Salonika (1387) were captured. It was only because of the assassination of Murad that the Turks did not expand further into Christian territory.

Murad's ambitions extended in other directions also; he conquered much of Anatolia from rival Turkish rulers such as the Karamanids. His successor, Bayazid I, continued to mop up the Turkish principalities and to extend his dominion in the Balkans. It was only when the Ottomans clashed with the Mongols—reunited under Timur—that there was any real opposition.

Terror out of the East

Timur the Lame (Tamerlane) was the last great conqueror in the tradition of Genghis Khan, Alexander the Great and Cyrus. His defeat of the Ottoman Turks in 1402 astonished the monarchs of Europe. For a century the Turks had menaced them, and this victory of an unknown Mongol from the East afforded all Christendom a welcome respite. But although Timur altered the destinies of Europe, little of his vast empire remained intact after his death.

In the summer of 1402 two great armies, both declared champions of Islam, met on a plain near Ankara. Bayazid I (called Yiderim, "the Thunderbolt"), Ottoman conqueror of Eastern Europe, was forced to do battle on his own ground by Timur, the Mongol overlord of the East. By sunset, despite the valor of their elite Janissary corps, the might of the Ottomans had been broken and their sultan taken prisoner. The battle of Ankara lost the Ottoman Turks Asia Minor; their royal family was either captive or fugitive, and they did not venture east again until the time of Mehmet II, conqueror of Constantinople. Moreover, by scattering the Turks, Timur inadvertently saved the Byzantine Empire and afforded all Christendom a welcome respite.

When Genghis Khan died, his vast empire had been divided among his descendants. Several principal states emerged, although one son held the title of Great Khan and was theoretically sovereign over the others. Chagatay, Genghis' second son, had taken as his domain Transoxiana, Khwarizm and Semirechye. After the death in 1294 of Kublai Khan, grandson of Genghis who extended the conquests to China proper, the Mongol empire disintegrated. The nomad warriors suffered the fate of all barbarian conquerors—they were absorbed into the culture of their subject populations and sapped of their own primitive ferocity and vigor. The Great Khans ruled in China as Chinese emperors until ousted by the Ming dynasty; in Persia the Hulagid Il-Khans were independent Moslem rulers; in the west the Golden Horde ruled from Saray in southern Russia over a Slav empire; and in their original home on the steppes the Mongol tribes, while retaining their primitive characteristics, had lost their cohesion and unity and fallen prey to civil war and feuds. It was from this latter group in Turkestan, a tribe only recently converted to Islam, that Timur emerged at the end of the fourteenth century to lead a Mongol revival that once more threatened the world.

Timur-i-Lang, or Timur the Lame, was born in April, 1336, near Kash in Transoxiana. His father was head of the Barlas tribe of Mongols who had come to Transoxiana with the Chaghatay khan, Mubarak.

The Chaghatay were divided into two groups; one settled in Transoxiana, the other lived outside Transoxiana and was nomadic. The nomads declared themselves independent in 1269, and the area they inhabited became known as Moghulistan. On the death of its governor in 1358, Transoxiana was invaded by the Khan of Moghulistan, Tughluk-Timur. Upon his advance to the Quashka-Darya River in 1360, the governor of Kash withdrew to Khurasan, letting Tughluk-Timur take Transoxiana almost unopposed.

The youthful Timur saved his valley and its cities from devastation by staying to face the Khan. Hoping to become the new governor of Transoxiana, he offered him his services. Tughluk-Timur, however, appointed his son Ilyas-Khoja as governor. Timur had allied himself with the powerful Jalayir clan to the north, by marrying Aljai, sister of Amir Husayn of Balkh. When Ilyas-Khoja allowed his generals to ravage all Samarkand Timur broke with the Moghulistan nomads and joined Amir Husayn in Afghanistan.

The brothers-in-law joined Jalal al-Din Mahmud, Khan of Sistan, and began gradually to acquire the motley following with which they were later to reestablish themselves in Transoxiana. (It was while a soldier of fortune in Sistan that Timur received the wounds that gave him his nickname.)

In 1363 Timur and Husayn retook Kash, forcing Ilyas-Khoja to flee toward the Ili River. They elevated a puppet Chaghatay khan to the throne, thus lending a specious legality to their position. They took Samarkand by treacherously luring the Sarbadar amirs out of the city and executing them.

After taking the capital, the collaboration between Timur and Husayn began to disintegrate. The death of Princess Aljai removed the final tie

Detail of a royal tomb in Samarkand. Timur transformed Samarkand, the capital of his empire, into the Rome of Asia.

Opposite Mongols building towers of enemy heads. This practise was intended as a salutary warning to restive subject peoples.

Timur traveling to Khivasan.

dynasty. All scholars, divines and artisans were taken captive and brought to Samarkand. With the reduction of Urganch and the submission in 1389 of the Jat khan, Khiza-Khoja, to the status of vassal, Timur had reunited the entire Chaghatay domain. A lifetime of conquest had begun.

The first years of Timur's military career saw the fall of Iran, which had degenerated into a number of minor states. In a series of campaigns he reduced the city of Herat, and then Khurasan and eastern Persia in 1383–85. His Persian campaign of 1386–88 started with the fall in the northwest of Tabriz, the great entrepôt of trade and one of the largest cities in the world at that time. After this he took Tiflis in Georgia, forcing King Bagrat to renounce Christianity and become his vassal. He then subjugated the prince of Erzinjan, justifying his campaign by the activities of the Karakoyunlu, a Turcoman tribe which had been plundering pilgrim caravans en route to Mecca. His efforts against the nomads were never entirely successful, it being difficult to force them into open battle.

Timur next turned to the Muzaffarid emirate of southern Persia, taking Isfahan unopposed. But the slaughter of the Tartar garrison by the townspeople resulted in his ordering a massacre of the inhabitants. Each soldier was given a quota of heads to supply, and when the Tartars withdrew an estimated 70,000 heads were piled outside the city. Timur then continued south toward Fars, which tendered its submission. However, learning of an attack on Transoxiana by Toktamish, Khan of the Golden Horde, Timur returned home immediately to face the new threat.

After defeating Toktamish in Russia, and wishing to add to his prestige as defender of Islam, Timur now concentrated his efforts on reducing the Moslem east to vassaldom. In 1392 he marched against those areas that conformed to the Shi'a version of the Moslem faith; after a campaign through Mazandaram to west Persia, their submission was assured. Tiflis in Georgia was taken again to ensure its continued compliance. During his absence revolts had broken out in Persia, particularly in the south. The rebellion there was ruthlessly repressed in 1393, and Persia was annexed to his empire.

This accomplished, Timur marched on Mesopotamia where Sultan Ahmad Jalayir still controlled Baghdad. Ahmad fled to Damascus, where he was given asylum by Barkuk, the Mameluke Sultan of Egypt. Baghdad capitulated without a struggle. On learning of Timur's maneuvers, Barkuk prepared to challenge him, moving north first to Damascus, then to Aleppo. But the conflict never materialized. At this point Timur learned of the renewed activities of the Golden Horde, and turned aside to meet it.

It was in fact through Timur's support that Toktamish had raised himself to the rank of khan. Though he himself was a descendant of Genghis Khan, he had accepted Timur as his suzerain. It was thus with great ingratitude that he withdrew

that bound them together. The intervening four years had seen intermittent hostilities between the two, but Timur's reduction of Balkh in 1370 resulted in Husayn's becoming a fugitive, and although Timur refused formally to sanction his execution he took no action when Husayn was subsequently killed in a blood feud.

After the fall of Balkh, Timur, now foremost chief in Transoxiana, was granted supreme command. For the first time in the 140 years since the death of Genghis Khan, the Tartar princes departed from the old code and chose a leader who was not a descendant of the Mongol Great Khan. Timur was made sovereign of the Chaghatay line of khans and proclaimed restorer of the Mongol empire. His accession was supported by the imams because he alone seemed able to restore order and to resist the northern hordes.

Timur's immediate problem was the establishment of internal security in Transoxiana. He dealt with it by gaining control of the territories adjoining his own, campaigning against Khwarizm in the west and Moghulistan in the east. After continued resistance he sacked Urganch in Kwarizm in 1387, razing it in 1388 and wiping out the local Sufi

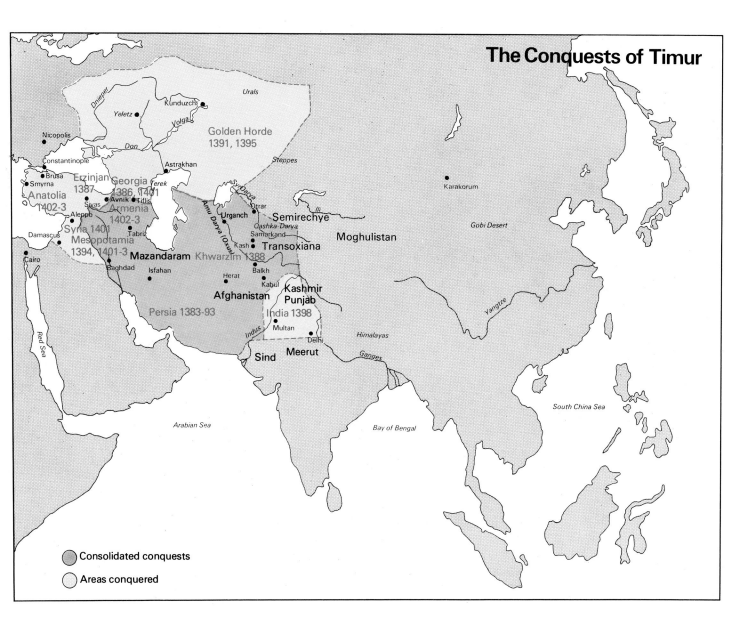

The Conquests of Timur

his homage and challenged the claims of the Amir of Transoxiana. Timur first embarked on a punitive campaign in 1391. Toktamish was finally brought to battle at Kunduzcha, east of the Volga, where he was defeated but not captured. Timur then divided the khanate among various Genghisid princes in an effort to prevent Toktamish, who was still at large, from uniting the Golden Horde against him. This done he had returned to Samarkand and his conquest of the Moslem east.

These latter campaigns were now interrupted by Toktamish's presence in the Caucasus. After a failed attempt to negotiate a treaty, Timur marched on the lands of the Horde, defeating Toktamish in 1395 on the Terek. He pursued him up the Volga, ravaging the area bounded by the Dnieper and the Don as far north as Yeletz. These blizkrieg campaigns, with their forced marches and surprise attacks, demonstrated three rules consistently followed by the great general: never to campaign in his own country; never to allow himself to be put on the defensive; and always to

attack as swiftly as possible. "It is better," he once said, "to be at the right place with ten men than absent with ten thousand." Returning eastward across the Kuban steppe, Timur demolished Astrakhan and the capital of the Golden Horde, Saray. This seriously damaged the northern trade route with the result that more trade passed through Transoxiana. In spring 1396 Timur returned to Samarkand where he spent the next two years beautifying the city and supervising the administration.

Timur made Samarkand the Rome of Asia. Like Augustus Caesar he could claim to have found a city of clay brick, and left one of marble. Palaces were constructed around great gardens; poplar-lined avenues led to open squares. Timur was never too engrossed in a campaign to overlook materials or works of art that might beautify the city. Academies and libraries were built and guilds authorized; there was even a menagerie for rare beasts, and an observatory. Turquoise buildings gleamed in the clear mountain air, the gold and

Baghdad, mighty entrepôt of the East. Timur captured it intact, but when the citizens proved treacherous he razed it to the ground.

age, and he affected a long beard. Although he limped with his right leg, only outside his borders was he spoken of as Timur the Lame. His most striking trait was the restless energy that characterized all his actions. He loved bravery, was intolerant of fools and liars, and drove himself as hard as he did his warriors.

To hold in check the unruly inhabitants of Central Asia, Timur became himself the law. He issued commands directly to his peoples. Newly acquired territories on the periphery were given to one of his sons or a high amir. Subject peoples were frequently conscripted into the army, and laborers and artisans impressed at need. Former rulers were brought to his court and honored, as long as they caused no trouble.

Under Timur a sophisticated communications network was maintained throughout the empire. Roads were kept open in winter and guard stations erected at intervals along them. These post roads enabled Timur to keep in touch with the most far-flung corners of his domains. Hard-riding couriers brought reports from governors, generals and secret service men: the information service was complete and swift.

The empire's wealth was not based merely on plunder. Trade hummed. Most of this was conducted overland and along the rivers of Asia. Merchants paid duty as well as road tax—a considerable source of income, as caravans coming from the Far East avoided Egypt, where the Mamelukes bitterly opposed any traffic with the Christians. For the merchants the single customs tax and an assured safe conduct for five months were a boon. Wherever possible Timur had kept his conquered cities intact. From Tabriz alone he gained revenues that were larger than the yearly revenues of the King of France. Theft was largely eliminated, each city magistrate or captain of the road guards being held responsible for his district.

Timur's empire was now considerable. Based in Transoxiana and eastern Turkestan, he controlled all Persia and was suzerain of the Golden Horde. The sixty-year-old warrior was not content to consolidate these gains however. In 1397 he ordered an invasion of India on the pretext that the Moslem sultans of Delhi were too lenient with their Hindu subjects.

The Indian campaign was typical of Timur's successes. He was ruthless and efficient, and he wanted treasure and vassals. For some time the local governors had ruled autonomously. Their small kingdoms thus constituted easy prey for Timur, who blazed his way across the Indus and into the Punjab where he reduced Multan.

In December, 1398, Timur was outside Delhi. After a brief sortie by the Indians he ordered the killing of all prisoners. The subsequent attack by the Indian forces, who carried the battle to the enemy, resulted in complete victory for the Tartars. The ruler of Delhi fled and Timur, on his entry into the city, offered protection in return for a huge indemnity. On his withdrawal, however, the

white lettering on their facades illuminated by the sun. Blue was the favorite color of the Tartars. Samarkand became known as Gok-kand, "the Blue City."

The chronicles of the time have described Timur as a tall, well-built man, with a massive head and high forehead. His hair turned white at an early

Tartar troops subjected Delhi to pillage and massacre from which it took more than a century to emerge. The treasure that was brought to Samarkand was immense.

From Delhi Timur turned north to the Ganges, taking Meerut and massacring its population. He fought his way back toward Kashmir, appointing a Moslem prince to rule the Punjab and Upper Sind as his vassal. He returned to Samarkand in 1399 by way of Kabul, leaving a devastated land behind him. To commemorate his victory he built a great mosque in three months. It was large enough, say the chronicles, to hold all the people of the court.

Even now the old man would not rest on his laurels. Western Asia once more attracted his attention. The death of Barkuk and the chaos resulting from the drug-induced excesses of Timur's heir, Miranshah, prompted him to mount a campaign in the west. Designating his favorite grandson, Mohammed-Sultan, as his heir in Transoxiana, he set forth late in 1399.

The rising power in the Levant was the Ottoman Empire. The Ottoman Turks had been pushed into Anatolia by the Mongol advance under Genghis Khan. Their composition is uncertain—it is quite possible they were not a single tribe, but a military brotherhood recruited for war against the infidels. They called themselves Ottomans or Osmanli after their leader and founder, Osman I (1270–1326). It is worth noting that the Ottomans were a strong European power before they began to expand in Asia Minor; as such, they did not overlap into the Mongol sphere of influence. Under Osman's grandson Murad I, they had crushed a Christian coalition at Kossovo in 1389. Under Bayazid I, Murad's successor, they defeated the last great crusade, headed by Sigismund of Hungary, at Nicopolis in 1396. The following year Bayazid laid siege to Constantinople. But his activities in the east and his grant of asylum to Timur's enemies were to draw the two empires into conflict. Thus the western kings, the Caliph in Cairo, the Protector of the Faithful in Baghdad and Bayazid, the Sword Arm of the Faith, came to form an alliance against the power of Central Asia.

The challenge was clear. Chieftains under Timur's protection had been ousted from Asia Minor, his sons' lands invaded and Baghdad taken from his governor. Moreover it is probable that Timur was now contemplating the invasion of China. He could not feel free to move east while the alliance in the west threatened his frontier.

The allied front formed an immense crescent stretching from the Caucasus to Baghdad. To meet it Timur had to march west more than a thousand miles over extremely difficult terrain. Awaiting him were a dozen separate armies: resurgent Georgians; a Turkish expeditionary force; Kara Yusuf, leader of the Karakoyunlu; a powerful Egyptian army in Syria; and in the south, Baghdad. If he attacked either wing of the crescent, the

other could close in on his rear. He could not force either of the two great sultans to give battle, while they were free to invade Asia at will.

Making Tabriz his base for operations, Timur assured himself of the neutrality of the Tartars of the Russian steppes. To Bayazid he wrote courteously, requesting that no aid be given to Kara Yusuf and Sultan Ahmad. Clearly Timur respected the power of the Turks and wished, even at this stage, to avoid a needless confrontation. Bayazid's reply was arrogant and defiant. A brief correspondence ensued, with the Thunderbolt promising, among other things, to violate Timur's favorite wife.

The Emperor's pavilion. Timur brought to his capital the best his conquered territories had to offer, and even established a zoo.

151

Coins of the Timurid Empire. Trade and commerce flourished both within the empire and with the West.

One by one the Tartar dealt with his opponents: the Georgians were crushed, the Karakoyunlu scattered; Sivas, the key to Asia Minor, was captured. In 1401 the Syrians were utterly defeated. First Aleppo, then Damascus fell. Baghdad was razed to the ground.

While Timur was besieging Baghdad, Bayazid was actually crossing from Europe to Asia in a leisurely fashion. Had he been more energetic, he would have found Tabriz undefended. As it was, Timur had marched from one end of the arc of his enemies to the other in fourteen months, eliminating all of Bayazid's allies before he even appeared on the scene. He then retired to Tabriz to receive reinforcements from Samarkand.

Experienced, highly trained and accustomed to victory, the Turkish host was confident. In the summer of 1402 it established its main camp at Ankara. Then Bayazid moved on into the hilly country beyond the river Halys: the Tartars were reported to be ahead at Sivas. Bayazid waited a week for word of them—but in vain. The Tartars had vanished, elephants and all. On the eighth day scouts reported a Tartar advance on Ankara from their rear. Timur, on finding the hills unsuitable for calvary, had doubled back, keeping the river between his army and Bayazid's. Now Timur forced the pace, covering the three hundred miles to Ankara in three days. There, basing themselves in the deserted Turkish camp, the Tartars diverted the small river that flows into Ankara to run behind their own position. They also destroyed the only other source of water for the oncoming Turks. Timur ordered the city to be invested, but on receiving news of Bayazid's arrival, raised the siege and prepared for battle.

The Turks had marched for a week in the Tartar wake, their supplies low. They arrived, weary, to find the Tartar installed in their own base. There was no water to be had except behind the enemy lines. They had no choice other than to attack. Bayazid was forced to launch his inferior cavalry against the masses of Asian horsemen. The battle was lost before the first sword was drawn.

Despite the fierce fighting, many of Bayazid's troops were induced by Timur's agents to change sides. The Turkish cavalry crumpled before the Mongol onslaught. The splendid Ottoman infantry had not struck a blow: without entrenchment they were exposed to successive cavalry charges and a rain of arrows and naphtha bombs from the backs of armored elephants. Some regiments fled while still they could. Others took their stand wherever they could find suitable ground. Bayazid held out on a hill with a thousand of his Janissaries, taking an axe himself and fighting grimly with his men. By sunset the rout was complete, and Timur was master of all the central lands of Islam. Bayazid was captured while trying to flee and taken to the conqueror. Although treated with civility, the Ottoman sultan was that evening forced to don his imperial regalia, seated at the Tartar victory feast, and compelled to watch his harem girls perform before the Mongol host.

In 1403, his pride broken, Bayazid died. Timur ordered that he be buried in the capital Brusa which was generously given, together with the original Ottoman heritage, to Bayazid's son Isa. Ottoman development however, was hindered during the following decade because of internecine strife between Bayazid's sons.

The defeat of Bayazid astonished the monarchs of Europe. For a century the Turks had menaced them. Suddenly they were utterly vanquished by the unknown Mongol from the East. All now made haste to pay their respects to the mighty power on their doorstep.

Timur spent the year 1403 plundering Anatolia. First he reduced Smyrna, which had held out against Bayazid. The resistance there of the Knights of St. John was buoyed up by the prospect of assistance from Rhodes, but the fleet that arrived shortly before the city's fall turned back when Timur fired the heads of his captives at them.

In the same year Timur's heir, Mohammed-Sultan, died. After holding a funeral feast at Avnik, he spent the next year campaigning in Armenia and Mesopotamia. Having eliminated India and cleared Asia, he returned to Samarkand, where his restless gaze turned eastward.

The foundation of the Ming dynasty in China at the expense of the Mongols was not to be tolerated. This, coupled with his desire to bring China within the community of Islam, meant that when the Ming emperor demanded the return of his envoy An Chi Tao together with tribute, Timur settled on a holy war against him. It was a race against time. Without the assurance of an heir to carry on his conquests, the failing Emperor insisted on departure as soon as the expedition was ready despite the severity of the winter. He managed to reach the frontier city of Otrar on the Syr-Daria, where he fell ill. There he made his last will bestowing the empire on his grandson Pir Mohammed Jahangir, and died on January 19, 1405. He was nearly sixty-nine.

On Timur's death the succession struggles which had so often proved the downfall of Islamic dynasties broke out. These were finally resolved in the assumption of power by Shahrukh, Timur's fourth and ablest son, who inaugurated an era of cultural achievement. The Timurid dynasty were men of peace and probably among the most enlightened monarchs of the day.

Timur's impact on his age cannot be overestimated, and derives not least from the terror nomads inspired in settled populations. His westward march changed the political constellation and altered the destinies of Europe.

He opened the transcontinental trade routes, blocked for over a century. He made Tabriz, instead of the more distant Baghdad, the center of Near East commerce; the upheavals following his death brought about the decline of the great Asian trade—one reason for the expeditions of Columbus and Vasco da Gama. To the north Timur crushed the Golden Horde, opening the way for the Russians to assert themselves as a free people. By scattering the Ottoman Turks he established himself as master of the Islamic world and saved a truncated Constantinople; but Europe was so weakened by dissension that the Turks recouped their power within fifty years. The Mongols were a declining power, the Ottoman star ascendant. The two were set on a collision course, that temporarily rocked the latter. But Timur's death caused the helmeted men, the warlike Mongol and Tartar elements of his army, to retire to their northern steppes. The more cultured southern element persisted, no longer a world power. His death was a blow to Islam, putting an end to all dreams of a universal Caliphate.

Timur was the last great conqueror in the tradition of Alexander, Cyrus and Genghis Khan. His beautification of Samarkand, his love of debate with scholars and divines, and his pre-

dilection for chess (which he played on an enlarged board with additional pieces) contrast strangely with his total ruthlessness, iron discipline, love of the nomadic way of life, and his illiteracy (although he spoke both Persian and Turkish). His greatness, however, must be said to lie in the effect he had on his contemporaries alone, for, with the exception of the Mogul dynasty in India founded by his descendant Baber at the beginning of the sixteenth century, Timur's successors had lost control of his domain within a century of his death.

GEOFFREY CHESLER

The Gur-i-mir mausoleum in Samarkand, built in 1402–04. The swelling domes of Muscovy and the Taj Mahal find their origin in turrets such as this.

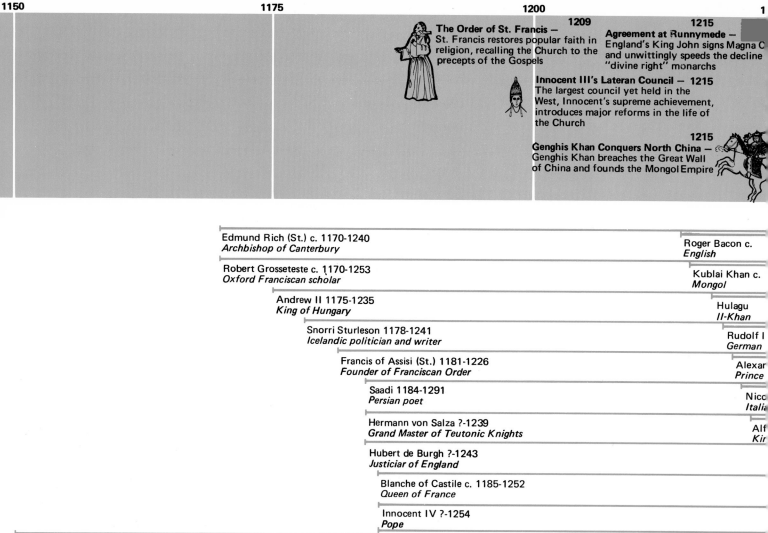

The Order of St. Francis — 1209
St. Francis restores popular faith in
religion, recalling the Church to the
precepts of the Gospels

Agreement at Runnymede — 1215
England's King John signs Magna C
and unwittingly speeds the decline
"divine right" monarchs

Innocent III's Lateran Council — 1215
The largest council yet held in the
West, Innocent's supreme achievement,
introduces major reforms in the life of
the Church

Genghis Khan Conquers North China — 1215
Genghis Khan breaches the Great Wall
of China and founds the Mongol Empire

Edmund Rich (St.) c. 1170-1240
Archbishop of Canterbury

Roger Bacon c.
English

Robert Grosseteste c. 1170-1253
Oxford Franciscan scholar

Kublai Khan c.
Mongol

Andrew II 1175-1235
King of Hungary

Hulagu
Il-Khan

Snorri Sturleson 1178-1241
Icelandic politician and writer

Rudolf I
German

Francis of Assisi (St.) 1181-1226
Founder of Franciscan Order

Alexar
Prince

Saadi 1184-1291
Persian poet

Nicc
Italia

Hermann von Salza ?-1239
Grand Master of Teutonic Knights

Alf
Kir

Hubert de Burgh ?-1243
Justiciar of England

Blanche of Castile c. 1185-1252
Queen of France

Innocent IV ?-1254
Pope

Gregory IX 1145-1241
Pope

Batu ?-1255
Leader of Mongol Golden Horde

Richard I (Coeur-de-Lion)
1157-1199 *King of England*

Louis VIII 1187-1226
King of France

Innocent III c. 1160-1216
Pope

Albertus Magnus (St) 1193-1280
German scholar at Paris

Simon de Montfort the Elder
c. 1160-1218 *French crusader*

Frederick II 1194-1250
Holy Roman Emperor

Genghis Khan 1162-1227
Mongol Conqueror

Ferdinand III 1199-1252
King of Castile

Philip II Augustus 1165-1223
King of France

Haakon IV c. 1204-62
King of Norway and Iceland

John c. 1167-1216
King of England

Birger Magnusson ?-1266
Swedish jarl (earl), regent

William Marshal, Earl of Pembroke ?-1219
Regent of Henry III of England

Henry III 1207-72
King of England

Dominic Guzman (St.) 1170-
1221 *Founder of Dominican Order*

Simon de Montfort c. 1208-65
Leader in English Barons' War

Stephen Langton ?-1228
Archbishop of Canterbury

Louis IX (St.) 1214
King of France

1185●
Victory of
Minamoto in
Japan

1204●
Philip II wins
Normandy

●1214
Battle of Bouvines: French
conquer Normandy and Poitou

1204●
Constantinople
falls to
crusaders

●12
Indus valley and Afghanist
conquered by Mongols

1217●
Fifth Crusade
begun

Abigensian Crusade begun ● 1208

1212●
Frederick
Hohenstaufen
elected
Emperor

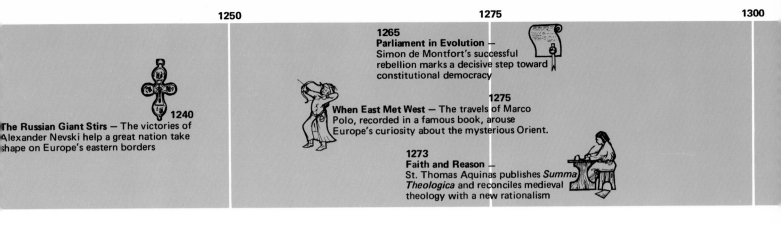

1250 **1275** **1300**

1240
The Russian Giant Stirs — The victories of Alexander Nevski help a great nation take shape on Europe's eastern borders

1265
Parliament in Evolution — Simon de Montfort's successful rebellion marks a decisive step toward constitutional democracy

1275
When East Met West — The travels of Marco Polo, recorded in a famous book, arouse Europe's curiosity about the mysterious Orient.

1273
Faith and Reason — St. Thomas Aquinas publishes *Summa Theologica* and reconciles medieval theology with a new rationalism

4-92
Jar

John XXII 1249-1334 *Pope*

-94
eror

Marco Polo c. 1254-1324
Venetian traveler

-65
ersia

Meister Eckhart c. 1260-1328
German theologian

apsburg 1218-92
eror

Sciarra Colonna ?-1329
Ghibelline leader in Rome

ski (St.) 1219-63
gorod and Vladimir

John Duns Scotus c. 1265-1308
British scholastic philosopher

no c. 1220-80
tor and architect

Guillaume de Nogaret c. 1265-1313
Chancellor of France

e Learned c. 1221-84
ile

Clement V 1265-1314
Pope

ael VIII Palaeologus 1224-82
antine Emperor

Dante Alighieri 1265-1321
Italian poet

mas Aquinas (St.) 1225-74
an philosopher

Giotto 1267-1337
Florentine painter

arles of Anjou 1226-85
g of Naples

Philip IV the Fair 1268-1314
King of France

Manfred c. 1230-66
Hohenstaufen King of Sicily

Osman I c. 1270-1326
Turkish Sultan

Otakar II 1230-78
King of Bohemia

William Wallace c. 1272-1305
Scottish rebel leader

Boniface VIII 1235-1303
Pope

Robert Bruce 1274-1329
King of Scotland

Peter III c. 1236-86
King of Aragon

Marsiglio of Padua c. 1275-1342
Italian political philosopher

Edward I 1239-1307
King of England

Diniz 1279-1325
King of Portugal

Cimabue c. 1240-1302
Florentine painter

Edward II 1284-1327
King of England

Alexander III 1241-86
King of Scotland

Ludwig IV of Bavaria 1287-1347
German Emperor

Llewelyn the Great ?-1282
Prince of Wales

Charles IV the Fair 1294-1328
King of France

Philip III the Bold 1245-85
King of France

Go-Daigo (Daigo II) ?-1339
Emperor of Japan

John Balliol 1249-1315
King of Scotland

● 1248
Seventh Crusade, led by St. Louis

● 1265
Battle of Evesham: death of Simon de Montfort

● 1276
Paper manufactured in Italy

● 1297
English Parliament acquires right to approve taxation

● 1226
er of Teutonic Knights
organized by Frederick II

● 1253-99
Venetian-Genoese struggle over trade in the Levant and Black Sea

● 1271
Yuan (Mongol) Dynasty established in China (Peking)

225
versity of
les founded

Florin first coined 1252 ●

● 1266
Battle of Benevento: Charles of Anjou takes Sicily from Germans

● 1282
Sicilian Vespers: French lose Sicily to Aragon

● 1236
Cordova, Moorish capital,
aken by Castile

Jerusalem taken by Egyptian Moslems
1244 ●

● 1258
Sack of Baghdad by Mongol Hulagu

● 1268
Battle of Tagliacozzo

● 1273
Accession of Rudolf I as Emperor ends German Interregnum (since 1254)

● 1291
Turks capture Acre

Golden Horde established ●
in southern Russia by Batu 1242

1245 ●
First Council of Lyons

● 1261
Constaninople fell to Greeks

Barons' War in England against Henry III 1270 ●
● 1264-5
Eighth Crusade, led by St. Louis

1274 ● Second Council of Lyons

● 1275
Edward I's Model Parliament

1320
"The Divine Comedy" — In composing his epic poem, Dante gives expression to new ideologies and helps create the modern Italian language

The Black Death — Trading vessels returning fourteenth-century Europe from Asian ports carry a new and deadly cargo: bubonic plague

1337
Europe's Century of War —
The English introduce longbows against the French—the beginning of the end for the feudal knight

Giovanni Boccaccio 1313-75
Italian writer

John of Gaunt 1340-99
Duke of Lancaster

Charles IV of Luxemburg 1316-78
Holy Roman Emperor

Geoffrey Chaucer c. 1340-
English poet

Urban VI c. 1318-89
Pope

John 1340-1416
Duke of Berry

John II 1319-64
King of France

Philip the Bold
Duke of

Peter I the Cruel 1320-67
King of Portugal

Cath
Itali

Bertrand Du Guesclin c. 1320-80
Constable of France

Bay.
Otto

William of Wykeham 1324-1404
English churchman and educationist

Louis I the Great 1326-82
King of Hungary

John Wycliffe c. 1328-84
English religious reformer

Chu Yuan-chang 1328-98
Founder of Ming Dynasty China

Edward the Black Prince 1330-76
Prince of Wales

Gregory XI 1330-78
Pope

Philip VI 1293-1328
King of France

Charles II the Bad 1332-87
King of Navarre

William of Ockham c. 1300-1342
English philosopher

Henry II of Trastamara c. 1333-79
King of Castile and León

Petrarch 1304-74
Italian poet

Timur the Great c. 1336-1405
Mongol conqueror

Etienne Marcel ?- 1358
Provost of Paris merchants

Charles V 1337-80
King of France

Stephen Dushan c. 1308-55
King of Serbia

Jean Froissart c. 1337-1410
French chronicler

Casimir III the Great 1310-70
King of Poland

Alexander V 1339-1410 *Pope*

Edward III 1312-77
King of England

Philip van Arteveld
Leader of Flemish

Cola di Rienzi 1313-54
Roman tribune

Gerard Groote 1340-84
Dutch Monastic reformer

1300 ●
Great Jubilee

● **1314**
Scots rout English at Bannockburn

1303 ●
Anagni stormed

1315 ●
Battle of Morgarten:
Ludwig IV recognizes Swiss confederation

1340 ●
Asia Minor controlled by Turks

1304 ●
Sea victory at Sluys for English

● **1325**
Aztec Empire established in Mexico at Tenochtitlan

Formation of Hanseatic ●
League **1344**

First Venetian trading ●
expedition to Flanders **1317**

Battle of Crécy **1346** ●

Naples overrun by Louis I ●
of Hungary **1347**

A New Dynasty for China — 1368
The Chinese under Chu Yuan-chang throw off the Mongol yoke and establish the native Ming dynasty

Father of English Poetry — 1387
By his *Canterbury Tales* Chaucer establishes the London dialect as England's literary language

1381
Wat Tyler "Captures" London — England's boy King averts civil war, but cannot ignore his subjects' demands for a larger voice in Parliament

Rival Popes — 1378
Christendom is divided for forty years while rival popes struggle for supremacy

Terror Out of the East — 1402
Timur creates the last Mongol world empire, halting the rise of the Ottoman Turks and altering the destinies of Europe

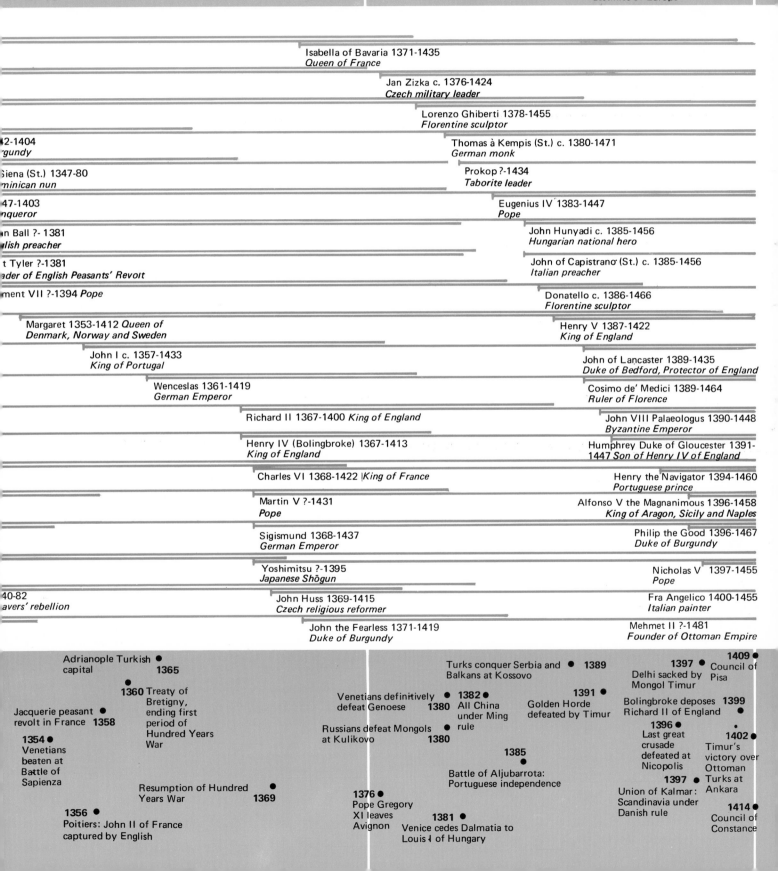

Isabella of Bavaria 1371-1435
Queen of France

Jan Zizka c. 1376-1424
Czech military leader

Lorenzo Ghiberti 1378-1455
Florentine sculptor

42-1404
rgundy

Siena (St.) 1347-80
minican nun

Thomas à Kempis (St.) c. 1380-1471
German monk

Prokop ?-1434
Taborite leader

47-1403
nqueror

Eugenius IV 1383-1447
Pope

n Ball ?- 1381
lish preacher

John Hunyadi c. 1385-1456
Hungarian national hero

t Tyler ?-1381
ader of English Peasants' Revolt

John of Capistrano (St.) c. 1385-1456
Italian preacher

ment VII ?-1394 *Pope*

Donatello c. 1386-1466
Florentine sculptor

Margaret 1353-1412 *Queen of Denmark, Norway and Sweden*

Henry V 1387-1422
King of England

John I c. 1357-1433
King of Portugal

John of Lancaster 1389-1435
Duke of Bedford, Protector of England

Wenceslas 1361-1419
German Emperor

Cosimo de' Medici 1389-1464
Ruler of Florence

Richard II 1367-1400 *King of England*

John VIII Palaeologus 1390-1448
Byzantine Emperor

Henry IV (Bolingbroke) 1367-1413
King of England

Humphrey Duke of Gloucester 1391-1447 *Son of Henry IV of England*

Charles VI 1368-1422 *King of France*

Henry the Navigator 1394-1460
Portuguese prince

Martin V ?-1431
Pope

Alfonso V the Magnanimous 1396-1458
King of Aragon, Sicily and Naples

Sigismund 1368-1437
German Emperor

Philip the Good 1396-1467
Duke of Burgundy

Yoshimitsu ?-1395
Japanese Shōgun

Nicholas V 1397-1455
Pope

40-82
avers' rebellion

John Huss 1369-1415
Czech religious reformer

Fra Angelico 1400-1455
Italian painter

John the Fearless 1371-1419
Duke of Burgundy

Mehmet II ?-1481
Founder of Ottoman Empire

Adrianople Turkish ● capital 1365

1360 ● Treaty of Bretigny, ending first period of Hundred Years War

Jacquerie peasant ● revolt in France 1358

1354 ●
Venetians beaten at Battle of Sapienza

Resumption of Hundred Years War 1369 ●

1356 ●
Poitiers: John II of France captured by English

Turks conquer Serbia and ● 1389
Balkans at Kossovo

Venetians definitively ● 1382 ●
defeat Genoese 1380 All China under Ming rule

Russians defeat Mongols ● rule
at Kulikovo 1380

1385 ●

Battle of Aljubarrota:
Portuguese independence

1391 ●
Golden Horde defeated by Timur

1376 ●
Pope Gregory XI leaves Avignon

1381 ●
Venice cedes Dalmatia to Louis I of Hungary

1409 ●
1397 ● Council of
Delhi sacked by Pisa
Mongol Timur

Bolingbroke deposes 1399
Richard II of England ●

1396 ●
Last great crusade defeated at Nicopolis

1402 ●
Timur's victory over Ottoman Turks at Ankara

1397 ●
Union of Kalmar: Scandinavia under Danish rule

1414 ●
Council of Constance

Acknowledgments

The authors and publishers wish to thank the following museums and collections by whose kind permission the illustrations are reproduced. Page numbers appear in bold, photographic sources in italics:

12 *Scala*
13 *Scala*
14 *Alinari*
15 *Mansell Collection*
16 *Scala*
17 (1) British Museum, London (2) *Scala*
18 *Scala*
19 (1) *Scala* (2) *Mansell Collection*
20 (1) *Scala* (2) Master and Fellows, Corpus Christi College, Cambridge (3) *A. F. Kersting*
21 (2) British Museum
22 *British Travel Association*
23 Bodleian Library, Oxford
24 (1) British Museum
25 (1) Master and Fellows, Corpus Christi College, Cambridge (2) British Museum
26 (1, 2) Master and Fellows, Corpus Christi College, Cambridge
27 British Museum
28 *Scala*
29 British Museum
31 (1) Cambridge University Library (2) Master and Fellows, Corpus Christi College, Cambridge
32 *Scala*
33 (1) Bodleian Library, Oxford (2) British Museum
34 Victoria and Albert Museum, London
35 (1) Master and Fellows, Corpus Christi College, Cambridge (2) Victoria and Albert Museum
36 British Museum
37 British Museum
38 (1) National Palace Museum, Taiwan (2) *Mansell Collection*
40 British Museum
41 (1) Bibliothèque Nationale, Paris (3) *Mansell Collection*
42 Bibliothèque Nationale, Paris
43 Victoria and Albert Museum: *John Webb*
44 (1) Master and Fellows, Corpus Christi College, Cambridge (2) Vatican Library
45 (1) *Lala Aufsberg* (3) *Archiv Gerstenberg*
46 *Novosti*
47 *Novosti*
48 *Novosti*
49 (1) *Society for Cultural Relations with the U.S.S.R.* (2) *Hulton Picture Library*
50 (1, 2) *Novosti*
51 (1, 2) *Novosti*
52 (1) Kungliga Biblioteket, Stockholm (2) *Foto Mas*
53 (1) British Museum (2) *Hulton Picture Library*
54 British Museum
55 *Mansell Collection*
56 (1, 2) Trinity College, Cambridge
57 (1) Cambridge University Library (2) British Museum
58 British Museum
59 *J. Allan Cash*

60 (1) Bodleian Library, Oxford (2) Cambridge University Library
61 Royal Library, Windsor
62 (2) *Archiv Gerstenberg* (3) Staatsbibliothek, Berlin
63 (1) *Jean Roubier* (2) *British Travel Association* (3) *Hulton Picture Library*
64 *Scala*
65 British Museum
66 *Scala*
67 Trinity College, Cambridge
68 Lambeth Palace Library
69 (1) *Scala* (2) British Museum
70 (1) Cambridge University Library (2) *Alinari*
71 Vatican Library: *Scala*
72 (1) Österreiches Nationale Bibliothek, Vienna (2) British Museum: *B.P.C. Publishing* (3) *A. F. Kersting*
73 (1) *J. Allan Cash*
74 Bodleian Library, Oxford
75 *Hulton Picture Library*
76 *Mansell Collection*
77 (1) *Giraudon* (2) University Library, Edinburgh
79 (1, 2, 3) Bodleian Library, Oxford
80 (1) Vatican Library (2) Vatican Library: *Clarendon Press, Oxford*
81 (1) *Swiss National Tourist Office* (2) *Mansell Collection*
82 Museo dell'Opera del Duomo, Florence
83 Bargello, Florence: *Scala*
84 St. Maria Novella, Florence: *Alinari*
85 (1) *Alinari* (2, 3) *Anderson*
86 (1) Cathedral, Florence: *Scala* (2) *Scala*
87 Palazzo Publico, Siena: *Scala*
88 St. Maria Novella, Florence: *Alinari*
89 (1, 2) *Alinari*
90 (1) *Foto Marburg* (2) *Central Office of Information: B.P.C. Publishing* (3) Bodleian Library, Oxford
91 (1) Courtesy Sir David Oglivy, Bt: National Library of Scotland (2) Crown copyright: *National Monuments Record*
92 British Museum
93 *Snark International*
95 (1) British Museum (2) Bodleian Library, Oxford
96 (1) *Hulton Picture Library* (2) *British Travel Association*
97 (1) British Museum (2) *Photo Bulloz*
98 (1) Lambeth Palace Library (2) British Museum
99 British Museum
100 (1, 2) *Hulton Picture Library* (3) *Mansell Collection*
101 Bildarchiv, Österreiches Nationale Bibliothek, Vienna
102 Galleria Nazionale, Palermo: *Scala*
103 St. Apollonia, Florence: *Alinari*
104 *Alinari*
105 (1) *Scala* (2) Biblioteca Laurenziana, Florence
106 (1) *Hulton Picture Library* (2, 3) Bibliothèque Royale, Brussels
107 (2) *Alinari*

108 (1) British Museum: *John Freeman* (2) *Alinari*
109 (1, 2) *John Freeman*
110 (2) *Alinari* (3) *Françoise Foliot*
111 (1) India Office Library (2) *Snark International*
112 British Museum
113 National Palace Museum, Taiwan
114 (1, 2) National Palace Museum, Taiwan
115 (1, 2) British Museum: *Photo Fleming*
116 (1) Percival David Foundation of Chinese Art (2) British Museum
117 British Museum
118 *J. Allan Cash*
119 *J. Allan Cash*
120 (1) *Giraudon* (2) Archiv für Kunst und Geschichte, Berlin
121 (1) *Mansell Collection* (2) British Museum
122 British Museum
123 British Museum
124 (1) *Mansell Collection*
125 (1) *Mansell Collection* (2) *Photo Bulloz*
127 (1) *Giraudon* (2) *Picturepoint*
128 *Mansell Collection*
129 (1) Bern Historisches Museum (2) *Giraudon* (3) British Museum
130 Bodleian Library, Oxford
131 Westminster Abbey, London
132 British Museum
133 (1, 2) British Museum (3) *Richard Burn*
134 (1, 2) British Museum
135 British Museum
136 (1) *Hulton Picture Library*
137 (1, 2) *Mansell Collection* (3) Kungliga Biblioteket
138 Bodleian Library, Oxford
139 Master and Fellows, Corpus Christi College, Cambridge
140 *Mansell Collection*
141 (1, 2, 3) *Mansell Collection*
142 (1) British Museum (2, 3) Henry Huntington Library, California: *B.P.C. Publishing*
143 *Mansell Collection*
144 (1) *Mansell Collection* (2) British Museum (3) New College, Oxford
145 (1) *Hulton Picture Library* (2) Victoria and Albert Museum
146 *R. Skelton*
147 *C. M. Dixon*
148 India Office Library: *Photo Fleming*
150 *R. Skelton*
151 *R. Skelton*
152 British Museum
153 *C. M. Dixon*

Managing Editor *Jonathan Mavrin*
Assistant Editors *Geoffrey Chesler, Francesca Ronan*
Picture Editor *Judith Aspinall*
Consultant Designer *Tim Higgins*
Art Director *Anthony Cohen*

Index